FLASH MX COMPONENTS MOST WANTED

Aral Balkan   Daryn Nakhuda
Todd Coulson   James Palmer
Jen deHaan   Mike Pearce
David Doull   Paul Prudence
Josh Dura   Bill Spencer
Peter Elst   Jon Steer
Jeremy Larkin   Jared Tarbell
Lifaros   Brandon Williams
Todd Marks   Todd Yard
Brian Monnone   Steve Young
Michael Montagna

friendsof

DESIGNER TO DESIGNER

Flash MX Components Most Wanted

ISBN-13 (pbk): 978-1-59059-178-9
ISBN-10 (pbk): 1-59059-178-X

Printed and bound in the United States of America (POD)

Trademarked names may appear in this book. Rather than use a trademark symbol with every occurrence of a trademarked name, we use the names only in an editorial fashion and to the benefit of the trademark owner, with no intention of infringement of the trademark.

Distributed to the book trade in the United States by Springer-Verlag New York, Inc., 233 Spring Street, 6th Floor, New York, NY 10013 and outside the United States by Springer-Verlag GmbH & Co. KG, Tiergartenstr. 17, 69112 Heidelberg, Germany.

In the United States: phone 1-800-SPRINGER, e-mail orders@springer-ny.com, or visit http://www.springer-ny.com.

Outside the United States: fax +49 6221 345229, e-mail orders@springer.de, or visit http://www.springer.de.

For information on translations, please contact Apress directly at 2855 Telegraph Avenue, Suite 600, Berkeley, CA 94705. Phone 510-549-5930, fax 510-549-5939, e-mail info@apress.com, or visit http://www.apress.com.

Authors

Aral Balkan
Todd Coulson
Jen deHaan
David Doull
Josh Dura
Peter Elst
Jeremy Larkin
Lifaros
Todd Marks
Brian Monnone
Michael Montagna
Daryn Nakhuda
James Palmer
Mike Pearce
Paul Prudence
Bill Spencer
Jon Steer
Jared Tarbell
Brandon Williams
Todd Yard
Steve Young

Technical Editor
Steve Rycroft

Editorial Proofer
Helena Sharman

Project Manager
Simon Brand

Technical Reviewers
Marco Baraldi
Alexandra Blackburn
Sally Cruikshank
Steve McCormick
Vibha Roy
Mike Sloan

Graphic Editor
Matt Clark

Cover Design
Katy Freer
Matt Clark

Index
Simon Collins

Author Agent
Chris Matterface

Commissioning Editor
Andrew Tracey

Managing Editor
Chris Hindley

CONTENTS

Introduction   1

Component 1   Event Calendar   7

Component 2   Text Editor   23

Component 3   XML News Ticker   33

Component 4   Tool Tip   43

Component 5   Sketch Pad   55

Component 6   Video Player   69

Component 7   Image Scroller   81

Component 8   Pattern Generators   93

Component 9   TabControl   105

Component 10   Sliding Panel   117

Component 11   ColorPicker   129

Component 12   Game Player Selector   143

Component 13   Particle Emitter   155

Component 14   Layout Manager   173

Component 15   Data Grid   187

Component 16   Tornado Movie Loader   195

Component 17   Image Modulation   223

Component 18   XML-to-ActionScript Parser   235

Component 19   Virtual Trackball   247

Component 20   Text Animations   261

Component 21   StringThing   281

Index   297

FLASH MX COMPONENTS MOST WANTED

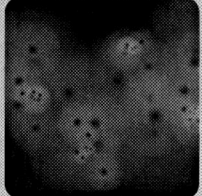

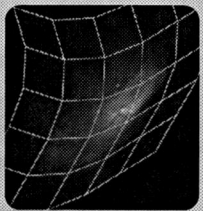

Introduction

Welcome to *Flash MX Components Most Wanted*.

In this book, and in the accompanying download, you'll find an ideal mixture of creative and functional components from some of today's leading Flash designers and developers. The beauty of packaging Flash MX components within a book is that we can offer the most comprehensive documentation possible. Each chapter combines an exhaustive reference resource with plenty of hands-on examples to form a rich, designer-oriented guide that will help you get the most out of all of the featured components. All the files you'll need for this book are easily downloadable at http://friendsofed.com/downloads.

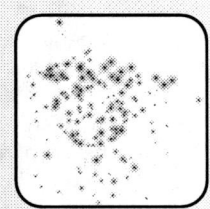

Components in Flash MX

A component in Flash can be thought of as an application within itself – completely independent and encapsulated functionality that's flexible enough such that it can easily be customized to take care of many different tasks. The most popular components are those that form the standard elements of a user interface (UI); for instance, the ScrollBar, ComboBox, ListBox, RadioButton, and CheckBox, amongst other ingredients that make up the typical UI.

There are also components that simplify the use of fairly complex functions and simulations. For example, creating elements of educational projects or graphical presentations, such as BarCharts and PieCharts, from scratch would be a rather large and daunting task. In fact,

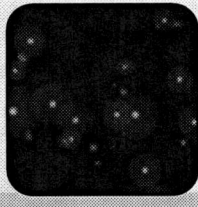

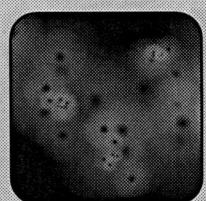

this is a natural extension of inheritance: creating bigger and more complex components from a foundation of smaller ones. For instance, when you write a program you'd usually divide a large task or problem into smaller modular operations; writing a search-and-replace routine for strings could logically be divided into a routine for searching a string and a routine for replacing a substring with another substring.

In general, we would usually try to break up our programs into many small, tangible sub-programs that can be put together in different ways to produce a number of unique applications. Indeed, modular programming is the essential philosophy behind components, and can be see as a necessary precursor to true object-oriented programming (OOP) techniques.

So, once you've created your required functionality and packaged it as a component, you can access all the properties and have complete control over this building block of design. You effectively avoid the need to 'look under the hood' at any of the hidden technical details (unless of course you want to!). The ability to simply *build*, *use*, *distribute*, *trade*, *buy*, and *sell* these friendly chunks of reusable functionality, with complete disregard to how they actually work, leads to an extremely productive and efficient workflow for the average developer/designer.

OK, so the advantages of components are pretty clear – they are, after all, a fairly logical concept, perhaps even a seemingly natural technical evolution. You might say that this is due to the fact that developers and programmers are a *strategically lazy* breed! On second thoughts, before the complaints arrive, we'd better amend that statement and suggest that it's because we're such an *inherently wise* community. Why create something many times, when you can do it correctly once, and then go crazy with 'drag and drop'? Although the idea of creating something once and then reusing and recycling it as much as possible is a rather obvious one, you might agree that many aspects of the design and development process, if not certain areas of life in general, could benefit by employing this model.

In this introduction we're going to familiarize ourselves with the installation and management of components in Flash MX using the Macromedia Extension Manager. This will provide a foundation for utilizing the amazing *Most Wanted* components that you'll find described in the rest of this book. We'll also suggest a few resources for learning about creating your own components. Most Flash components give the user full control and the ability to customize their appearance and functionality. As simple to use as they are (you can simply drag and drop them onto the stage, and they're pretty much ready to run!), this background information regarding their installation is an important first step on the road to learning the true potential of components.

Downloading, installing, and managing Flash components

Once you are convinced that components are the *way of the future*, you might be left wondering where to get them. Macromedia has provided an *Exchange* for this very purpose, where you can browse through numerous components and download them for your own use. You can peruse the collection at www.macromedia.com/exchange, and once you've found a component that you need, you can simply download an MXP file – you can use this to install the component in Flash MX via the Macromedia Extension Manager.

Macromedia Extension Manager

The Macromedia Extension Manager is included with Macromedia Studio MX, or can be downloaded for free from www.macromedia.com/exchange/em_download/. The Extension Manager provides a means to install, uninstall, and manage all of your components:

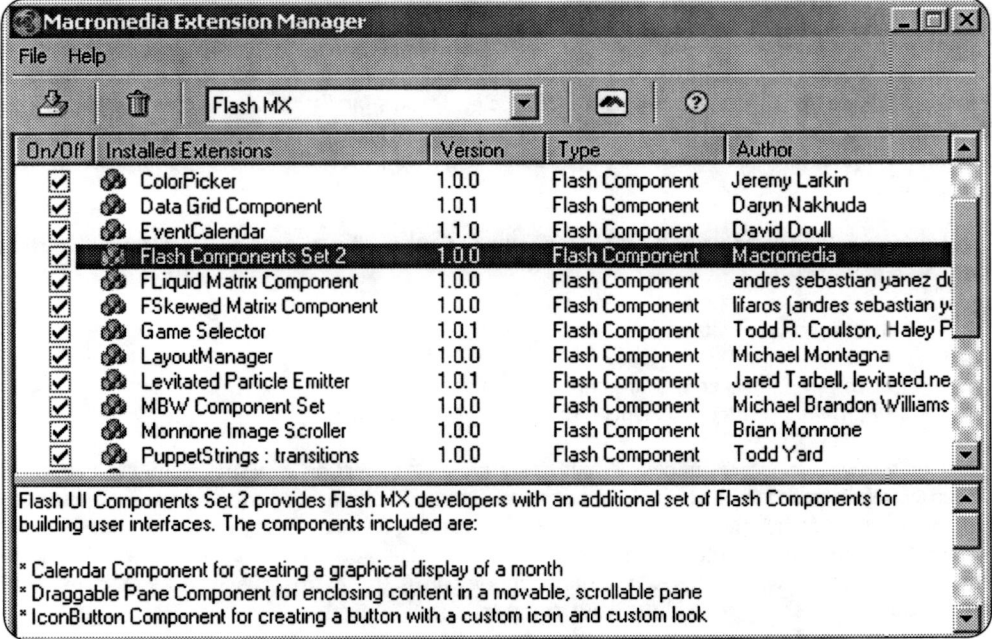

After downloading and setting up the Extension Manager, you're ready to install your components. Flash MX components are typically packaged within an MXP file; once you've downloaded your required component, or extracted it from this book's accompanying download, simply double-clicking on the MXP file, accepting any disclaimer or copyright notices, and restarting Flash MX is enough to install it. The component will then automatically be available in the Components panel (Window > Components), ready for you to drag, drop, and use:

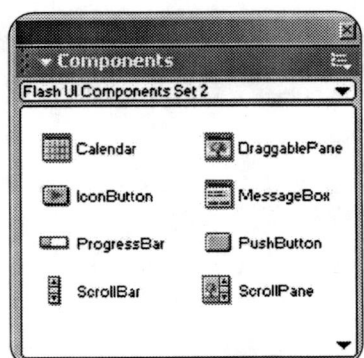

3

More advanced readers will probably be interested in how to package components as MXP files for use with the Manager – those curious might want to download the relevant documentation at http://download.macromedia.com/pub/exchange/mxi_file_format.pdf, which gives an overview of the XML structure used to create MXP files.

Resources for Flash components

In addition to the Macromedia Flash MX Exchange (www.macromedia.com/exchange), the Macromedia Designer & Developer Center (www.macromedia.com/desdev/) is a great place learn more about components. Here you'll find an abundance of articles, forums, and tutorials on creating and using Flash MX components, as well as interesting information on many other related topics and features. A useful introduction to creating components can be found at www.macromedia.com/support/flash/applications/creating_comps/.

Of course, a quick web search will reveal a number of other sites geared towards spreading the word about components:

- www.flashcomponents.net
- www.illogicz.com
- http://componenthq.entclosure.com/
- www.urbanev.com/components.html

In particular, www.flashcomponents.net features a growing collection of visual elements that can easily be added to projects and customized – some of the tutorials here (www.flashcomponents.net/tutorials.cfm?nav=4) are certainly worth reading, especially Jonathan Kaye's excellent introductory article (www.flashcomponents.net/tutorials/triangle/triangle.html). Last, but in no way least, the MX Component Creation forum at www.were-here.com/forums/index.php is the perfect place to meet other designers and developers, and share ideas about your components.

Of course, one of the greatest resources that exist will be your own imagination and motivation to customize or create components to perform specific tasks – hopefully some of the exciting designs in this book will inspire you to get out there and start creating!

Styles used in this book

We use some simple layout conventions to make things clearer throughout the book:

- We'll use the following styles to introduce **new terms** and to stress *important points* in the text.

- We use `this style` for code that appears in text. Similarly, file names will appear in this style: `HappyHappyJoyJoy.swf`.

- When we're indicating anything that you need to input as text, you'll see these styles: "type `FunkyMonkey` into the Target field".

- URLs will be shown in this style: www.friendsofed.com

- Menu path descriptions will appear like this: File>Open>Monkey>Banana, while keyboard stroke sequences will be displayed in this style: F4 and CTRL+ALT+DEL.

```
Blocks of code
Will appear in this style,
And we'll also use
This style to highlight new code,
Or code that deserves your attention.
```

Support at friends of ED

This friends of ED book is fully supported at www.friendsofed.com, and you can also visit our support forums for help, inspiration, or just to chat.

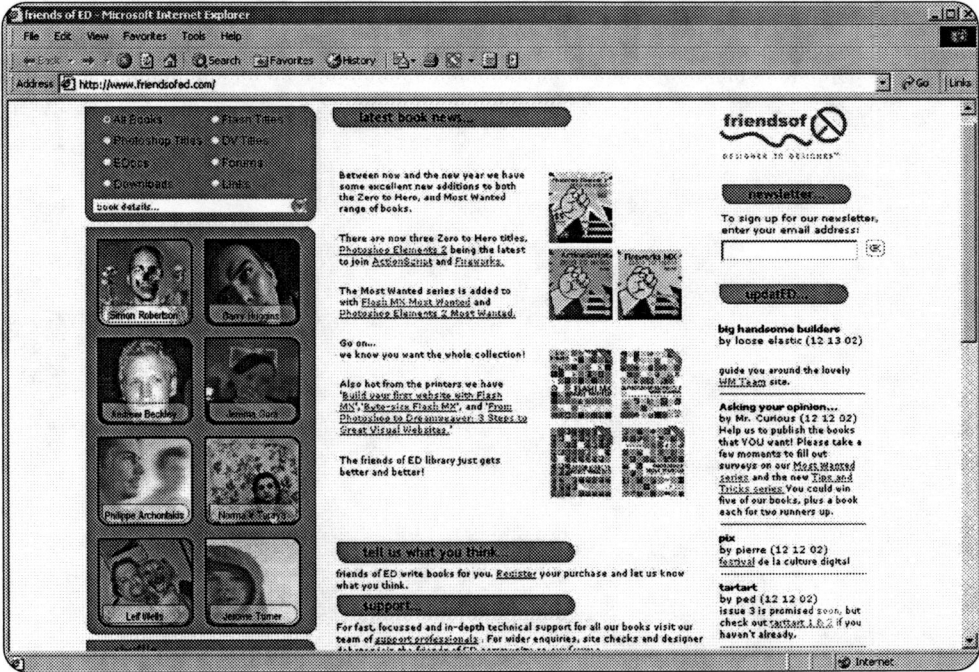

Additionally, if you run into any trouble – maybe have a problem with a certain file or tutorial – we're right here for you. Leave a message on the forum or drop a mail to support@friendsofed.com – we'll get you sorted in no time. Even if you don't have problems, let us know what you think of this book, or if you've got any ideas for future books. E-mail feedback@friendsofed.com or fill out the reply card at the back of the book – we'd love to hear from you!

David Doull

David is an Australian freelance Flash developer specialising in building applications and games in Flash.
Examples of his work and plenty of fun Flash games can be found at his business site artifactinteractive.com.au. Within the flash community he is best known for his sitessmallblueprinter.com and urbanev.com

He has been a finalist in the Flash Film Festival three times and has picked up a Macromedia Site of the Day for his Flash 3D interactive house plan tool at smallblueprinter.com

David has contributed to a number for friends of ED books ,including the Flash Usability Guide.

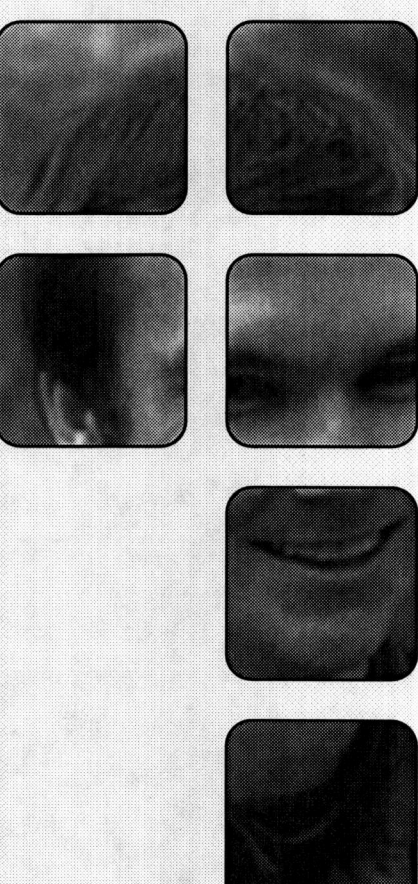

Component 1
Event Calendar

Want to add an events calendar to your site without typing a line of code? This component is a robust event calendar application, which allows you to easily store, display, and edit your own interactive calender.

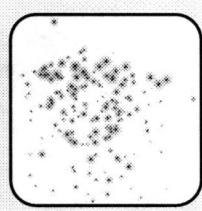
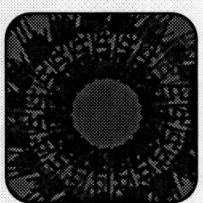

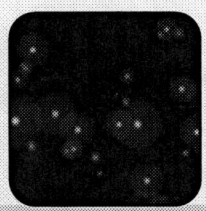

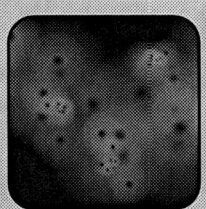

The origin of the word **computer** comes from as far back as the 1600s when it was actually used to refer to people who calculated the yearly calendar. So it seems somewhat appropriate that our first Flash component in this book is a computer generated calendar.

The event calendar component that we'll be looking at in this chapter gives us a simple way to add all of the functionality that you'd associate with an event calendar to our website. It's effectively a mini-application that you can drag and drop into your Flash designs allowing you to store, view, and edit events against dates in a calendar. The event data can be stored on your local PC as a shared object (in Flash MX, local shared objects are analogous to the *cookies* that your web browser utilizes) or on a server as an XML document.

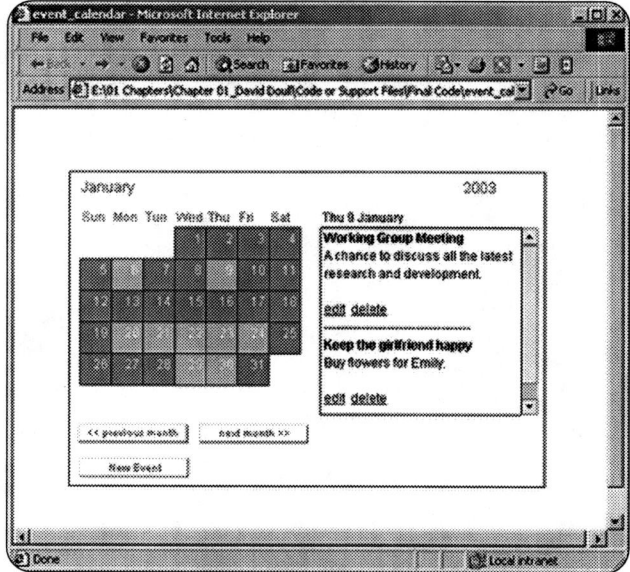

This component could be used on a website of a social club to display a calendar of upcoming events, or on an intranet to show the times for team meetings and seminars. Perhaps even on a corporate site to provide a calendar of upcoming product demonstrations – I'm sure you can think of even more ideas for its use. Essentially, it can be used anywhere that you want to display information associated with dates.

This event calendar component is ideally suited to an environment in which only a few people will be updating the calendar, and a larger group of people will be viewing it. It has intentionally been built to be as flexible as possible. If you only have FTP access to your server then you can set it to work in that environment, but if you have access to server-side scripts, such as ASP or PHP, then you can make use of that functionality to enhance the component (more on this later).

It's worth noting that the Macromedia Flash UI Components Set 2 also contains a calendar component, but this is just a simple user interface element, comparable with a drop down list. It will of course display a calendar interface, but doesn't store, manage, or display data. With this chapter's component we have a full calendar application that can integrate with server-side XML data, allowing you to browse and manage a calendar of events – now let's learn how to use it!

Using the Event Calendar

The best way to understand how the component works is to try it out. If you have installed the events calendar component from its `EventCalendar.mxp` file, found in the relevant directory in the download that accompanies this book, then it should appear in the Components panel (see the introductory chapter of this book for full installation details) Create a new a Flash file and drag the event calendar from the Components panel onto the stage. Otherwise, you can simply open up the file event_calendar.fla, again from the download, and just drag the component from the Library (Window > Library or F11) of this FLA onto the stage:

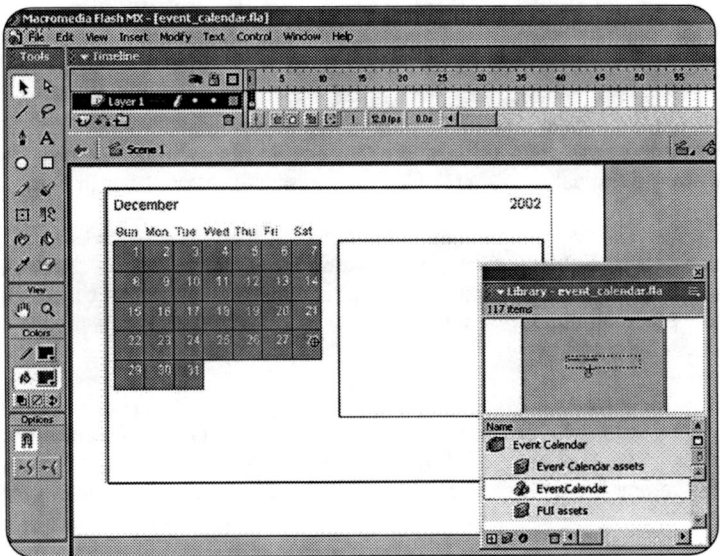

You should now see a preview version of the calendar on the stage. This is a simplified version of the calendar to give you a feel for how it will look when you run your Flash file. Note that if you don't see the preview version then you need to have Flash MX set to show live previews – select `Enable Live Preview` from the Control menu.

Select the events calendar on the stage and open up the Property inspector (Window > Properties) – this window, along with the Component Parameters panel, is extremely useful when dealing with components. Here you should see the three main parameters for the component. If you don't see these, make sure you've clicked on the `Parameters` tab:

This component also has a number of ActionScript methods that can be set through function calls – these are described at the end of this chapter. Right now however, we'll move on to study the component parameters in more detail.

Setting the parameters

As we can see from the Property inspector, the component has three parameters that can be set to customize its basic functionality:

- Allow users to edit – This first parameter can be either `true` or `false`. If it is `true` then users will be able to add, edit, and delete events within the calendar. If it is set to `false` then these options won't be visible and users will only be able to view the calendar. This option will be useful if you only want certain people to be able to add or edit the events. For example, on a website you may want an administrator to be able to add events, but the general public only able to view the events.

- Store data – This defines how the events data is stored. There are three options: `local`, `xmlStatic`, and `xmlDynamic`. The `local` option means that the data will be stored on the users' hard drives as a Flash MX shared object. As their names suggest, the two XML options involve storing the data as an XML file – we'll discuss these options in detail later in this chapter.

- Show current day – This final parameter can be either `true` or `false`, and relates to whether the event details for the current day are shown by default when the component is first accessed. The default value is `false`, which means that the events detail text box is initially blank. If this is set to `true` then the events detail text box will display the events for the current day. If there are no events for the current day then it will be blank.

Let's have a look at the events calendar in action. Leave all the parameters at the default settings and test the movie (Control > Test Movie or CTRL/COMMAND+ENTER). You'll see the current month displayed, as well as an empty text box. The text box will display the details for any events on any day you select. At this stage you don't have any events specified, so the details box will of course be empty!

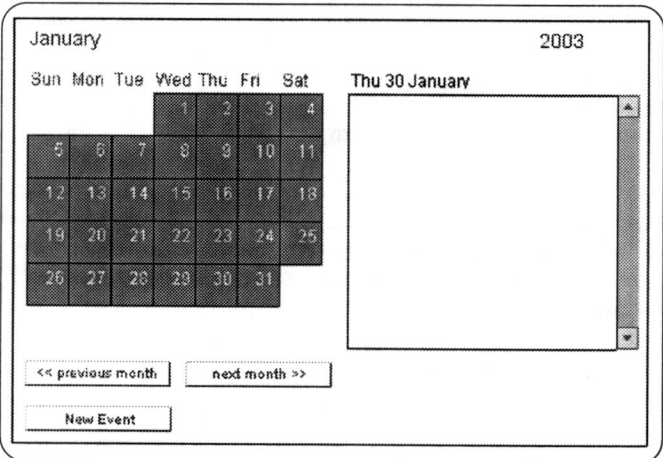

Adding events

Now let's add some events to our calendar. Click on the New Event button and the new event window will be displayed on the right hand side, as shown below. Note that if you can't see the New Event button, make sure that the allow users to edit parameter is set to `true` (the default value):

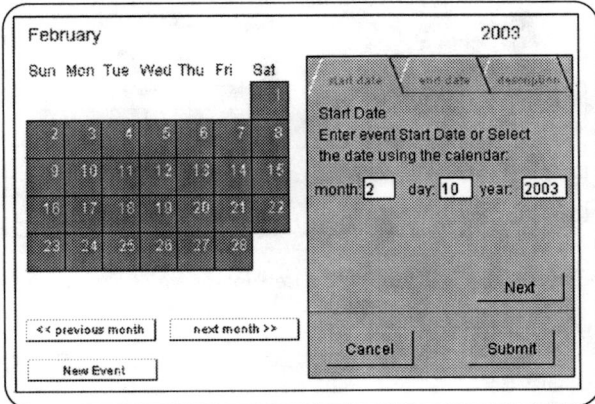

Creating a new event is a three-step process:

1. First you enter the start date for the event. By default, this will be set to the last day you clicked on in the calendar. You can either type in the date or select the date using the calender. Simply clicking on a date on the calendar will automatically fill in that date into the input boxes.

2. Click Next and do the same thing for the end date. If the event is a single day event then either leave the end date blank or enter the same date as the start date for the end date. Otherwise, if the event lasts longer, just click on the date in the calendar that the event will finish:

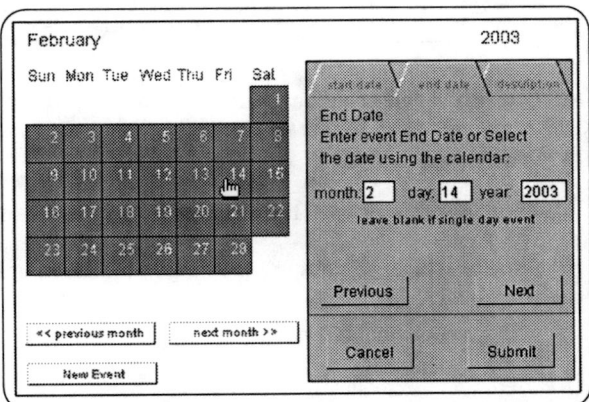

3. Finally, you can fill in the title and description for the event by clicking on the Next button again, or by selecting the description tab at the top: (see overleaf)

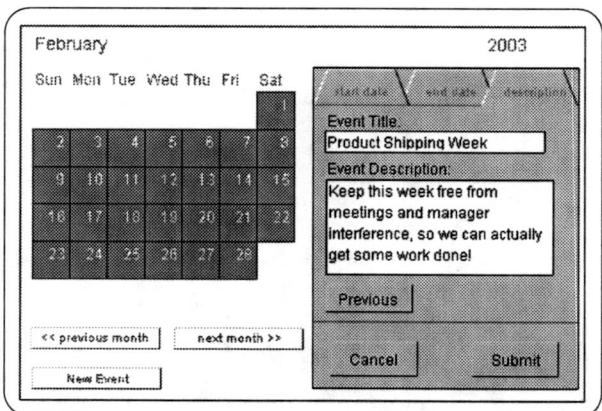

On pressing Submit, your meeting will be highlighted in the calendar (in this case, we demonstrate a week-long event):

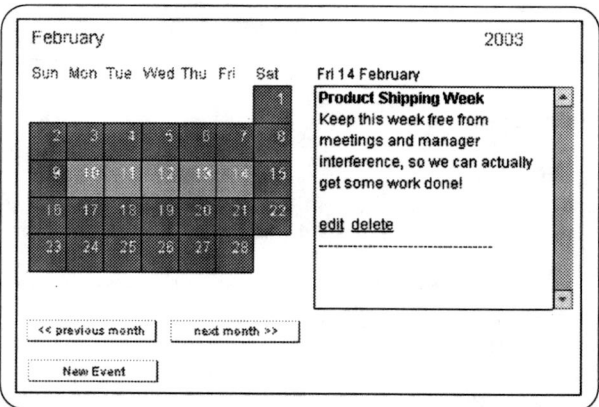

The Event Description text box also supports basic HTML formatting, so you can use formatting tags such as <B>, <I>, <FONT COLOR>, and <FONT SIZE>, as well as hyperlinks <A>. For example, you could type something like this into the event details text box:

```
Oh no, not <I>another</I> <B>boring</B> strategy meeting!
```

This will result in the text of the specified formatting appearing in the event details window:

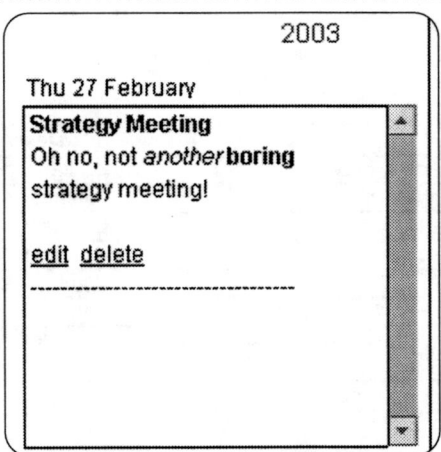

Modifying the component style

The default color for the calendar cells is blue, for the simple reason that I like blue and was tired of the dull grey that is often used in components! However, you aren't forced to keep them blue because this component supports global style formatting, which means you can easily set the colours to whatever you desire.

Create a new layer on the main timeline for your ActionScript, and call it something that reflects this (actions, for example). Now add the following two lines of code to the first frame of this new layer, via the Actions panel (F9):

```
globalStyleFormat.cell=0x666666;
globalStyleFormat.applyChanges();
```

Test it out and you will find that the calendar cells are now gray!

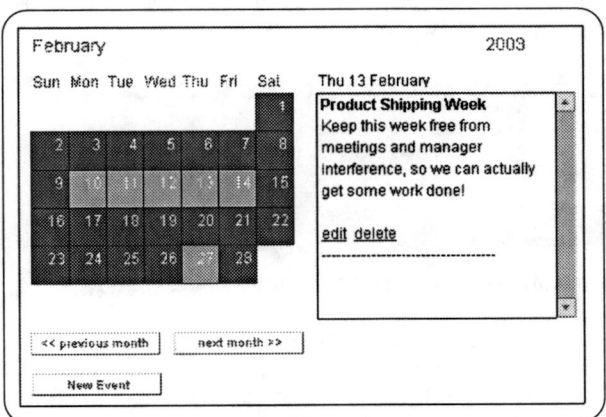

OK, so that wasn't too exciting – but these aren't the only changes you can make. The ScrollBar used on the event calendar text box is the standard Macromedia ScrollBar component and, accordingly, you can use the formatting options listed in the scrollbar reference. There are also a number of formatting options specific to this component:

Property	Description
globalStyleFormat.background	Background color
globalStyleFormat.dayNumber	Calendar cell number color
globalStyleFormat.cell	Calendar cell color
globalStyleFormat.cellBorder	Calendar cell border color
globalStyleFormat.cellHighlight	Highlighted cell color
globalStyleFormat.eventWindowBorder	Border color for the event entry window
globalStyleFormat.eventWindowBackground	Background color for the event entry window
globalStyleFormat.popupWindowBackground	Background color for the popup window

The component also has a method that lets you change the divider between different events in the event details text box. By default, a number of dashes (-----------), appears after the description for each event, to separate the details for multiple events on the same day:

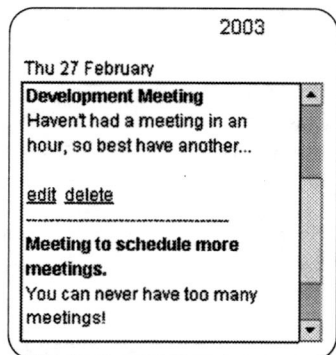

But you can change it to any string using the setEventDivider(). To see how this method, and some of the style properties mentioned above work, open up the file changing_colors.fla. First of all, note that we've given our component an instance name of myCalendar, as shown below, so that we can specifically link it to the setEventDivider() method:

The first frame of the actions layer contains the following code:

```
globalStyleFormat.face = 0x8098B0;
globalStyleFormat.highlight = 0xC0CCD8;
globalStyleFormat.highlight3D = 0xC0CCD8;
globalStyleFormat.darkshadow = 0x000000;
globalStyleFormat.shadow = 0x4E657C;
globalStyleFormat.arrow = 0x333333;
```

```
globalStyleFormat.foregroundDisabled = 0xC0CCD8;
globalStyleFormat.scrollTrack = 0xC0CCD8;
globalStyleFormat.focusRectInner = 0xDBDCE5;
globalStyleFormat.focusRectOuter = 0x9495A2;
globalStyleFormat.background = 0xEAEEF2;
globalStyleFormat.border = 0xFF6666;
globalStyleFormat.cell=0xFF66FF;
globalStyleFormat.cellHighlight=0x999933;
globalStyleFormat.eventWindowBorder=0xFF66FF;
globalStyleFormat.eventWindowBackground=0xC0CCD8;
globalStyleFormat.popupWindowBackground=0xC0CCD8;
//
globalStyleFormat.applyChanges();
//
myCalendar.setEventDivider("+++++++++++++++++");
```

This code results in a number of changes to the look of the calendar – test the FLA movie then check out the results:

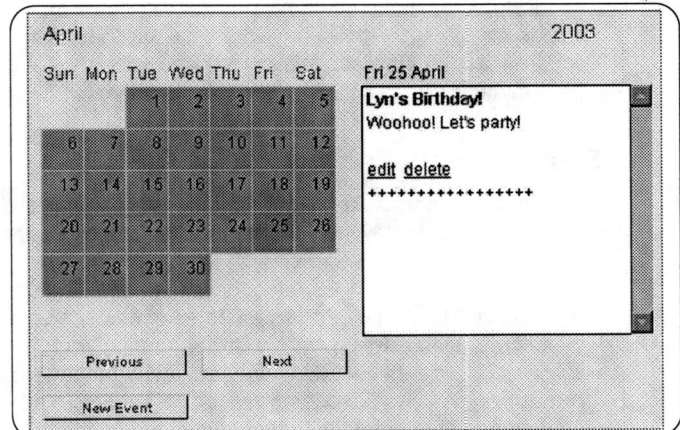

Naturally, you can also graphically modify, or skin, the elements of the component within the Library to take on whatever look and feel you desire! Remember, we briefly covered the process of skinning our components in the previous chapter.

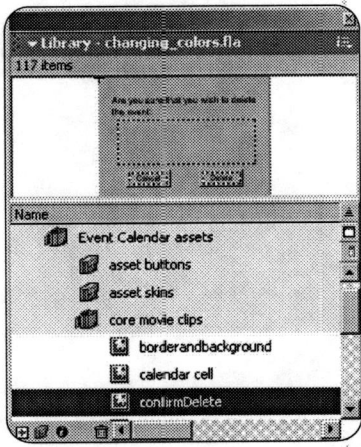

15

Storing data

If you've tested the event calendar component a couple of times, you may have noticed something interesting – Flash remembers any events that you've created. Even if you completely shut down your computer and restart, the events will still be there, provided you are testing the same Flash file.

This is because the method used to store the event data is set to `local`, through the store Data parameter. What this means is that the data is stored on your hard drive in what's known as a **shared object**, effectively a Flash cookie, which is a small file that permanently stores data on your computer. Obviously, this is useful for testing the component but you should be aware that this doesn't allow you to share your events calendar with other users. If you put the calender on a website with the data store set to local then every user that accesses the site will have a different calendar stored locally on their own computer. If you change your calendar then you are only changing it on your computer, not on the website.

This local data store may be useful if you want to provide users with their own personal calendar application. Indeed, it could be a useful tool for users in an office environment who don't have access to a desktop calendar application, or it may be used in an environment where only one computer is being used, such as a public kiosk terminal. However, in most cases you are going to want to use either a static or dynamic XML method to store your event data.

Storing events in a static XML file

The simplest solution to providing your events data to all users is to store the data within a file on the web server. For the events calendar, we can store data in an XML document that we load into Flash when the calendar is first displayed.

If you have FTP or network access to your web server, but don't have the rights to run server scripts or a database, then this is probably the option for you. All you have to do is create an XML document that contains all the event data, and set the component's store Data parameter to `xmlStatic`. The component will then look for a file called `events.xml` in the same folder as the Flash file and will load this into the calendar.

Let's take a look at an example of using a static XML file with the component – first, open up `events.xml` from the `xml_static` example folder from the download. This is a simple XML document containing some sample events data – take a look at the structure of this file by opening it up in your favorite text editor:

```
<<XML>> (events.xml)
1  <events>
2    <item id="0">
3      <title>Group Meeting</title>
4      <description>A chance to discuss how the project is going</description>
5      <startDate>2003-1-23</startDate>
6      <endDate>2003-1-23</endDate>
7    </item>
8    <item id="1">
9      <title>Planning week</title>
10     <description>Lots of planning and some research and development</description>
11     <startDate>2003-1-7</startDate>
12     <endDate>2003-1-11</endDate>
13   </item>
14   <item id="2">
15     <title>Mike&apos;s Birthday</title>
16     <description>The party starts here!</description>
17     <startDate>2003-1-28</startDate>
18     <endDate>2003-1-28</endDate>
19   </item>
20 </events>
```

You could probably create this document by hand in a text editor, but you don't need to. If you use the calendar with allow users to edit set to `true` as well as store data set to `xmlStatic` then you will have an extra button, called `Create XML`, next to the New Event button when you test the Flash movie – take a look at `xmlStaticDemo.swf`. With this example, when you have entered or updated your events, click on the Create XML button and it will display a text box containing the XML for the events data:

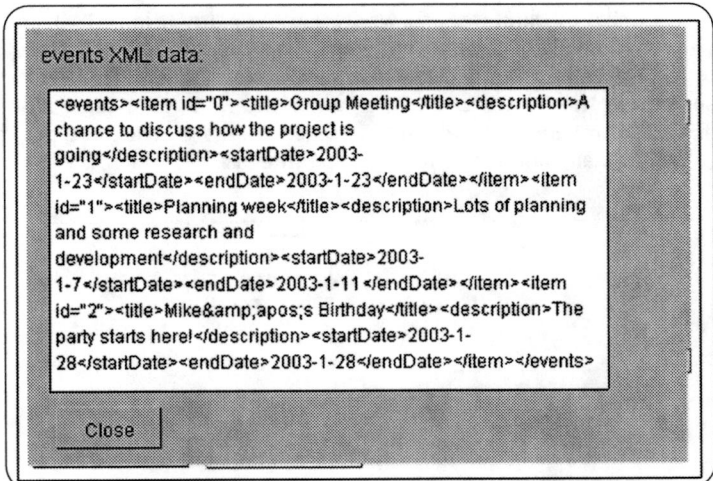

You can then select, copy, and paste this into a text editor and save as `events.xml`, then upload `events.xml` to your web server and your event calendar will be updated. Remember to save the `events.xml` file in the same folder on the web server as your SWF file. Using this method, you will need to replace the events.xml file every time you make a change to the events calendar.

This method will suit situations where most users will be browsing the calendar and the events don't need to be updated very often. In this scenario, you'd have two different web pages containing the SWF:

- One page will have the allow users to edit option set to `false` – this is the page that most users access, so they can view the calendar but not change it.

- The second page will have the allow users to edit option set to `true` – this is the page that the administrator can access to update the calendar.

However, uploading to the server every time you change or add an event may prove a little tedious. If you have the rights to run scripts and create files on your server then you should definitely look at the next option.

Storing events in a dynamic XML file

If you have the rights to run server-side scripts on your web server, such as PHP, Perl, or ASP scripts, then you can eliminate the need to upload the XML data. Instead, we can send the event data to a middleware script that writes directly to a file on the web server.

Many web-hosting providers allow users to run PHP scripts on their account. If you haven't used it before, you should check with your hosting provider to find out if you can run PHP scripts. You can also find out more about PHP, as well as download it to test on your own computer, from the PHP site www.php.net.

To use this data store method you need to set the store data parameter of the event calendar component to `xmlDynamic`. As with the previous method, we store the event data in an XML document that we load into Flash when the calendar is first displayed. The difference here is that instead of the Create XML button, we have a Save Data button. Clicking this will send the events data formatted as an XML document to a server-side script that replaces the events data with the updated XML data. So every time you click Save Data, the `events.xml` file gets updated. Here's a schematic diagram that shows the communication flow between Flash in the web browser, the PHP sever script, and the XML data:

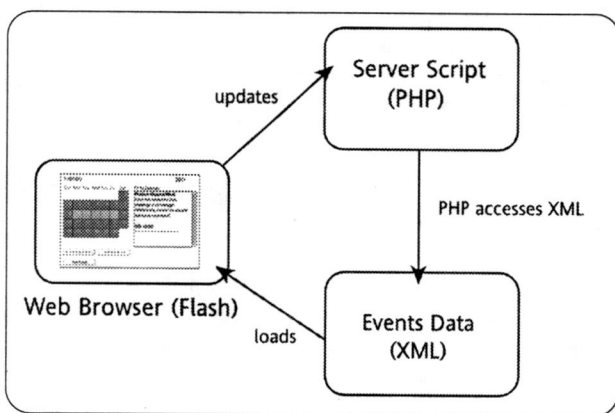

For those interested, it might be worth checking out either *Foundation PHP for Flash* (ISBN 1-903450-16-0) or *Advanced PHP for Flash* (ISBN 1-904344-03-8), both available from friends of ED.

In the `xml_dynamic` folder of this chapter's example files (in the download), you'll find the PHP script file `generatexml.php` – this will take the XML data and save it on the server as `events.xml`. If you wish to use a scripting language other than PHP, then you'll of course need to create your own script that takes the submitted XML data and saves it to the web server – but the general principles used here are the same.

For reference, the code for the `generatexml.php` PHP file is shown below:

```php
<?php
$filename = "events.xml";
$fp = fopen( $filename,"w");
fwrite ( $fp, "$HTTP_RAW_POST_DATA" );
fclose( $fp );
?>
```

By default, the component sends the data to a script called `generatexml.php`. If you want to change the name of the script that is called, then you can use the `setXMLscript()` method of the event calendar component. This should be passed a string containing the name of the script that will save the XML data. For example, if your server-side script for saving the data was called `savedata.cgi` and the components instance name is set to `myCalendar`, then the code would be as follows:

```
myCalendar.setXMLscript("savedata.cgi");
```

To finish this chapter, we'll provide an overview of the other public methods that are available when using this component.

Component methods

The component has a number of methods that may be useful. All are used in the form:

```
componentInstanceName.methodName()
```

These methods are also documented in the Reference panel within Flash, accessible once the component has been installed.

Command	Description
`generateXML()`	**Method**; generates the XML for the current events calendar. This is equivalent to clicking on the `Save Data` button if in `xmlDynamic` mode, or clicking on `Create XML` if in `xmlStatic` mode. **Parameters**: none **Returns**: nothing
`getDisplayedMonth()`	**Method**; returns the name of the currently displayed month (for example, March).

Command	Description
	Parameters: none
	Returns: string
getDisplayedYear()	**Method**; returns the name of the currently displayed year (for example, 2003).
	Parameters: none
	Returns: string
getEventDivider()	**Method**; returns the string used to divide the event descriptions.
	Parameters: none
	Returns: string
getEventsFilename()	**Method**; returns a string representing the name of the XML document containing the events data. By default this is set to events.xml.
	Parameters: none
	Returns: string
getXMLscript()	**Method**; returns a string containing the name of the server script that the XML events data is sent to. By default this is set to generatexml.php.
	Parameters: none
	Returns: string
resetMonth()	**Method**; redraws the currently displayed month.
	Parameters: none
	Returns: nothing
setButtonTitles(nextTitle,prevTitle)	**Method**; sets the names of the Next and Previous month buttons.
	Parameters: string, string
	Returns: nothing
setEventDivider(mystring)	**Method**; sets the string used to divide the event descriptions.
	Parameters: string
	Returns: nothing
setEventsFilename(mystring)	**Method**; sets the name of the XML document containing the events data.
	Parameters: string
	Returns: nothing
setTextFormatting(myTextFormat)	**Method**; sets the text formatting for main text fields.
	Parameters: a TextFormat object
	Returns: nothing
setXMLscript(myString)	**Method**; sets the name of the server script that is called to save the XML event data.
	Parameters: string
	Returns: nothing

Command	Description
showDay(integer)	**Method**; displays the event details for the specific day of the current month. **Parameters**: integer (day between 1 and 31) **Returns**: nothing
showNextMonth()	**Method**; advances the calendar one month forward. **Parameters**: none **Returns**: nothing
showPreviousMonth()	**Method**; moves the calendar one month backward. **Parameters**: none **Returns**: nothing

Josh Dura

Josh started his career like many web developers have done before him – designing simple HTML pages with little graphics here and there. About 3 years ago, Josh started coding ColdFusion and learning some basic OOP skills, which drew him to ActionScript. Josh currently works for ReadyHosting.com out of Richardson, Texas, doing their web and graphic/print design work. On the side, he looks after his own site, www.joshdura.com. He also currently owns and runs Dura Media, LLC (www.duramedia.com) with his brother Daniel.

"I dedicate this book to my brother, because he was really the one who introduced and walked me through the computer world. I would also like to personally thank Shauna Dudley, Keran McKenzie, Brian Monnone, Samuel Granato, everyone from Flashkit, Actionscripts.org, and Were-Here, and everyone who posts on my weblog. Last but certainly not least, Mom and Dad. Without you, this would have never been possible."

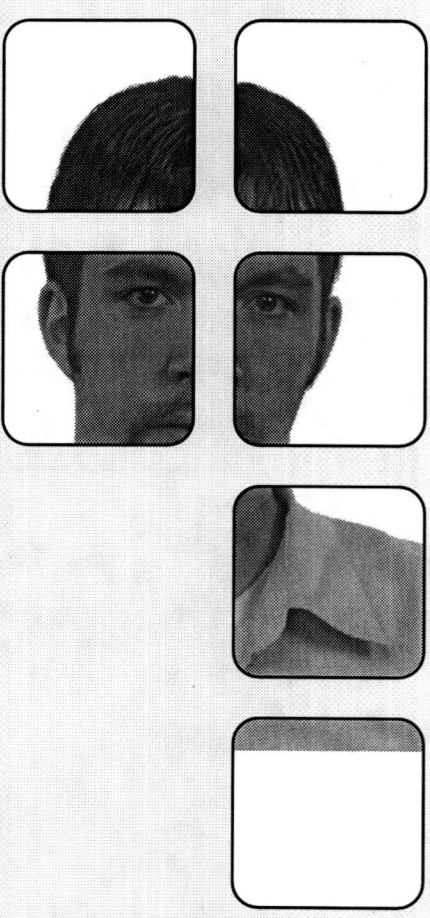

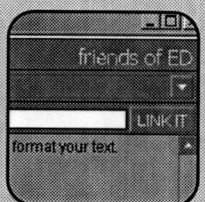

Component 2

Text Editor

This component enables you to quickly and easily include all of the functionality of a Rich Text formatter in your projects. In addition, you can convert your formatted text into HTML to cut and paste into your applications.

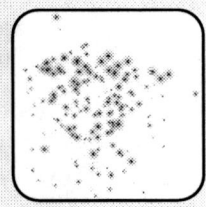

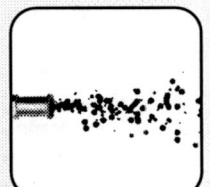
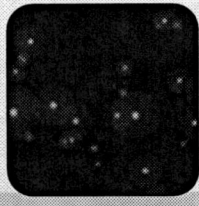

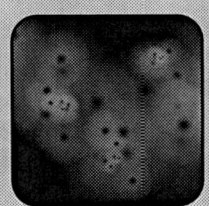

Recently we've seen many great examples of Flash application development on the Internet:

- Colin Moock's Address Book Application - www.macromedia.com/desdev/mx/flash/articles/addressbook.html
- PhilterDesign Flash Blog RSS Reader - www.philterdesign.com/dev/flashFeeds/
- Ericd.net's Flash Forward Guide - www.ericd.net/guide/
- Face Card - http://host.mp4.com
- Macromedia Pet Market - www.macromedia.com/desdev/mx/blueprint/
- Broadmoor Hotel Reservation System – www.ihotelier.com/onescreen/onescreen.cfm

Those who designed these applications were, in many cases, required to hand code their own interface elements: date pickers, list boxes, tabbed windows, scroll bars, check boxes, and so on. Flash MX components make design and development of projects in Flash as simple as many of the visual authoring environments, such as Microsoft Visual Studio for example. When you drag the component on to the stage, all functions, classes, and parameters contained within it are instantly available to be manipulated either dynamically at runtime or manually during the design phase.

Now that we can actually integrate our components with different ActionScript commands, and create our own prototypes for each component, it's pretty straightforward to dynamically customize components through code. Component design and implementation is one of the most powerful, though sometimes underestimated, elements of Flash MX. It allows programmers and designers to implement movie clip objects that provide a plug-and-play input and output mechanism for any Flash movie. This will allow Flash to move closer to being a tool for not only motion graphic design, but also a full-featured application development environment.

The TextFormat object is another feature of Flash MX that Macromedia have done a very nice job developing. It includes all the basic text editing characteristics that you can find in the Flash authoring environment: bold text, italicize text, underline text, bullet text, various fonts, font sizes, and so on. Accordingly, some of my early experiments with Flash MX involved applying and implementing components and the TextFormat object. Slowly, I realized it would be possible to create a feature-rich text editor interface, utilizing these two great features: components and the TextFormat object. In this chapter, I'll be discussing the set up and use of my text editor component.

When I began designing my component, there were a few examples that sparked my interest. One example was Stuart Schoneveld's rich text/HTML editor, which illustrated some of the features that I required of my own design. However, I decided from the start that every piece of code I wrote would be my own. The actual coding of the Text Editor only took about 5 days (between a full-time job and freelance work) and was surprisingly fairly straightforward.

Using the text editor

As is usual with the components in this book, you can open up the text editor by installing the textEditor.mxp file via the Macromedia Extension Manager, or by simply opening up TextEditor.fla from the download. In either case, after dragging the component from the Components panel or the Library, it will appear in full on the stage:

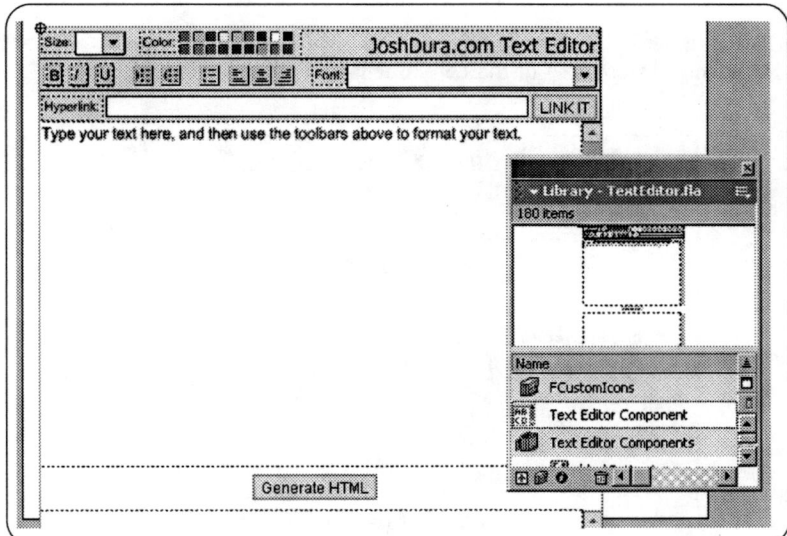

Setting the parameters

Through the parameters tab of the Property inspector, you can customize two properties:

The first option of the component is the Title – this changes the main title of the text editor to whatever you want it to be, so you can customize the component to fit your particular application. The second available customization is the Visible? Option, which just sets the visibility of the component to true or false. For the moment, just stick with the default values and go ahead and test your movie (Control > Test Movie):

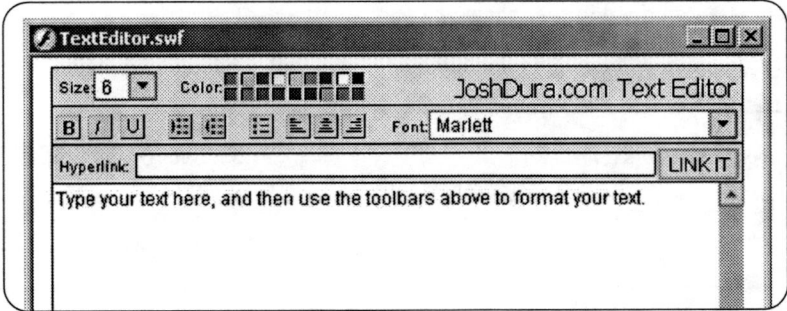

The user interface is rather intuitive, so just spend a moment familiarizing yourself with all of its elements. The features included in this release of the component include the following:

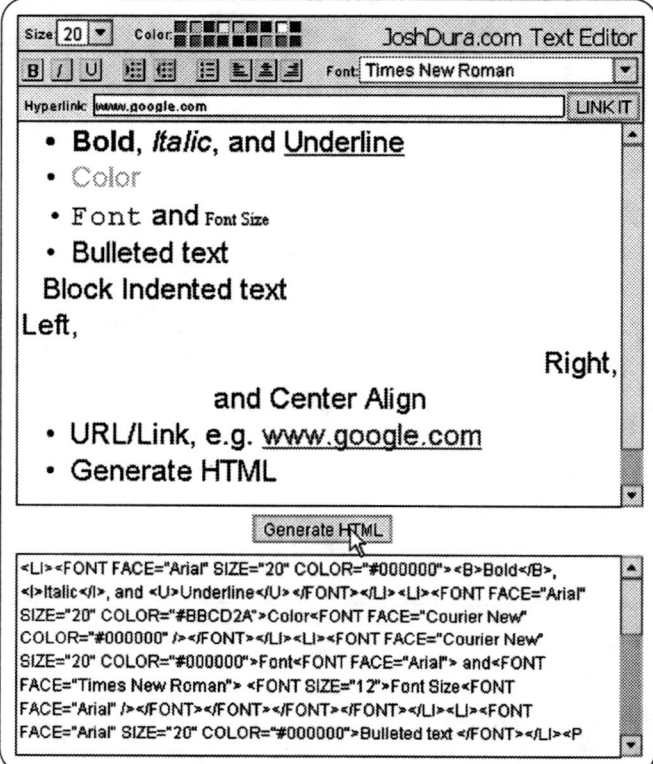

Customization via ActionScript

Now that we're comfortable with the basic use of this component, we're ready to move on to a slightly more advanced topic. Probably the best way to edit the look and feel of the text editor is to use ActionScript. With this component, I've included a number of additional public methods — all are used in this form and are described in the following table:

```
componentInstanceName.methodName()
```

Method	Description
setButtonBackground()	Set the background color of the buttons on the toolbar.
setButtonBackgroundActive()	Set the active button background color (when the button is pressed and stays down).

Method	Description
setButtonContentColor()	Set the button content color (inside the button).
setButtonDarkShadow()	Set the dark shadow color of the buttons.
setButtonLightShadow()	Set the light shadow color of the buttons.
setEditorBackground()	Set the editor background color (the editable text area).
setScrollBackground()	Set the ScrollBar's background color.
setTextColor()	Set the text color of any text on the toolbar.
setTitle()	Set the title of the text editor.
setToolbarBackground()	Set the background color of the toolbars.
setToolbarBorder()	Set the border color of the toolbars and the rest of the text editor.

These methods are very easy to use – one line of code will cover each property. Open up TextEditor_customize.fla from the download to see some of these methods in action. First of all, notice that I've given the text editor component an instance name of textEditor1. Next, take a look at the code on frame 1 of the actions layer:

```
textEditor1.setTitle("friends of ED");
textEditor1.setButtonBackground(0x5B84AD);
textEditor1.setButtonBackgroundActive(0x84A3C2);
textEditor1.setButtonContentColor(0xFFFFFF);
textEditor1.setButtonLightShadow(0xADC2D6);
textEditor1.setButtonDarkShadow(0x336699);
textEditor1.setTextColor(0xFFFFFF);
textEditor1.setToolbarBackground(0x5B84AD);
textEditor1.setToolbarBorder(0x666666);
textEditor1.setEditorBackground(0xADC2D6);
textEditor1.setScrollBackground(0xADC2D6);
```

Now hit CTRL/COMMAND+ENTER (PC/Mac) to test this movie – it should look like this: (see over page)

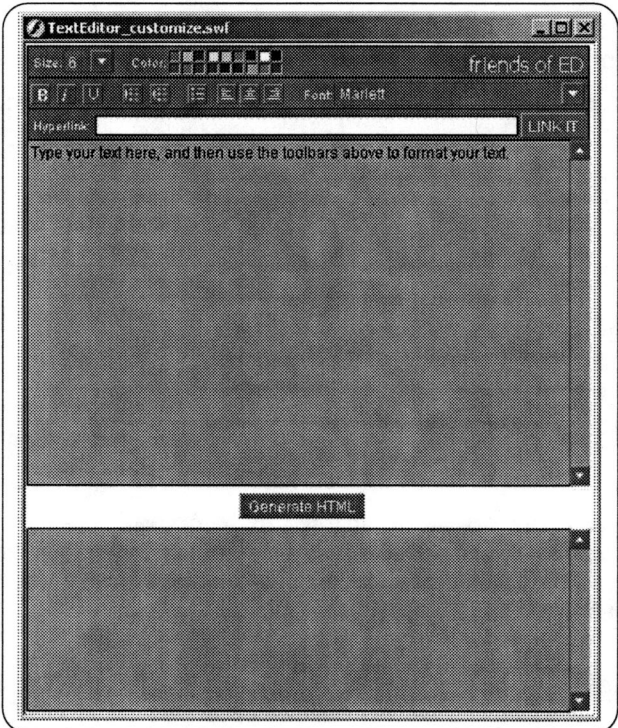

So, all you have to do to customize any bit of this is just change the hexadecimal color values specified for each method. Similarly, for the `setTitle()` method, you just change what is inside the parentheses to your desired title.

Additionally, if you want to change the background color of the toolbars, those are editable in the main component document. The Scrollbars and ComboBoxes are the default Macromedia components, so if you use the ActionScript reference that Macromedia has given for those, they should work as normal. As for the color selector, you can easily edit the color selections by editing the symbols of the specific colors. Then in the ActionScript of the main component (double-click on its icon in the Library and then look at the code on frame 1 of the Actions layer), change the RGB value for the code of the relevant changed color button:

```
474  colorButton1.onRelease = function(){
475      Selection.setFocus(textIns_txt);
476      Selection.setSelection(begin, end);
477      myTextFormat = currentFormat;
478      myTextFormat.color = "0xFF0000";
479      textIns_txt.setTextFormat(begin, end, myTextFormat);
480  }
481
482  colorButton2.onRelease = function(){
483      Selection.setFocus(textIns_txt);
484      Selection.setSelection(begin, end);
485      myTextFormat = currentFormat;
486      myTextFormat.color = "0x00FF00";
487      textIns_txt.setTextFormat(begin, end, myTextFormat);
488  }
```

Finally, you can in fact graphically edit any of the symbols within the component (for instance, buttons and icons on the toolbar) directly through the Library. For example, buttons like Bold, Italic, Underline, Align, and so on, all have the background button as a symbol, so when you change that, it changes all of them. If you want to make all of the buttons have a different background color, light shadow color, dark shadow color, and so on, all you have to do is edit one symbol in the Text Editor Components folder in the Library, and they will all change.

Text editors in the real world

There are many different potential uses for this application in a real world business environment. I have already been contacted by a couple of businesses asking me to customize the code of this component to fit their application needs. One use would be as a HTML editor for basic entries into a newspaper classified ad system. The user could simply enter in the classified ad that they want displayed, format it through the options the customer chooses, and then submit the ad. Before the ad could be submitted, Flash would need to convert the text into basic HTML (HTML 1.0 is the only version Flash supports at present) and then the application could submit the ad through a basic PHP mail form.

Another use would be to use this component as an editor for intranet pages - maybe a company requires an application that allows even inexperienced employees to create basic HTML pages. The webmaster could then either write a script to automatically insert this code into a template, or they could insert it in the template manually.

As you can tell, there are any number of uses for this component in the real world, and with future upgrades it could become a very powerful tool indeed.

Taking it further

The future of this component holds numerous opportunities. I've been coming up with ideas to extend the simple text editor every day, so keep an eye on my website www.joshdura.com for updates. Features that I'd like to add in future releases include the following:

- Scalability – so that the buttons and ScrollBars keep their size as you scale the component
- Internal ActionScript reference and complete documentation
- Export/Save to a file
- Import of XML and text (.txt) files
- Better Color Selector
- Image Input
- Smart cut and paste (which maintains formatting)

Building this component forced me to learn how to utilize Object Oriented Programming (OOP). When applied correctly, OOP can provide you with a much cleaner and more robust component. Instead of having functions scattered throughout the movie, they are grouped together making it easier for you, the developer, to make changes to different environment variables, which in turn can affect the visual layout and functionality of the component. It also increases the ease with which you can allow the component to be changed at runtime by other users, or during the design process by designers using your component.

For reference, here's a list of excellent Flash OOP resources:

- Flashcoders list – http://chattyfig.figleaf.com/
- Robin Debreuil OOP Tutorial – www.debreuil.com/docs/ch01_Intro.htm
- Object Oriented Programming with ActionScript – www.wheelmaker.org/
- Samuel Wan – www.samuelwan.com/information/
- Branden Hall – www.waxpraxis.org
- ActionScript.org – www.actionscript.org

While creating this component, I found out how fun it actually is to construct something reasonably large-scale like this (once you get the hang of the scripting!). I'd like to seriously recommend and encourage anyone out there to just jump head first into the world of component creation.

Jon Steer

Jon has been working as a web developer for nearly five years, after graduating from Durham University with a degree in Economics. He is technical director of Durham Associates Ltd (www.da-group.co.uk) a marketing communications company in the north-east of England and admits to being far happier working with code than with pretty pictures! His main focus is server side technologies, especially PHP and mySQL, and he is always looking for different ways to put these to work. Jon lives near Durham with his wife and two daughters to whom special thanks go for their enormous support and encouragement.

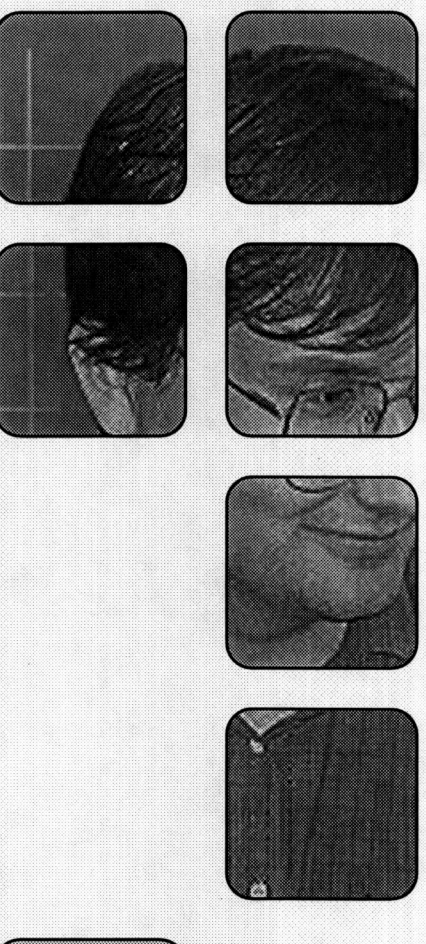

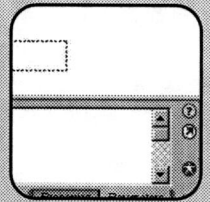

Component 3

XML News
Ticker

This component provides a very flexible ticker. The content can be read from an XML file or generated by a server side script. The appearance of the text and the speed and direction of scroll are all customizable using simple paramaters. More advanced parameters include easing of movement and fading.

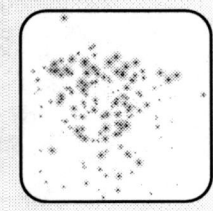

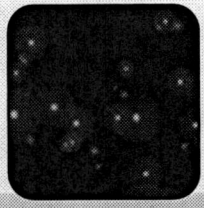

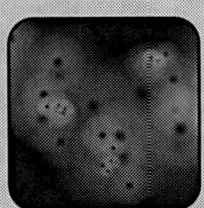

Websites today need to hit the visitor with up-to-date information. This serves a number of purposes. Firstly, it shows the visitor that the site is well maintained and that the content is likely to be always relevant. It also encourages the visitor to bookmark the site and keep coming back to read the latest information. The impact of an up-to-date site will leave visitors with a positive impression of your site – and that has to be good for business!

One of the most common forms of continually updated information is of course news. Whether it's your favorite football team's latest result or a press release announcing the launch of the latest killer software, delivering up to the minute news is what the web does best.

The news section of a website, listing the latest newsworthy information, and driven by your chosen server-side scripts and database is all very well – but how do you drive people to that part of the site, and how do you use this rich source of information across the whole site?

This is where the news ticker comes into play. A ticker provides a dynamic way of showing the user a number of punchy headlines to draw them into the main news area of your site. The ticker can do all this in a fairly small area by rotating or ticking through the latest headlines.

So the benefits of using a ticker are pretty obvious, and in fact there are a number of ways of implementing one, so why choose Flash? In many ways, it's simply down to personal preference and where your skills lie. However, as we shall soon see, a Flash MX component is an ideal way to have a single object to manage our content.

The simplest way to create a ticker is probably using the <MARQUEE> HTML tag introduced by Microsoft (see http://msdn.microsoft.com/workshop/author/dhtml/reference/objects/marquee.asp for more information) and supported by recent versions of Mozilla. The drawbacks are that many browsers don't support it and it isn't very controllable. This approach also requires you to include the headlines you want to display and the associated links directly in the HTML page. To pull this information out of a database and place it in the page will require a bit of server-side scripting on your page.

The next step up is probably a JavaScript-based ticker. If you do a quick web search, you will find quite a number of tickers written in JavaScript ranging from the very basic to the overly complex. Browser compatibility can also be a problem here and only the best JavaScript implementations will be universally browser friendly. Like the marquee approach, most tickers of this type will need the headlines defined as variables in the JavaScript code on the page. Mixing client-side and server-side scripts in this way can lead to sticky problems!

Then we have Java. Again, a quick search of the web will throw up a number of Java applet tickers of varying usefulness – some will require the headlines and links set as parameters, but some will read the data from external sources and do the job very well.

So why Flash? Well, my Java coding isn't really up to it and I've always found Java applets to be slow and unreliable at the best of times. Flash provides a straightforward way of reading in data from XML files, which is ideal for this purpose. Although we won't really be pushing the boundaries of technology with this component, it will have some neat animation and display features. Packaging the ticker as a component gives enough control for most scenarios right at the fingertips of the designer, via the component parameters. Anyone needing to tweak the ticker a bit further can just dip into the code and make whatever changes are required.

Using the XML ticker

With the design of this component, I've attempted to provide a wide enough range of options for many different uses, and also a foundation for more advanced ticker systems.

Let's take a look at a simple example of this component in use – open up newsTicker.fla from this chapter's source files in the download. Here you'll see that I've already dragged a few instances of the component from the Library onto the stage and set the width and height of each instance using the Property inspector. Now select any instance of the ticker component on the stage and take a look at the available parameters in the Property inspector:

Setting the parameters

We can also read and edit these parameters in full from the Component Parameters panel (Window > Component Parameters):

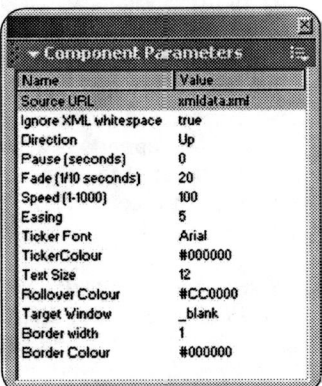

Now, the only parameter that we actually need to change for the component to work is the SourceURL parameter which must point to a valid XML file. In the `newsTicker.fla` example file, I've preset this parameter to `xmldata.xml` – this refers to the XML file that contains the data we want to load into our ticker. Note that in this case the URL specifies an XML file located in the same directory as the Flash file. We'll look at the structure of the XML in the next section.

Now go ahead and test this Flash movie (Control > Test Movie) to get a feel for the finished result:

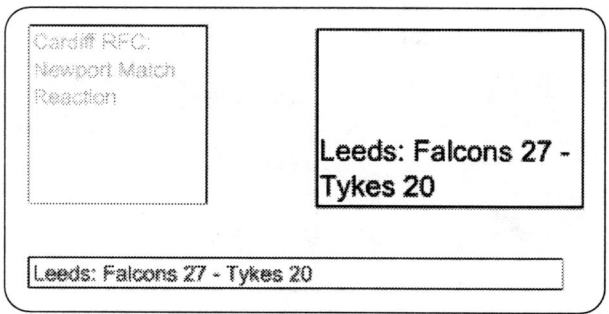

OK, I've probably overloaded this movie with tickers, but I'm sure you get the general idea of how useful they can be. Each headline will move into the ticker area one at a time and pause for a specified number of seconds before being cleared to make way for the next headline. When all headlines have been used the ticker loops back to the first headline. Let's now return to the Flash authoring environment to look at some of the other options that are available, ensuring that we understand exactly how the ticker functions.

The Speed and Direction of the ticker scrolling can both be set using parameters. The speed can range from 1 to 1000 – this number determines how many times each second the position of the ticker is updated. The direction of movement can be one of Left, Right, Up, or Down, with the default being Left.

As well as the speed of the ticker, the movement can also be controlled using the Easing parameter. A value of 0 means no easing and the ticker moves at a constant speed. A value greater than 0 will cause the ticker to slow down as it approaches its final position, a good value for this parameter is around 10. Note that a value of 1 will cause the ticker to stay in the same position as it switches between headlines.

The Pause parameter controls the number of seconds that the ticker will wait once it has reached its final position. After pausing, the ticker will fade over a length of time set using the Fade parameter.

The ticker supports headlines that wrap on to multiple lines. If the headlines are longer than the width of the ticker at the chosen text size then they will wrap on to multiple lines, as long as the ticker is tall enough to accommodate the extra lines. This is more likely to be used when the ticker is placed as a column and the direction of movement is either up or down.

You can also customize the appearance and size of the ticker text through the TickerFont, TickerColour, Rollover Colour, and Text Size parameters. The appearance of the ticker itself can be specified simply by changing the width and height of the component, keeping in mind the size of the text and the possible length of the headlines that you are likely to use. Note that the TickerFont requires that the font used must be embedded in the movie and set as Export for ActionScript in the linkage properties of the font in the library. The default font, Arial, is already embedded within the component.

XML data

As I have alluded to above (and its name is another big giveaway!), the XML news ticker component gets its content data using XML. There are two pieces of information required for each ticker item: the text of the ticker item itself and the URL to navigate to if that headline is clicked on. The structure of the XML is fairly basic – for instance, take a look at the sample XML file that we used in the previous example:

```xml
<<XML>> (xmldata.xml)
1  <xmlticker>
2      <tickeritem>
3          <headline>Leicester: Bristol deny Tigers</headline>
4          <link>http://www.sportnetwork.net/main/s103/st13765.php</link>
5      </tickeritem>
6      <tickeritem>
7          <headline>Leeds: Falcons 27 - Tykes 20</headline>
8          <link>http://www.sportnetwork.net/main/s102/st13825.php</link>
9      </tickeritem>
10     <tickeritem>
11         <headline>Cardiff RFC: Newport Match Reaction</headline>
12         <link>http://www.sportnetwork.net/main/s170/st13817.php</link>
13     </tickeritem>
14 </xmlticker>
15
```

The base node is `<xmlticker>`, and the only child node parsed is `<tickeritem>`. In turn, the only child nodes of `<tickeritem>` that are acted on are `<headline>` and `<link>`, both of which are text nodes. The component parses the XML data and creates two arrays – one for the headlines and one for the links. The source XML file is controlled by the SourceURL parameter that we mentioned earlier – this can be any URL under the same domain name as the Flash movie.

Loading from an external data source

If you want to use a news feed from an external source such as a news provider (for example, see www.moreover.com) then you will need to use a server-side script on the same server as your Flash movie to act as an intermediary. The script reads the data from a URL on the news provider's site and passes it on to the Flash movie. The data is now deemed secure by the Flash movie as it appears to be coming from the same domain as the movie.

If the XML data from a remote site is correctly formatted for use by the component, then we can use a simple server script (PHP, ASP, Perl, and so on) to read the data from the remote site and feed to the Flash movie that calls it. The name/URL of this script should then be used as the sourceURL parameter of the component. For example, the following PHP script would enable us to pull data from the URL www.mynewsprovider.co.uk/xmlnews:

```php
<?php
        $news_url = "http://www.mynewsprovider.co.uk/xmlnews";
        readfile($news_url);
?>
```

This use of a script as an intermediary will also be necessary if the XML files that you are generating or pulling from a news provider are not compatible with the XML structure required by this component. It is a fairly simple task in most server-side languages to parse an XML file and then create a new XML file that meets the requirements of the component.

In fact, there are two ways that this component can be used to present current headlines from your news database. The first is to point the source URL at a server-side script, such as a PHP script like that mentioned above – this will query the news database and retrieve a number of headlines and links. The script can then format the data according to the appropriate XML structure and return it to the Flash movie. This way is ideal for small-to-medium levels of traffic, but for very busy sites it can lead to a lot of queries and place a heavy load on the database.

A more suitable method for high traffic sites is to run the server-side script as a scheduled process at regular intervals. This could be every ten minutes or every hour, or even every day depending on how often the news database is updated. The script will perform the same query and format the results in the same way as mentioned previously, but instead of returning the XML data to the Flash movie it stores the XML data in a file on the server. The Flash movie can then request the static XML file to get the latest snapshot of the database. Using this method, the load placed on the server is much smaller as the query is only performed once.

How it works

Without going into too much detail, it's worth discussing how the XML news ticker component actually works. Accordingly, in this section we'll show the main operations of the ActionScript that makes up the component. For those interested, you can examine the inner working of the component by double-clicking on its icon in the Library and then studying the script on frame 1 of the code layer. Here, you'll see that nearly all of the component's operations are broken down into individual functions to make the code easier to read and easier to extend. The following flow diagram represents this ActionScript:

For completeness, let's briefly describe each of these functions:

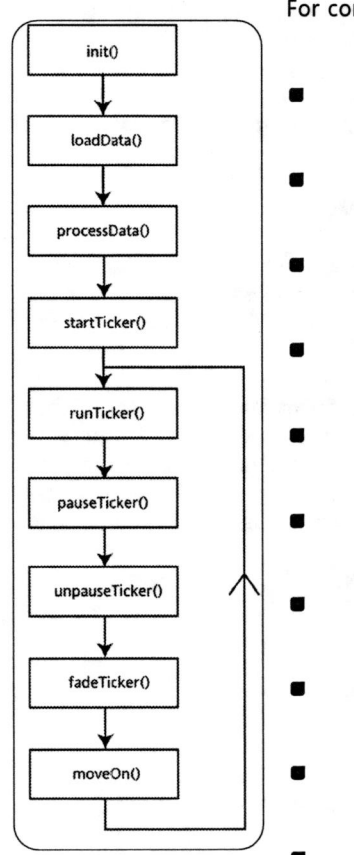

- `init()` – Sets up the basic properties of the ticker, the text functions, and creates the mask.

- `loadData()` – Creates an XML object and uses it to read from the source URL.

- `processData()` – Called by the `onLoad` event of the XML object, reads the data into two arrays.

- `startTicker()` – Sets the `setInterval` function to call `runTicker()` repeatedly.

- `runTicker()` – Moves ticker until headline reaches end, then calls `pauseTicker()`.

- `pauseTicker()` – Sets the ticker state to paused, uses `setInterval` to call `unpauseTicker()` after the required length of time.

- `unpauseTicker()` – Sets up another `setInterval` handler to call `fadeTicker()`.

- `fadeTicker()` – Fades ticker item by reducing alpha to 0 then calls `moveOn()` and returns the ticker state to play.

- `moveOn()` – Updates the text with the new headline and returns it to starting position.

- `runTicker()` – Continues as before...

There is also a method stopTicker() that isn't used, but could be called from elsewhere in the Flash movie to stop the ticker. Calling startTicker() would then restart the ticker from the first headline. Take a look at newsTicker_buttons.fla in the download – a bonus example file that demonstrates how to incorporate the news ticker with start and stop buttons using these two methods.

Adding more public methods with which the component could be controlled pragmatically from the host Flash movie would be a useful way to extend the functionality of this component.

Taking things further

There are many ways in which this component could be developed, and these fall into two general areas: improving the *look* of the ticker and enhancing its *flexibility*.

Some examples from my 'to do' list for improving the look of the ticker component include:

- As well as the four directions currently available, there could be many more transitions. For example, having the text starting as a speck and growing as if moving towards the viewer.

- More control over the look of the ticker itself would be useful. At present, the border around the ticker can be controlled using parameters; it would be easy enough to add parameters to control the background colour of the ticker, and even to add a background image loaded from an external file.

Finally, here are a couple of ideas for improving the flexibility of the XML ticker:

- Override parameters in the XML file – to allow more control over the ticker without editing the Flash file, a second type of child node could be added to the base `<xmlticker>` node that could include parameter names and new values for those parameters. When the XML file is read into the Flash movie, the new parameter values could be applied.

- More support for Flash sites – the current component is perfect for mainly HTML sites but could be made friendlier for Flash sites if the `onPress` action for the headlines was more easily customizable. If it was possible to set variables, move between frames, or even request the full news story as XML when a headline is clicked, then the component could easily be used in Flash-based news sites. Instead of opening a browser window to view a web page for the full story, the user could see the full story within the same Flash file as the ticker.

Brandon Williams

Michael Brandon Williams is a freshman year mathematics major at New York University. His mathematics focus has been real analysis, graph theory, combinatorics, and number theory. His computer science experience is based on programming design, object-oriented programming, and problem solving. In his spare time, he helps run the math forum at Were-Here (www.were-here.com) under the name of ahab, and works for Eyeland Studios (www.eyeland.com) as a games programmer.

Component 4
Tool Tip

The three D's of why this component is good: Drag, Drop, Done. After installing the tool tip simply drag it from the Components panel, drop it to the movie clip you want to have a tool tip, and be done with it. With such an easy to use, versatile component how could you not afford to give some of your elements more explanation for the user?

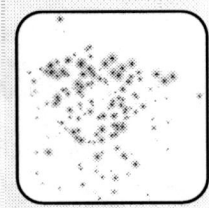

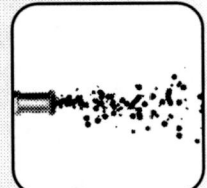
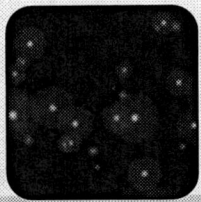

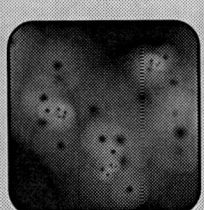

One of the most practical parts of any application is a tool tip. It allows you to attach small pieces of information anywhere, and do so without cluttering the screen. You can use a tool tip on anything from buttons that seem slightly ambiguous by themselves, to navigation hotspots that might need a little bit more explanation than what meets the eye. You can even incorporate them with other components, for instance you might add a tool tip message to the DraggablePane component (from the Flash UI Components Set 2) to ensure that users are made aware of the fact that they can drag the pane to wherever they choose.

In fact, this tool tip component can handle any practical amount of information; so don't be scared to cram an entire paragraph in the tool tip if it fits your needs – you can even try to come up with some less obvious applications for this component, like strategy hints in a Flash game or adding editorial comments in a Flash Text Editor. For the moment, let's take a look at the basic usage of the tool tip component.

Using the component

You can install the component using the Macromedia Extension Manager by opening the file MBW_Component_Set.mxp, which you'll find in the download that accompanies this book (or simply look in the Library of this chapter's example FLAs). Once installed, you'll find the component, FtoolTip, in the Components panel of the Flash MX authoring environment under MBW Component Set.

In most scenarios, you need only drag and drop an instance of the tool tip from the Components panel or Library onto the stage. If you already have the component, movie clip, button, or whatever you want to attach it to ready, then drop the component on top of its target and it will snap onto the target's top left corner:

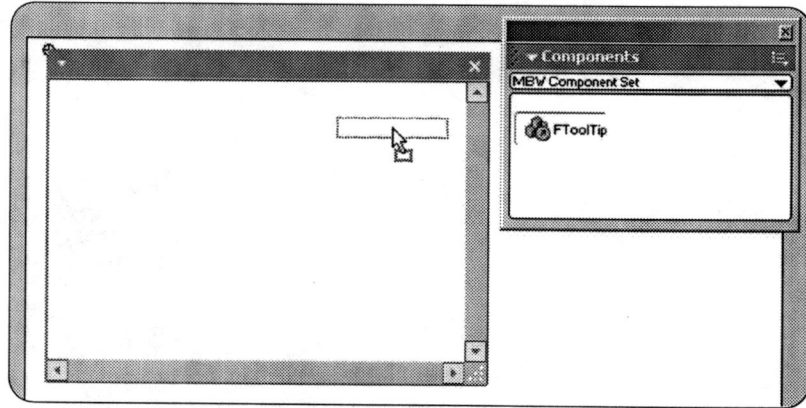

Once you've done this, and you test your movie, you've automatically given that movie clip the default tool tip:

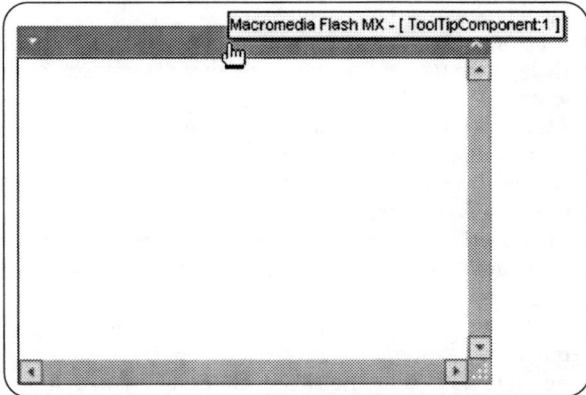

You can change a tool tip's target by either dragging and dropping it onto another movie clip, or editing the tool tip's parameters – more on this in the next section. As you can see, by default the tool tip takes on all the attributes that a standard Windows tool tip does. In the simplest cases, you can make use of the tool tip by changing only the text that appears in it (via the Tool Tip Text parameter – see below). However, to get the most out of your tool tip you'll probably want to set up and customize some of the other component parameters too. And for more adventurous modifications, you can even use ActionScript – we'll look at the necessary techniques in a later section on customization.

Setting the parameters

Once you have a component on the stage, you can edit a number of its attributes through the Property inspector or the Component Parameters panel. Select Window > Component Parameters:

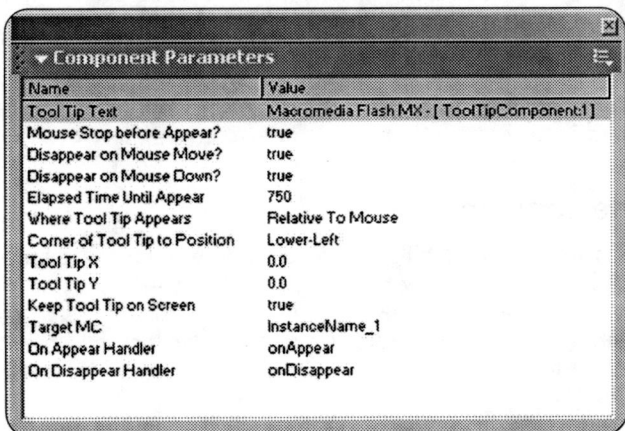

These parameters are described overleaf:

- **Tool Tip Text** – A string specifying the text that shows up in the tool tip.
- **Mouse Stop before Appear?** – A Boolean value that determines if you want the viewer to have to keep their mouse still over the target before the tool tip appears.
- **Disappear on Mouse Move?** – A Boolean value that determines if you want the tool tip to disappear when the mouse moves.
- **Disappear on Mouse Down?** – A Boolean value that determines if you want the tool tip to disappear when the mouse is pressed.
- **Elapsed Time Until Appear** – The amount of time, in milliseconds, that must pass before the tool tip appears. Note that this value is measured from the point when all pre-imposed conditions are met.
- **Where Tool Tip Appears** – This value determines from what point the tool tip's position should be measured from. If you chose `Relative to Mouse`, then the tool tip will appear at a certain distance from the mouse. On the other hand, choosing `Relative to Target` makes the tool tip appear a certain distance from the target's center (see also the **Tool Tip X** and **Tool Tip Y** parameters, below).
- **Corner of Tool Tip to Position** – This parameter specifies which corner of the tool tip you want to position. For example, Windows usually positions the lower-left corner of the tool tip just a little above the mouse.
- **Tool Tip X**, **Tool Tip Y** – These two numeric values determine that 'certain distance' specified earlier. If you want the lower-left corner of the tool tip to be right at the mouse cursor, you would use `Lower-Left` for the previous parameter, and `0.0` for both of these parameters.
- **Keep Tool Tip on Screen** – A Boolean value that determines if you want to prevent the tool tip from falling off the screen. Using `true` for this parameter will keep the entire tool tip on the visible screen.
- **Target MC** – Instance name of the movie clip that you want to be associated with the tool tip.
- **On Appear Handler** – Name of a function that you want to use as a callback with this component. The function is called every time the tool tip appears. A possible use might be to have a sound play when a tool tip appears, which would be defined in the function handler.
- **On Disappear Handler** – Similar to the On Appear Handler, except the function you specify in this parameter is called when the tool tip disappears.

The best way to familiarize yourself with how these parameters work is to try specifying some different values and test your movie to see the effect they have – go on and have a little play around.

Customizing the tool tip

The tool tip parameters are ideal for getting the component up and running, but you might find that you want to do your customization remotely through ActionScript – and this component comes with a number of specific properties and methods that can be used for this very purpose. In the following sections, we'll concentrate on programmatically modifying the look and feel of our tool tip, giving examples throughout. But first, here are a couple of relevant tips:

- **Code hint menu** – Assuming that a tool tip is already on the stage, if we gave it an instance name with the suffix `_tt` (for example, `myToolTip_tt`), this will allow us to bring up a menu of all the available methods and properties of the component in the Actions panel, much like for the default macromedia objects. After typing in your instance name, simple add a period (.) to bring up the actions menu:

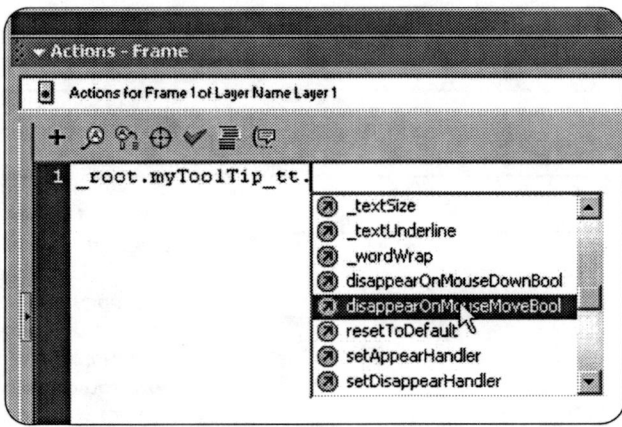

- **Reference documentation** – The tool tip component comes complete with ActionScript documentation of all the methods and properties. Take a look in at MBW Component Set > FToolTip in the Actions or Reference panels:

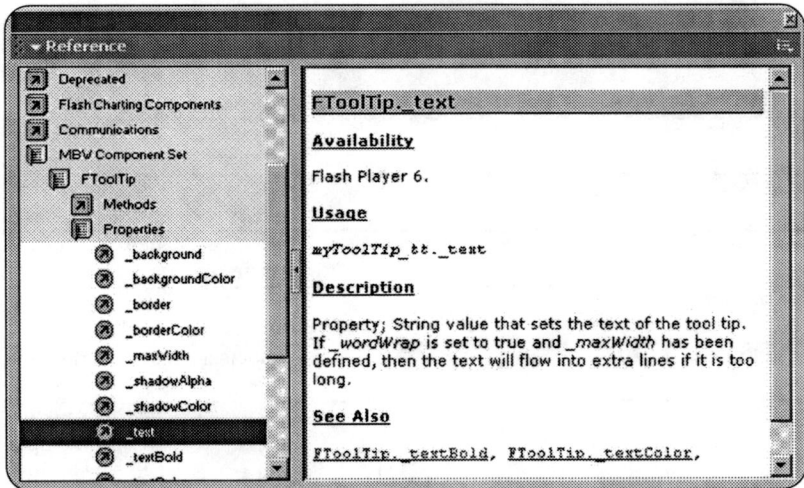

Component properties

The properties of the tool tip that you can change are as defined in the following table:

Property	Description
_background	A Boolean value that determines if you want to have a background color behind the text for the tool tip.
_backgroundColor	A hex value of the form 0xRRGGBB that determines the color of the tool tip's background.

Property	Description
_border	A Boolean value that determines if you want to have a border around the text for the tool tip.
_borderColor	A hex value of the form 0xRRGGBB that determines the color of the tool tip's border.
_maxWidth	A numeric value that determines the maximum width a tool tip is allowed before the text flows into another line.
_shadowAlpha	A numeric value between 0.0 and 100.0 that determines the alpha of the tool tip's shadow. You can use 0.0 for this property if you do not want to have a shadow.
_shadowColor	A hex value of the form 0xRRGGBB that determines the color of the tool tip's shadow.
_text	A string value that determines the text that shows up in the tool tip. There are no bounds on how much information can be put in the tool tip. If you wish the tool tip to have a fixed width with overflowing text wrapping to extra lines, refer to the _maxWidth and _wordWrap properties.
_textBold	A Boolean value that determines if you want bold text.
_textColor	A hex value of the form 0xRRGGBB that determines the color of the tool tip's text.
_textItalic	A Boolean value that determines if you want italicized text.
_textSize	A numeric value that determines the size of the tool tip's text.
_textUnderline	A Boolean value that determines if you want underlined text.
_wordWrap	A Boolean value that determines if you want text to overflow into multiple lines. If this property is set to true, then the value of _maxWidth determines how wide text is allowed to grow before it flows into a new line.

We can use these properties to customize the appearance of our tool tip. To see a demonstration of this, open up the file ToolTipSample01.fla from the download. Note that the tool tip attached to a button on the stage has been given the instance name info_tt. Now take a look at the ActionScript on frame 1 of the Actions layer of this FLA:

```
info_tt._background = true;
info_tt._backgroundColor = 0x00BB00;
info_tt._border = true;
```

```
info_tt._borderColor = 0x00;
info_tt._textColor = 0x00;
info_tt._shadowColor = 0x005B00;
info_tt._text = "A tool tip with a green background and shadow, Xand a
black border and text."
info_tt._wordWrap = true;
```

On testing this example, you'll see that these properties give the tool tip a green color scheme, and change the tool tip text from that specified manually in the component parameters:

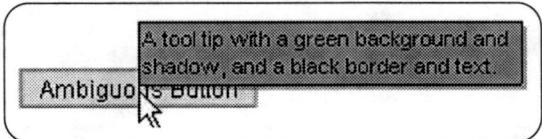

Component methods

As we mentioned earlier, we also have a set of methods with which we can customize other features of the component. One cosmetic attribute that was neglected in the properties was the font of the tool tip's text. This is a slightly complicated issue in Flash, so you must use a method to change the font. These methods are shown in the following table:

Method	Description
disappearOnMouseDownBool (bool)	Takes a Boolean value that determines if the tool tip should disappear when the mouse is pressed.
disappearOnMouseMoveBool (bool)	Takes a Boolean value that determines if the tool tip should disappear when the mouse is moved.
resetToDefault ()	Resets all the properties of the component to the default, except for the tool tip's text.
setAppearHandler (handler, timeline)	Changes the On Appear Handler of the tool tip. You must pass the string value of the function's name, as well as the reference path to the timeline that the function lives on.
setDisappearHandler (handler, timeline)	Changes the On Disappear Handler of the tool tip. You must pass the string value of the function's name, as well as the reference path to the timeline that the function lives on.
setFadeBool (bool)	Takes a Boolean value that determines if you want the tool tip to fade in and out. To use this option you must be using an embedded font – see the setFont () method. If you are not using an embedded font then the tool tip will still appear, but will not fade.

Method	Description
setFadeSpeed(speed)	Takes a numeric value between 0.0 and 100.0 that determines how fast the tool tip fades in and out.
setFont(font_name,embed)	Takes a string for the name of the font you want to use, and a Boolean value for determining if you are using an embedded font or not. To embed a font create, select the New Font... option in the Library menu and give it an appropriate linkage name (make sure that you give a name for the linkage different from the actual name of the font).
setShadowOffset(x,y)	Takes two numeric values, and offsets the tool tip's shadow by the specified amount.
setShadowVisibility(bool)	Takes a Boolean value that determines if the tool tip's shadow should be visible.
setTargetMC(reference)	Takes either a string value or movie clip reference. If you pass a string, then the target of the tool tip is set to the movie clip in the _parent timeline relative to the component with the name passed. If you pass a movie clip reference, then that movie clip is used as the target for the tool tip.
setTimeDelay(milliseconds)	Takes a numeric value that determines the amount of time, in milliseconds, that the component waits before it appears.
startDragToolTip()	Call this method to have the tool tip drag with the mouse when it appears.
stopDragToolTip()	Call this method to have the tool tip stay in one place when it appears.
waitForMouseStopBool(bool)	Takes a Boolean value that determines if you want the mouse to stay still over the target before the tool tip appears.

These methods give us a lot to play with! Assuming we're keeping the color scheme and settings that were defined earlier, let us add some more scripted modifications – these can be found in ToolTipSample02.fla. This time, we will remove the restriction that the tool tip disappears when the mouse moves or is pressed – so now the only way to get rid of the tool tip is to roll off the target. Also, we make it so that the mouse does not need to stay idle for the tool tip to appear. We will also reset the font to Courier New, but not embedded (yet). Although not really practical, for this demonstration I'm also going to have the target of the tool tip be _root, which means it will be triggered when you roll over anything on the stage. Finally, the time delay for the component will be extended so that it takes slightly longer for the tool tip to show up:

```
info_tt._background = true;
info_tt._backgroundColor = 0x00BB00;
info_tt._border = true;
info_tt._borderColor = 0x00;
info_tt._textColor = 0x00;
info_tt._shadowColor = 0x005B00;
info_tt._text = " Now i can roll over any object on the stage to
➥activate the tool tip."
info_tt._wordWrap = true;
//
info_tt.disappearOnMouseDownBool (false);
info_tt.disappearOnMouseMoveBool (false);
info_tt.setFont ("Courier New", false);
info_tt.setTargetMC (_root);
info_tt.setTimeDelay (1000);
info_tt.startDragToolTip (true);
info_tt.waitForMouseStopBool (false);
```

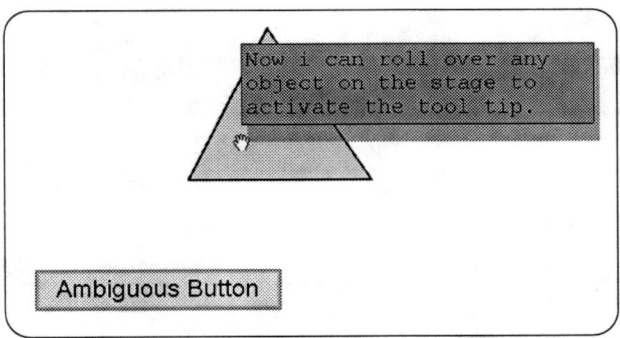

Next, if you want to have the tool tip fade in and out, you must embed a font, as noted before. Refer to `ToolTipSample03.fla` to see this in action. I've already installed a font in this example FLA, but for reference, you simply open your Library's menu and click on New Font. Make sure to give the font a different symbol name and linkage name from its actual name – conflicting names will cause Flash to use the shared fonts incorrectly. After giving the font a linkage name, you can then set the font in the component by passing this linkage name to the `setFont()` method, with `true` for the second parameter this time. Take a look at the example code on frame 1 of the Actions panel in `ToolTipSample03.fla`:

```
info_tt.setFont ("my_embedded_font", true);
```

Once a font is embedded and set in the component, you can enable fading and set the fade speed as follows:

```
info_tt.setFadeBool (true);
info_tt.setFadeSpeed (6.0);
```

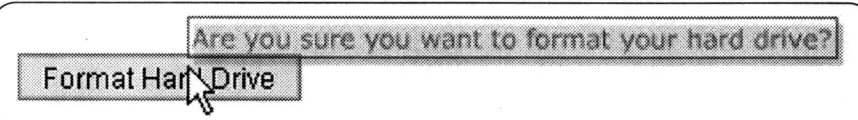

Style format properties

As a final bonus, there is one more feature of this tool tip: provided with the original UI Components is a class for handling style formats of components. You can create an `FStyleFormat` object, set the various common properties that all components share, and apply it to a component or a number of components. The tool tip component is compliant with the `FStyleFormat` object and the `globalStyleFormat` object. For completeness, here is a list of properties that can be used:

Property	Description
`background, face`	Hexadecimal color value of the form `0xRRGGBB` that determines the color of the background (since both `background` and `face` describe the back part of the tool tip, either property can be used to mean the same thing).
`embedFonts`	Boolean value that determines if you are using an embedded font.
`shadow`	Hex value of the form `0xRRGGBB` that determines the color of the tool tip's shadow.
`textBold`	Boolean value that determines if the tool tip's text is bold.
`textColor`	Hex value of the form `0xRRGGBB` that determines the color of the tool tip's text.
`textFont`	String value that determines the font of the tool tip's text.
`textItalic`	Boolean value that determines if the tool tip's text is italic.
`textSize`	Numeric value that determines the size of the tool tip's text.
`textUnderline`	Boolean value that determines if the tool tip's text is underlined.

You can either use an `FStyleFormat` or `globalStyleFormat` object to apply changes to the tool tip. For example, look at the code in `ToolTipSample04.fla`, in which I've changed to the green color scheme that we were using earlier, but this time using the `FStyleFormat` object (as well as a rather ludicrous font size!):

```
format = new FStyleFormat();
format.addListener(_root.info_tt);
format.background = 0x00BB00;
format.textColor = 0x00;
format.textSize = 20;
format.shadow = 0x005B00;
```

```
format.applyChanges();
info_tt._text = "A tool tip using the FStyleFormat object.";
info_tt._wordWrap = true;
```

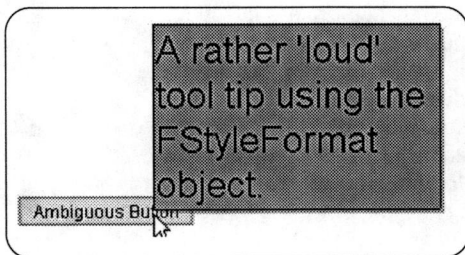

Similar modifications can also be achieved using the globalStyleFormat object.

Once you know how to customize the component, you must realize that you can use it anywhere. The beauty of components is their encapsulation into small applications that are completely independent from everything else. They are abstracted as much as possible so that they can handle any situation you think of to use them in. Don't be afraid to use a tool tip deep within a timeline hierarchy, with large amounts of text, or in any other crazy situation you can conjure up.

Steve Young

'Who is this guy?' I hear you ask. Well, allow me to introduce myself. I'm a 28 year old designer and Flash developer living in the sunny town of Coatbridge, near Glasgow, Scotland. I originally started out as a Product Designer, having studied at Glasgow School of Art, but somehow found myself in the New Media industry, like most of my peers I just seem to have 'fallen into' New Media. Up until recently I've spent the last 2 years of my life working (if you can call it that) at Flammable Jam with Hoss Gifford and some of the other top designer/developers in Scotland. Check out my site at www.gimpster.net

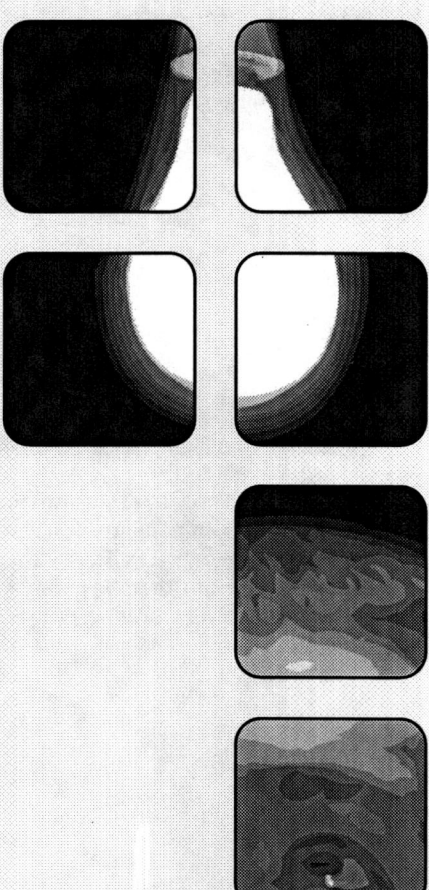

Component 5

Sketchpad

Ever fancied one of those Flash drawing pad things? Well now you and your clients can have one! Just check out this sketchpad component!

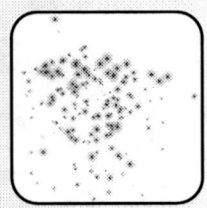
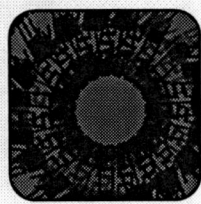
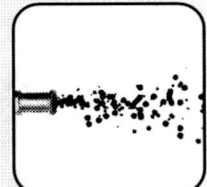
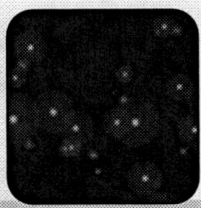

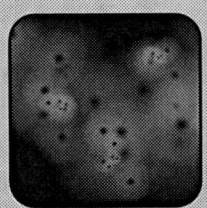

Ever since I can remember, drawing has been really important to me. When I was a kid I was always drawing monsters, cars, and... well, just monsters and cars as it happens. I was highly focused on monsters and cars! Then, at high school, I really got into the whole 'art thing' and was constantly drawing self-portraits (nobody else would sit still long enough!) and working on my portfolio to get into art school. Ironically though, once I started art school I seemed to stop drawing, real drawing anyway. Since I was studying in a design field rather than something like fine art, I spent my time drawing thumbnail sketches and little schematics before going down to the workshops where I'd turn these sketches into 3D prototypes.

Recently, I've been telling myself that I really need to start observational drawing again. However, sadly, I never seem to find the time for drawing just for the sake of it. Although I do draw every day, it's more functional – for instance, at the start of every new project I produce numerous thumbnail sketches before I get anywhere near a computer. On top of that, I've been going a bit crazy with D.I.Y. and home improvements lately, so I've been crudely sketching one room at a time before I get the old tools out. Way back when I was into drawing monsters and cars, little did I know how useful drawings would be in everyday life.

At work, digital sketchpads have always been a firm favorite – clients would often say vague things like, "We'd like one of those drawing things on our site!" Of course, since the client is always right, we'd have to oblige. Not ones for being labeled a one-trick pony, our design team would always try and do something a little different, a variation on a theme if you like, so the client gets their 'drawing thing' and we stretch ourselves and come up with something a bit out of the ordinary – everyone's happy!

A good example of this is the idea of a digital Zen Garden I came up with for one of our clients, 7-26. Take a look at www.7-26.com:

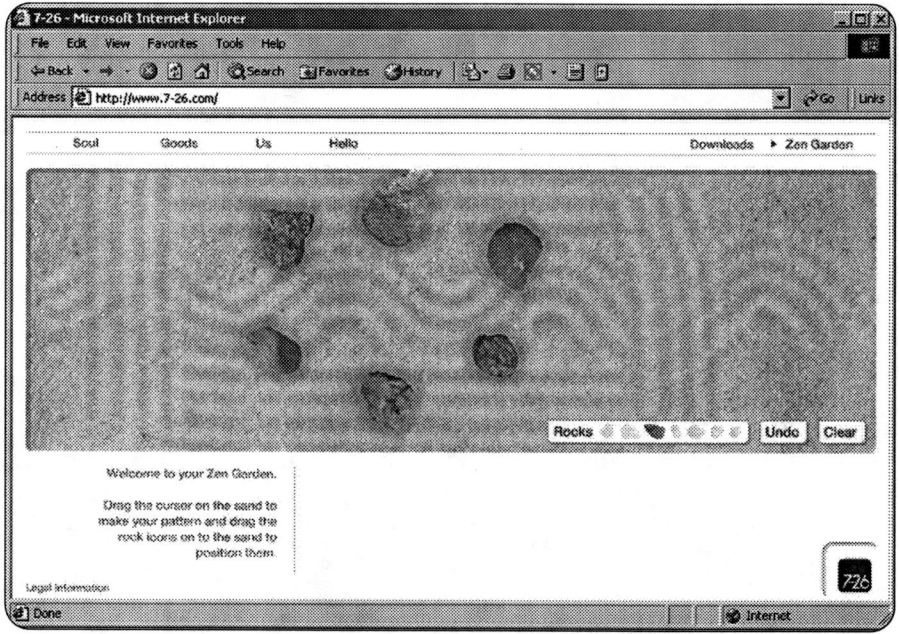

The Zen Garden is basically a drawing pad but instead of having 'digital paper', we use digital sand, and instead of a pen we use a rake. Simple! It's been so successful that now clients have started saying, "We'd want one of those cool Zen things on our site". Arrrgh!

So, things started to click early on, "Why don't we start creating assets we can simply re-skin and resell?" Bingo! Rather than going back to the drawing board (excuse the pun!) every time, it makes perfect sense to create libraries of code and components that you can use on many different projects.

"Waste not, want not!" a gravitationally-challenged friend of mine once said. If you don't already **recycle** and **reuse** your code, now's the time to start! And of course, this is where components in Flash MX really come into their own! Rather than creating custom-made code for every project, it's worth investing a little extra time and effort into creating a component. The next time a client wants one of those 'springy button thingies' or one of those 'dynamic image viewers', instead of using up hours, days, or even weeks rehashing your old code (because by this time you've forgotten how you did it and you didn't bother to comment your code the first time!), you simply drag and drop a component and re-skin a few buttons. You've just saved yourself a whole heap of trouble, and better still – your clients think you're a genius who never sleeps!

Now you can spend your day surfing, playing games, even drawing monsters and cars if you so desire, and you'll go home on time for a change totally stress free. I plan to streamline my entire life in this way. Just a couple of words of warning – don't tell your boss, he'll only increase your workload and you'll be back to square one. Secondly, and most important of all, don't tell your clients – or mine, for that matter!

Here's a little tried and tested formula I like to use:

```
if (noOfComponents>=1) {
    fun = true;
    stress = false;
    components = "Easy money!";
}
```

So, since a digital sketchpad is quite a useful accessory (or even toy!) to have on a website and clients really love them, I thought it would be quite handy to create a component that you can just drag from your Library, drop on top of a movie clip, and customize the interface to suit your needs. Ultimately, you'll save yourself a day or so, and your client will hopefully be over the moon!

Before Flash MX came along, any drawing toy created in Flash would work by duplicating movie clips (a simple dot, for instance), placing them on-screen using the mouse co-ordinates, and stretching their X and Y scales to the next mouse co-ordinates. This worked quite well, but was never really fluid enough for me. It was also pretty darn intensive on the processor. Typically, drawings would be made up of a series of straight lines, and this was very noticeable when quickly drawing circular shapes. Now, with the brilliant drawing API in Flash MX, such previous annoyances can be eradicated, allowing a much smoother, more realistic drawing experience.

Using the sketchpad

OK, that's enough with my meandering preamble. It's time to get to grips with the sketchpad component, and see how it works – trust me, it's a piece of cake!

Let's dive right into using the component – we'll learn how to set it up shortly. Open up the file `sketchpad_sky.swf`, and you'll see the component in action:

So, with this example of the component, you can see the sketchpad user interface at the top of the Flash movie, and the background is a JPEG image of sky and ground (we'll learn how to change the background shortly). The controls are very user-friendly, but it's worth taking a moment to familiarize yourself with them:

You can name, save, and playback your drawings with the first control, select your brush size using the slider in the second option, pick your color with the color pad, and undo or clear if you make any mistakes. Note that you should press and hold the Undo button to dynamically undo your work (try it out!), but if you want to wipe the slate clean and start again, hit Clear. Now you're ready to start drawing!

Setting it up

Now that we're comfortable with using the component, let's see how to set it up – open up `sketchpad.fla`. The first thing we want to do is attach the sketch pad to a movie clip to give it a background image. This could be anything from a plain old white pad, to a picture of one of your friends that you want to graffiti over. So, take a look in the Library of `sketchpad.fla`, and you'll see I've included some images to play around with:

As well as the sky image that we used in the first example, in `sketchpad_sky.swf`, there are a couple others. Now drag the `brick_wall` JPEG onto the stage and align it in the center of the stage. This picture will make as good a background as any, but first we need to convert it to a movie clip so that our sketchpad component can link to it. So, with the bitmap still selected, hit the F8 key to convert it to a symbol (or select Inset > Convert to Symbol…):

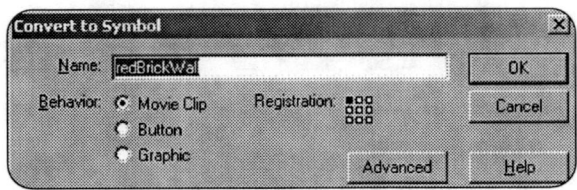

In the resulting dialog box, make the image a movie clip, give it an appropriate name, make sure that the registration point is top left, and hit OK. Now, with your new movie clip selected, we want to give it an instance name. Go to the Property inspector and type in a suitable name – actually, it doesn't really matter what you call it, as you'll see in a moment (no spaces though):

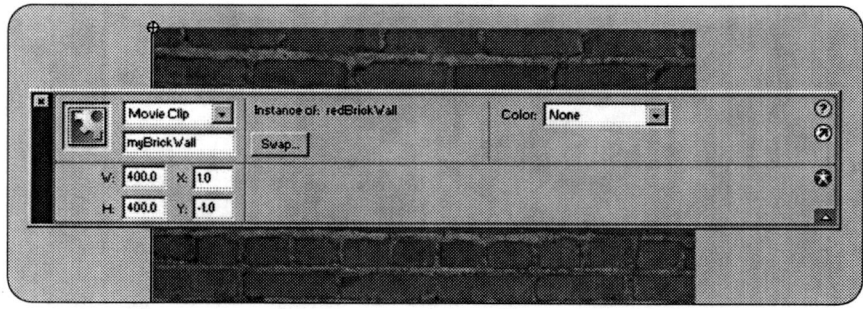

This movie clip is going to be your new canvas. Before we go any further, stay in the Property inspector and go to the Color drop-down menu. Change the alpha value of your movie clip to 99%. This is another industry secret – if you don't do this and you start to sketch over the top of your bitmap, it'll be a little buggy and start doing irritating 'twitches'. Don't ask me why, though! This applies to all bitmaps when you bring them into Flash – this is worth keeping in mind for future projects!

While I'm in such a generous tip-giving mood, notice that I've set the frame rate in all my example Flash files to 31 frames per second:

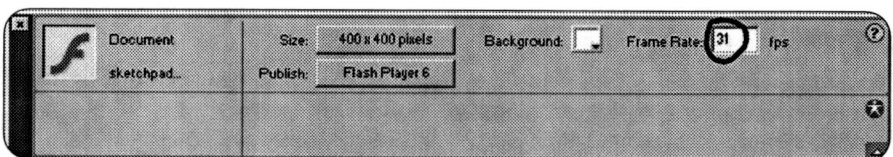

30 fps will assure nice and smooth drawing, but unless I set it to 31 fps it won't run at 30fps on a Mac. Why? Well, again, I don't know, but just take my word for it – it doesn't! For the record, the movie size is set to 400 x 400 pixels, but this can be anything you want.

OK, enough sidetracking, we're now ready to add the component. Go back to the Library where you'll see the component – it's called sketch. Drag and drop it onto the top of your newly created canvas, and it should snap neatly to the top left hand corner of the canvas, just like a ScrollBar attaches itself to a text field, for instance. Next, with the component itself selected, look back in the Property inspector and select the Parameters tab (alternatively, you could go to the Component Parameters panel):

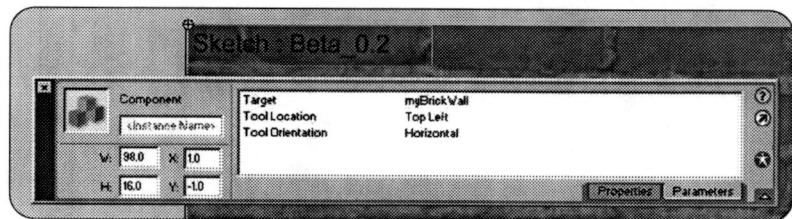

Component parameters

In the Property inspector, you can see the three parameters and the default values that have been assigned to them. These parameters are pretty self explanatory:

- Target – automatically assigned as the instance name of your 'canvas' movie clip (pretty clever, eh?)

- Tool Location – puts the interface in one of the four corners of your canvas, so select one of the 4 possible values (Top Left, Top Right, Bottom Left, or Bottom Right), or just keep the default value.

- Tool Orientation – two possible values, Horizontal and Vertical

Specify your parameters and you're ready to roll. Hit CTRL/COMMAND+ENTER (PC/Mac) to test your movie:

Pretty neat, huh?

Graphical customization

No doubt you'll want to customize the look and feel of the interface buttons to fit in with the existing design of your site. No problem! In the Library, you'll find a folder called `Sketch_interface`. Open it and you'll see five movie clips: `brushSize`, `clearBut`, `colourPicker`, `undoBut`, and `recorderBit`:
(see over)

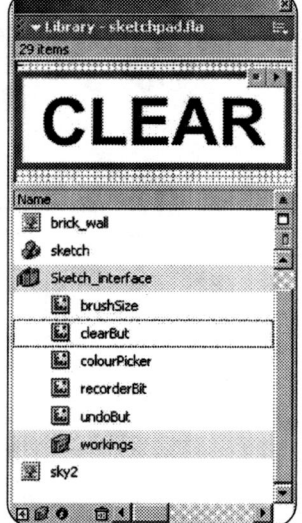

Both `clearBut` and `undoBut` are very straightforward to customize. Just double-click on either one to open, and you'll find very self-explanatory layers and frame labels:

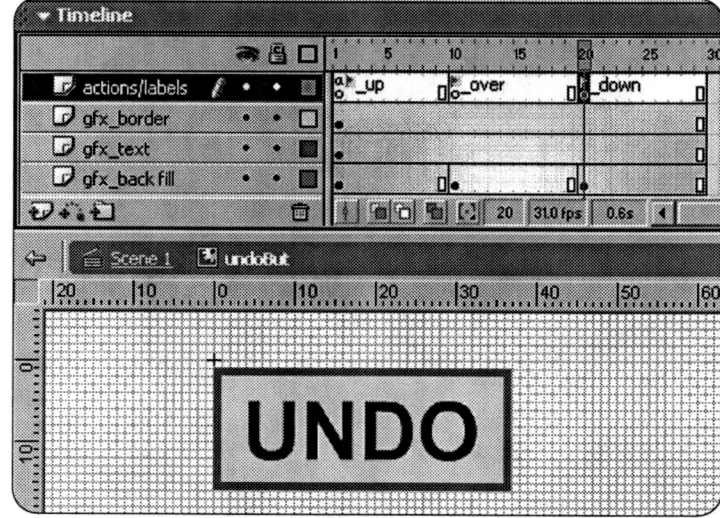

The three layers beginning with gfx are the graphics layers. The layer gfx_back fill is the background color of the button and has three main keyframes representing the Up, Over and Down button states. You can simply change these frames to whatever you'd like, I've used very basic color changes. The other two gfx layers contain a border and a text field which lets the end user know what the button does. Once you're happy with how your button looks, save your file and move on to the next button. Easy!

The `brushSize`, `colourPicker`, and `recorderBit` movie clips are a little more complicated. They all contain essential ActionScript that sets important variables. I have endeavored to comment my code to make things easier to understand when you want to alter these elements, and typically try to make my code as self-explanatory as possible, using actual words rather than obscure two letter variable names – this is a good standard practice if several people are likely to work on the same file, and optimization isn't of utmost importance. Also note that, coming from a design background as opposed to a programming one, I've relied on the technique of attached scripts throughout this component, rather than a single centralized program. Starting with the `brushSize` movie clip, I'll briefly talk you through how to customize each of these more complex clips.

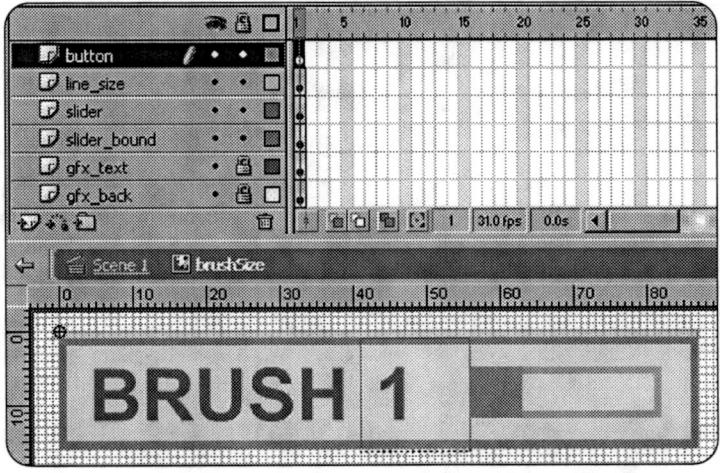

The `brushSize` movie clip has six layers. The bottom two layers (gfx) are again just graphics layers, and can be changed without fear of breaking the functionality of the sketchpad. The next layer up is called slider_bound and works in conjunction with the layer slider. These layers are the most important in this element and require a little more care when changing how they look because their size is directly related to the `lineSize` variable. The wider you make the slider_bound element, the further the slider element can be dragged. It's very important that both slider_bound and slider are aligned together on the left. As the slider is dragged to the right, the `lineSize` increases. The value of `lineSize` is displayed in the layer line_size and lets the user know what size of line they're about to draw.

The top layer, button, is also very important – once you've got your button looking how you'd like, resize the movie clip on the button layer to the same size as your background. All this does is disable the sketchpad by setting the `padActive` variable to `true` or `false`, depending on whether you're over it or not while you set the `lineSize` variable. If you look inside this button movie clip, you'll see what I've done. You could set this with just a standard button, but this is a much better solution, in my opinion. I just don't like having a button appear active unless it's going to do something when pressed or clicked.

Now let's take a look at how we might go about customizing the `colourPicker` clip – double-click on it in the Library to open it up. This one's probably a little more complicated than the `brushSize` element. Yet again, I've prefixed all the graphics layers with gfx – you can adjust these elements according to your own design requirements, as before.

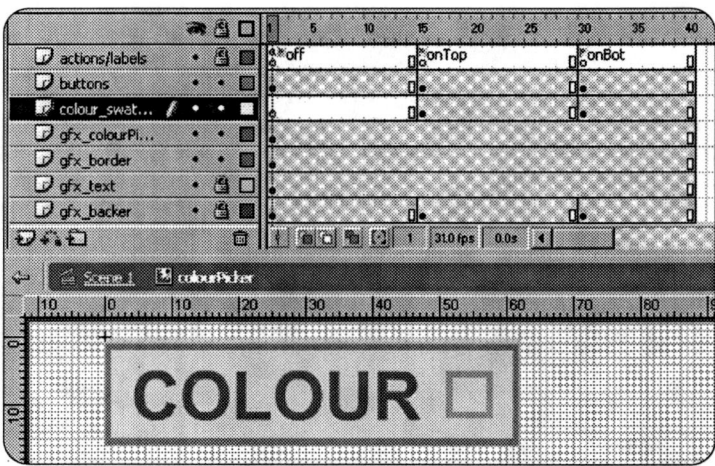

You'll also notice that I've got three frame labels: off, onTop, and onBot. The latter two contain exactly the same elements, except that one expands down (onTop) for when the interface is located at the top of the pad and the other, you guessed it, expands up (onBot) for when the interface is on the bottom.

In the colour_swatches layer, I've got 14 different colors – you can have as many as you want, just adjust your design accordingly. Each swatch has some code on it – click on one and have a look in the Actions panel:

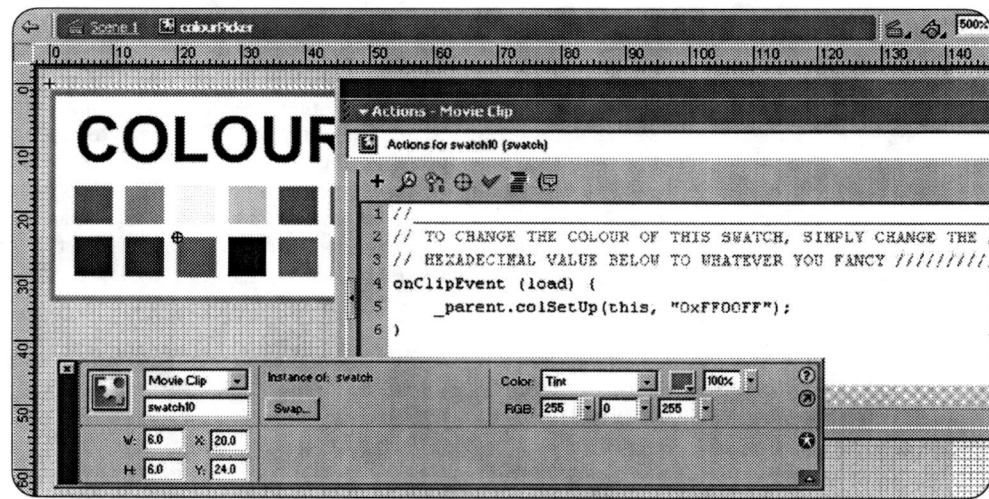

This code calls a function located on frame 1 of the actions/labels layer, which there's no need to touch. All you need to do to change the color of the swatch is change the hexadecimal value to that of the color you want. You don't have to change the color property of the swatch itself as the function does it when you publish, but you might want to for clarity in the authoring environment. To do this, just go to the Property inspector and from the Color drop-down menu select Tint and choose your color. Remember, if you've changed the sizes or added more swatches, you'll need to adjust the buttons on the buttons layer. The button on the frame labeled off should be resized to be the same as your background, and then make sure that the buttons on frames onTop and onBot are sized appropriately in relation to the background.

Last but not least, let's take a look at the recorderBit movie clip. As usual, the gfx layers can be altered to fit your existing design:

The text on the status_text layer is simply to let the user know what's happening when the record or play buttons are pressed, change the style or wording as required. The layer input_text contains a very important input text field that allows the user to rename, save, and replay drawings. Again, you can change the style of this text but don't change the text type (Input Text) or variable name, or you'll break the component. After any amendments, remember to resize the buttons accordingly.

Now here's a tip for the more adventurous scripters – one of the neat features of this component is the recorder. For this, I utilized the shared local object functionality of Flash MX, which basically stores data locally on the users machine as a text file (*.sol). You can find the relevant code towards the end of the actions/labels layer:

```
1  _parent.playBack = true;
2  localObject = SharedObject.getlocal(recordMe);
3  tempData = new Array();
4  tempSize = localObject.data.howBig;
5  for (i=0; i<tempSize; i++) {
6      tempData[i] = localObject.data.sketchData[i];
7  }
8  _parent.wipeClean();
9  _parent.storedData = tempData;
10 howBig = tempSize;
11 inc = 1;
```

By typing a name into the input field on the recorder and clicking the red record button, your work of art (remember Godzilla, earlier in the chapter!) will be stored locally on your computer. It's worth noting here that I haven't limited the amount of 'ink' (that is, the number of the lines the user can draw), so if you want to save a very complex drawing, it's going to use a lot more hard drive space than you'd imagine – be prepared to increase your allocated Local Storage space!

For those interested, I've previously used shared objects to great effect on a recent project I worked on for a local architects' firm in Glasgow (www.coopercromar.com). Believe it or not, they actually asked for 'one of those cool Zen designs', and this virtual Bonsai Tree is what I came up with:

This is essentially another obscure take on the sketchpad – the user prunes their tree by clicking on the leaves. Whatever is done to the tree, by the user, is stored in an array, which is then stored locally on the users hard drive. Along with this array, I store the time of their visit. On their next visit to the site, I load the locally stored data, compare the current time to the previously stored time and then I re-grow some of the leaves accordingly. It takes a full month for the tree to fully re-grow. Pretty cool, eh? Of course, this is not just about me showing off my portfolio – the point is that your imagination is the only limit to how far you can customize the sketchpad component, or any of the other components in this book for that matter. That's that beauty of components – so dive right in and start streamlining the way you work!

Jen deHaan

Jen is a Flash designer/developer and has been involved in the writing and technical editing many books about Flash, ActionScript and ColdFusion. She primarily uses Flash MX, and is most interested in Remoting with ColdFusion, drinking large amounts of coffee, handhelds, and building components. Jen has a degree in Art education, and certification in New Media. You can find her on the web at www.ejepo.com and www.flash-mx.com.

Jen lives in Toronto with her husband Peter and two cats. Special thanks to the friends of ED team and Peter for all of their support.

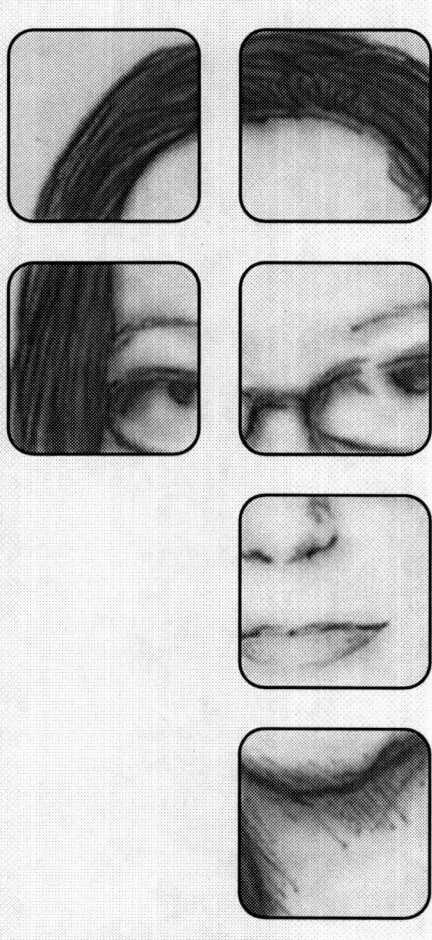

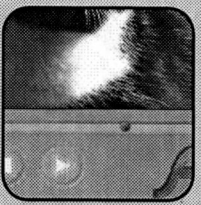

Component 6
Video Player

This component is a simple player that can control the playback of any kind of movie clip in your Flash movie. The Video Player has a stop, play, and pause button, as well as a close button and toggle to scroll through the content. It has the look of a traditional video player so that your end user will be accustomed to the intuitive controls. And of course, this player is easily skinnable so it can be customized to match the look of any website.

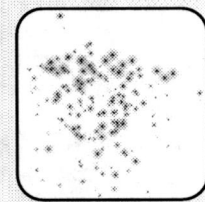

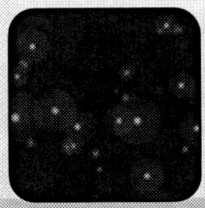

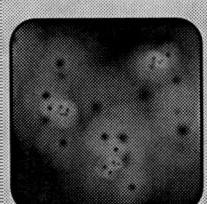

The Video Player component is a fairly straightforward tool that allows you to play and control your videos or movies online without having to rebuild control buttons or redo and resize any interface graphics. It attaches to movie clip instances and, at runtime, will customize its dimensions to the size of your movie clip instance. This enables you to put any kind of content into a player, and allows your visitors to control playback and close the player altogether when finished.

The main way that you'll probably want to graphically customize this component is by *skinning* the buttons and body of the player. By making your own graphics in an editor like Fireworks or Photoshop, you can easily make this player match the look of your own website. You only need to match the size of the graphic assets in this component, and then swap the existing graphics (making sure that you maintain the same registration points).

When working with video in Flash, it's worth remembering that most computers usually cannot handle clips greater than four or five minutes in length, since the data is loaded into the Flash Player RAM. If you have difficulty publishing, playing, or importing the video clip, it's most likely too long and you should break the video into smaller chunks or use a more robust solution for displaying your videos, such as Macromedia Director MX (www.macromedia.com/software/director/).

Before building any component, it's usually a good idea to create a specification – having a plan for what you are setting out to do can save a lot of time in the long run while constructing your component. Accordingly, before I even sat down at my computer, I wrote a spec outlining the functionality and design of the Video Player, with the ultimate aim of minimizing the development time, and making the whole design process less of a headache.

The initial specification for this component is as follows, and it should give you a good idea about what the Video Player component is all about, and a general idea of how and why it was constructed. If you've already used this component, you can probably tell that the original ideas did not change too much from this spec:

- **Name:** FVideoPlayer

- **Function:** To stop, pause, and play movie clips in a Flash movie.

- **What it will look like:** The player will have the look and feel of a small, brushed-metal style device (like a virtual PDA), and will be easily recognizable as a movie player, with clear stop and play buttons. It will also be simple to customize through easy to skin graphical elements.

- **What it does**: The component will attach to movie clips on the stage, and then play the content of those clips. It will scale itself to accommodate different sizes of movie.

- **Potential problems**: Accommodating for the potential sizes and shapes of different movie clips that the component attaches to is one area that requires some specific attention. The player must accommodate large, small, tall, short, wide, and narrow variations of movie sizes, and it should not alter its size such that it is too narrow for the controls to fit, or enlarge bitmaps so they become too grainy.

As you can see in this spec, it can be useful to make a quick sketch on paper (or with a tablet) to generate an overall idea of what the component will look like – this effectively gives you a design to work towards.

Importing video into Flash MX

To test or use the Video Player component, we need to have some video images imported into our Flash movie. For this reason, it's worth taking a moment to outline the general process. It's actually very easy to get your video files into Flash, but even if you're already used to working with video in Flash MX, be sure to read about converting your video files to movie clips, towards the end of this section.

1. In a new Flash document, select File > Import to Library... and the Import to Library dialog will open – from here you need to browse to your required video file and select it by double-clicking (there are a couple of sample video files included in this chapter's code folder in the download).

2. The Import Video dialog box will now open up – select the Embed video in Macromedia Flash document option, as shown opposite:

3. Next, the Import Video Settings dialog box will open. These settings are used to adjust the quality, keyframe interval, scale, synchronization, and video-to-Flash frame ratio (additionally, if your clip has audio, you will see a check box that enables you to choose whether or not to import the audio track):

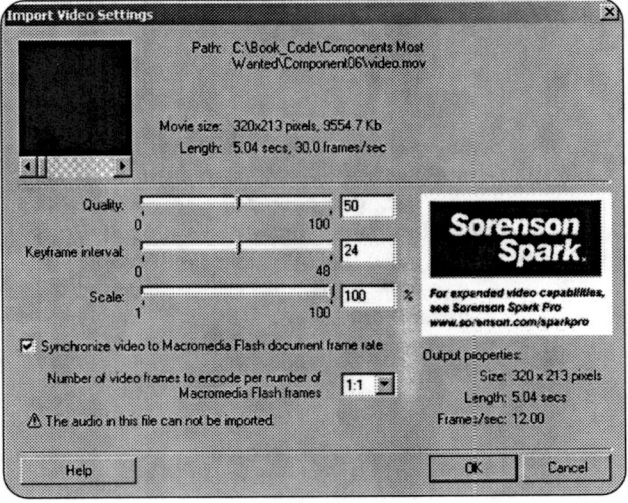

71

- Quality – This slider controls the amount of compression, 0 being high compression, and 100 being the lowest level of compression. You will see a significant difference between different quality settings. For instance, anything below a setting of 50 will be very blocky. In order to achieve an acceptable quality level for your video, it is likely you'll need to use a higher setting (greater than 70).

- Keyframe interval – This slider sets the interval that keyframes are set at in your video. A value of 48 inserts fewer keyframes than a setting of 1, so a setting of 0 does not insert keyframes and is therefore more similar to a setting of 48 than a setting of 1. If your video has a lot of quick changes or movement, you should try a lower keyframe interval (but not 0!).

- Scale – This setting changes the frame size of the movie.

- Synchronize video to Macromedia Flash document frame rate – By selecting this option, the imported video will be adjusted by dropping frames to match the frame rate of your Flash document so that your video stays in sync with Flash. Each frame of the video will play in sync with Flash if you leave this option unselected. Dropping frames can lead to lost content (including any code within those dropped frames!) so you should use caution when selecting this option.

- Number of video frames to encode per number of Macromedia Flash frames – This setting sets a ratio between the frame rate of the Flash movie and the imported movie.

4. After setting your import options and clicking OK, open your Library (F11), and you'll see the video file listed as Embedded Video, as seen opposite:

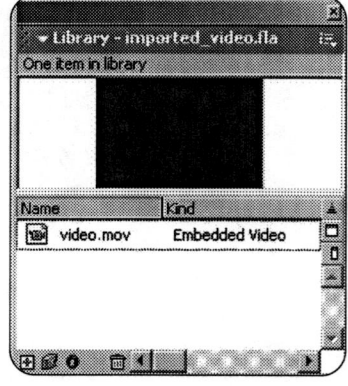

5. Next, since the Video Player does not play embedded video directly, you will need to convert it to a movie clip by following these simple steps. Select Insert > New Symbol, choose the Movie Clip option, give your clip a suitable name, and hit OK:

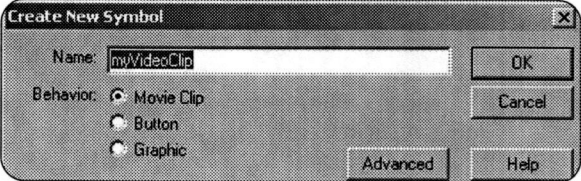

6. With the new movie clip instance now open, drag your video from the Library onto the stage of the movie clip. A dialog box will open informing you about the number of frames that need to be added to play the video – just click on Yes:

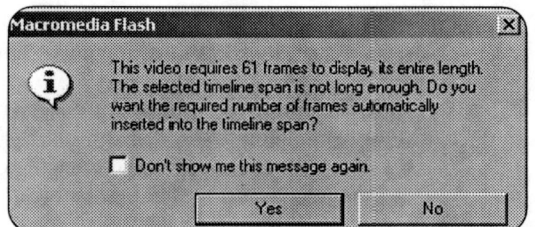

7. Now select the video instance and change the co-ordinates to (0,0) using the Property inspector:

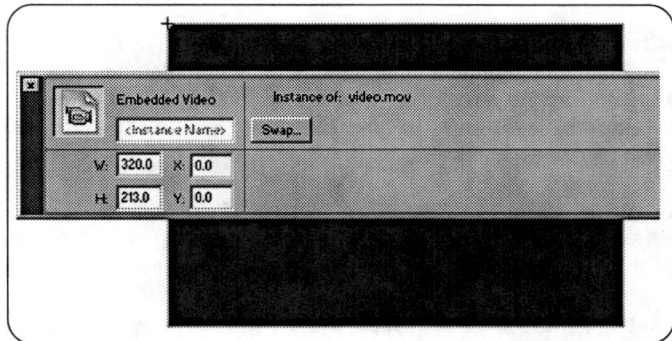

In this step, we've specifically set the registration point of our movie clip to (0, 0). If you don't do this, then when you use the clip with the Video Player component, it will not be placed in the correct location in relation to the other graphics in the component.

8. Now return to the main stage – you'll find your newly created movie clip in the Library, ready to be dragged onto the stage and viewed through the Video Player component:

Tips and tricks for video compression and editing

Before moving on to the component, let's consider some important points about video compression. You might find it quite difficult to make a particular video 'look good' or have an acceptable file size after it has passed through Sorenson Spark video import process. Most of the time, if you run into quality problems, it's simply because you have a video that is difficult to compress. Accordingly, here are some basic points about video compression and editing:

- **Never recompress compressed video** – When compressing something that has already been compressed, you lose detail and quality in your footage through *artifacting*, so make an effort to use a master (uncompressed) copy. If you don't have access to the original file, use a copy that has the least amount of compression.

- **Trim your video carefully** – Keep in mind that you should trim any empty space at the beginning and end of your video, and crop it as much as you can; it all adds up! Also, make sure to disable any audio track if it's not needed.

- **Reduce noise** – If you have access to digital video software like After Effects, you can try reducing the noise and/or changing color levels and balance. Sometimes this makes a significant (and beneficial) impact on the file size of your movie. Higher end compressors (like Cleaner 5 from Discreet, Sorenson Squeeze, and Flix) have controls to handle noise level reduction and smoothing. These can also reduce your file size.

- **Reconsider the cross-fades** – The fewer of these effects you have, the better the compression (and therefore file size!). Lengthy transitions or fade-outs are difficult to compress because anything with a lot of movement or pixel changes is difficult for software like Spark to handle.

- **Test your settings, and then test again!** – If you are happy with your video after it has been compressed, try lowering the quality setting even further. Attempt to discover the optimum setting that offers the lowest possible file size while maintaining an acceptable quality level for your project. If you are using more advanced software for compressing your video, it's a good idea to look into the finer points on topics such as data rate, video keyframing, and VBR/CBR.

Using the Video Player

You can install this component through the Macromedia Extension Manger in the usual way, by double-clicking on the `video_player.mxp` file (alternatively, just open up `FVideoPlayer.fla` and drag it from the Library). After restarting Macromedia Flash MX, the Video Player component will be found in the Components panel under the name FVideoPlayer in the drop-down menu.

Assuming you've already created a movie clip containing a video to use with this component, and it's on the stage already, drag an instance of the FVideoPlayer component from the Components panel and onto your movie clip. Otherwise, refer back to the section on *Importing video into Flash MX*, or just use the movie clip in `imported_video.fla`. The Video Player icon component will immediately 'snap' to the top left corner of your movie clip, like this:

Now select the component icon and look in the Parameters tab of the Property inspector. When the component snaps to movie clip, it will automatically enter the clip's instance name into the target movieclip field (however, if your movie clip doesn't have an instance name, the default name, InstanceName_1, will appear):

If you haven't selected a movie clip, or you have tried to attach the Video Player to the wrong kind of instance (such as a button), you will be warned when you try to test or publish the Flash movie. Note that in the Property inspector you can also change the initial volume the clip is set at and whether or not your movie clip will loop (these parameters are discussed shortly). Although this is a limited set of parameters, there are other ways that you can control the component using ActionScript (also discussed later on).

Finally, when you test your movie (CTRL/COMMAND+ENTER), the video will appear at runtime within the user interface of the component:

The Video Player component will automatically change to fit the dimensions of your movie clip. But remember, the player has been constructed to play movie clips as opposed to embedded video. Therefore, if you have imported your video into Flash and it's on the stage as such, you will need to insert the video into a new movie clip symbol before it can be attached to the Video Player (see earlier section on *Importing video into Flash MX*). So if your video does not stop when you test your movie and press the stop button, it could be because you are using an embedded video with the player instead of a movie clip instance. Make sure you place your video inside a new movie clip instance by going to Insert > Symbol and selecting Movie Clip. Then drag your video onto the stage, and place it at (0,0) inside the movie clip symbol.

Being able to play movie clips in the player gives us more options than only being able to play embedded videos. Anyway, it's much easier to change a video into a movie clip than it is to change a movie clip into a video. This also allows you to create your own effects and control video using the MovieClip object, and then you can play those movie clips in this player.

There are a few important things you should consider before choosing the movie clips you are going to present in the player. First of all, very small videos will scale in a different way to large videos. 160x120 pixels are the smallest dimensions with which the player will retain regular spacing between the elements. If your clips are smaller than this, the player will remain the same size as it would for a 160x120 video, regardless of the clip. The component is constructed this way so the controls and assets remain legible even if the video itself is very small (refer to the issue that I highlighted as a *potential problem* in my spec outline, earlier in the chapter). This means that the panel and controls may seem oversized in comparison to a very small clip.

The Video Player also supports 'irregular' dimensions, such as particularly tall, wide, or narrow movie clips. However, the rounded edges of the player will seem slightly distorted due to stretching. All other elements of the player will retain their original sizes.

Component parameters

The parameters assigned to the Video Player component are modified through the Property inspector – these settings are explained below:

- Target movie clip – This is the target movie clip instance that the Video Player will attach to and play at runtime.
- Initial Volume – This numerical value (0 - 100) sets the initial volume of any sound in movie clip and move the volume slider to the appropriate position.
- Looping – If this property is set to `true`, it will cause the movie clip to play continuously; `false` means the movie will stop when it reaches its last frame. This can also be changed during runtime using ActionScript (see below).

ActionScript interface

You can use ActionScript to control the Video Player in the following ways:

Method	Description and Usage
`getLoop()` loop:	Used to return a Boolean that tells whether or not the movie clip is set to loop: `trace(this.myPlayer.getLoop());` If the movie is not set to loop, this will return 0 (`false`), and 1 (`true`) if it is looping.
`getVol()`	Used to return the current volume setting of the movie clip: `trace(this.myPlayer.getVol());`

`pauseVid()`	Used to pause the movie clip on its current frame when it is called during runtime. The code for a button that pauses the movie might look something like this:
	
	`this.button.onRelease = function() {`
	`        this._parent.myPlayer.pauseVid();`
	`};`

`playVid()`	Starts playing when this is called during runtime. Used in the same way as `pauseVid()`.

`setLoop()`	Used to change the current volume setting to a new value. You could test this in the following way:
	
	`trace("before "+ this.myPlayer.getLoop());`
	`this.myPlayer.setLoop(1);`
	`trace("afterwards " + this.myPlayer.getLoop());`

Method	Description and Usage

setVol()	Used to change the current volume setting to a new value. You could do this in the following way, and then check the value of the new volume:
	
	`this.myPlayer.setVol(92);`
	`trace(this.myPlayer.getVol());`

stopVid()	Stops the movie clip when this is called during runtime. Again, used in the same way as pauseVid() and playVid().

Refer to the file `FVid_properties.fla` in this chapter's code folder – this example will give you an idea of how to use some of these properties to control the Video Player component from external buttons.

Skinning the component

Luckily, you're not stuck using the graphics provided with this component. You simply have to change some of the graphics in the Library, and you can have an entirely different feel. This way, you can easily customize the component to look good in relation to your own designs. Since you are not changing instance names or ActionScript, the functionality of the component will remain exactly the same.

After dragging the component to the stage, open up the Library and take a look at all of the elements that make up the Video Player's user interface. You can customize, or 'skin', your movie by changing the graphics in the Component Skins folder (the movie clips containing these graphics are found in the Other Assets folder):

Skinning a component is very straightforward. There are two graphics for the stop button, and four for the play/pause button. You will need to make a graphic for the back panel, the toggle, and then the bar that the Video Player's playhead moves along. Create your graphics to match the dimensions of those in the Library. When creating the graphics for the back panel of your player, remember that any movie larger than 320x240 pixels in height or width (or both) will distort the image and probably cause it to look 'fuzzy'. You might also want to try using your own logo to match your site in the lower right corner.

When you are changing the graphics, an easy way to quickly get the job done is by swapping the symbols or bitmaps – simply right-click the graphic contained in the movie clip, and selecting Swap Bitmap.... Alternatively, you can directly edit the graphics in the component, or delete and replace the symbols for bitmaps. Whichever way you choose to handle this, you'll want to make sure you don't change the registration points of each graphic. Some are centered on the stage, and others are intentionally placed at (0,0). If this is altered, there will be a very noticeable misplacement of the component's assets when you publish your movie. Similarly, you'll run into problems if you change the dimensions of the graphics to any great extent since the component arranges the assets on the panel in relation to one another. A skinned component can be seen on the next page – for more insights into the skinning process, open up and test FVideoPlayer_skin.fla.

Taking it further

Not only can you change how the Video Player looks, but also how it works by selecting the component instance in the Library, double-clicking on its icon, and choosing Edit.... This will open up the component so that you can change the ActionScript that makes it run. Here you can extend the VideoPlayerClass or add new properties using addProperty() to suit your individual needs. You might want to add properties for things such as:

- isPlaying – the video is currently playing
- isStopped – the video is not playing
- isUnloaded – the movie has been unloaded from memory (the close button was pressed)

Or, if you change the size or nature of the graphics you might need to alter how the player's movie clips are placed when they attach to the component.

The original aim of this component was to provide a video player that offered a standard look and feel that could be skinned by designers to match their own websites. The intuitive and user-friendly nature of this component should really enhance the usability of any site in which it is incorporated. Simply remember to insert your embedded video into a new movie clip and set the x and y co-ordinates to (0,0) before publishing your Flash movie.

This is the first version of this new Video Player. If you are interested in future adaptations of this component, check out www.flash-mx.com for information, links, and downloads.

Brian Monnone

Brians personal website is www.monnone.com
Brian is the Senior Multimedia Producer/Developer for
Tocquigny Advertising in Austin, Texas USA. Tocquigny
Advertising received the Austin Business Journal's Top 25
Web Developers #1 position for 2002-2003 in web design
and development in Austin. He has been computing for
over 17 years and has found himself doing what he loves
to do, "making really cool stuff".

Brian works on projects with AMD, Dell, HP, USAA,
GlobalScape, and a host of other companies, creating Flash
demos, websites, videos, and other types of multimedia.
Brian has won awards for his works and many accolades
for his personal site. Nestled in the hills, he finds
inspiration for his work and plenty to do with his wife and
children. He enjoys creating interactive content and hopes
to become a filmmaker in the future .

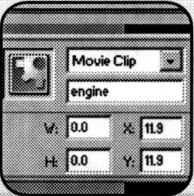

Component 7
Image Scroller

Use this component in web designs, menus, presentations ,or just about anything you can come up with. This is an image scroller that interacts with the mouse and is unlike any other. This dynamic image scroller is flexible, easy to use, and highly customizable.

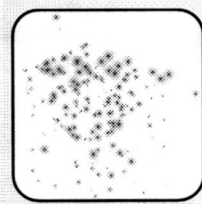

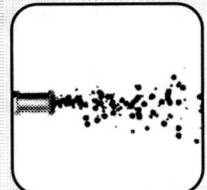
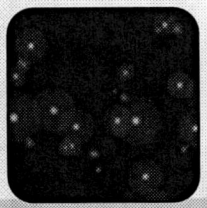

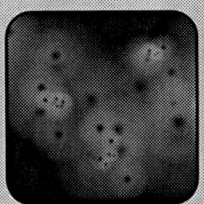

Every great Flash component should have one thing in common when it comes down to it – they should help us to create something with as little effort as possible. A component that is easy to use is one that increases productivity and shortens project timelines. In a nutshell, components make developing in Flash faster and easier. But not all components are created equal; the difference between a great component and a not so great one is the ability to be able to manipulate it in precisely the way you want so that it fits into your project – flexibility is the key.

So what exactly is this component all about? Well, as its name suggests, it allows you to scroll through various images using the mouse movements to control the motion. With a little imagination, this can be used for a variety of things, from an online photo album to a complete Flash navigation system. In fact, the image scroller component is dynamic in every sense of the word – it has the ability to dynamically load both Flash movies (SWF) and JPEG images. It does this with the help of an XML file that we can edit to determine which files will be placed in the scroller, and where.

You'll soon see that relying on XML in this way means that the image scroller component is a snap to use. With this system, you have the ability to add as many images or SWFs as you wish simply by editing the XML document. You can also choose whether to make the loaded objects URL links, buttons that interact with the loaded Flash movies, or just plain eye candy. It's also worth stressing that you don't have to be an XML guru to use this component – I'll explain everything we use with XML along the way, and in the first section of this chapter, *How it works*, I'll provide a little background to how the Flash and the XML files work together. With this complete knowledge of how the image scroller functions, you'll be all set to get the best out of it.

As a teaser of what's to come, it's worth taking a look at the component in action – in your web browser open up `index.html` from the this chapter's examples folder in the download:

Here, the image scroller is loading in some sample images and Flash movie (located in the `images` folder). Now spend a moment familiarizing yourself with the controls – if you move your mouse cursor to the center of the scroller, it will stop scrolling, but moving it up or down from there allows you to scroll in either direction. Additionally, note the extra dynamic and interactive features of the component – the JPEG images have been turned into links to various sites, and the loaded Flash movies can move you to different frames within the parent movie.

Of course, the version you see here uses all the default settings – any number of the parameters can be changed, as you will see later in the chapter. This scroller component also has the ability to adjust the transparency of the all loaded objects, as well as the background of the loaded images. You can also adjust the size and color of the background, and you can specify the degree of rotation for the loaded objects. This component has adjustable parameters that enable you to adjust the height and width of the scroller itself, and the loaded objects. Last but not least, you have the ability to adjust the speed and the spacing between each loaded object.

How it works

If you've already installed the component by opening up the `monnone.mxp` file from the download, you're ready to open up Flash, drag it onto the stage, and use it. But before we do that, it's worth spending some time looking at the XML file that makes possible the dynamic image loading – remember, by editing the XML doc we can decide how many objects we want in the scroller, and what we want them to do. We'll avoid an in-depth explanation of XML with Flash here – again, it's important to emphasize that you *do not need to be an XML expert to use this component*. Because the image scroller uses only a small amount of XML, even the novice user should have no problems getting to grips with its use.

XML stands for Extensible Markup Language and, in a nutshell, XML provides a technique for containing structured information in documents. For further background information on XML, take a look at www.xml.org and www.xml.com. Additionally, because XML must interact with some other type of language or program, like Flash or PHP, you may want to also check out: http://www.macromedia.com/desdev/topics/xml.html or http://www.flashdeveloper.nl/g_flash_xml_faq.html to get more familiar with XML and Flash. The *Flash MX Designer's ActionScript Reference* available from friends of ED (ISBN: 1-903450-58-6) also provides an excellent guide to using XML with Flash MX and ActionScript.

Now let's get down to the business of describing how the XML fits in to the use of this component. Open `myImages.xml`, found in this chapter's code folder in the download, with Notepad or your favorite text editor program:

Each line in the above code within the `<myMenu>` tags represents an object to load into the image scroller component, and its associated attributes. In this example file, there are six objects that will be placed in the scroller. To add more objects to the scroller, you can simply copy and paste the `<myItem>` node, and change the image or Flash movie names and paths. Let's take a look at what's going on.

The JPG or SWF is identified through the `theImage` variable. It's obviously crucial to ensure that your path is correct when creating new objects. For example, the first entry specifies the path and file name `images/image1.jpg` – notice that in the same examples folder where you found `myImages.xml` you'll see the `images` folder, which in turn contains the file `image1.jpg`. Also note that wherever you decide the destination for your final Flash movie, just make sure that the `myImages.xml` is in the same directory as the main SWF, and the loaded objects are given the appropriate path *relative* to that location.

The next variable, `theUrl`, determines what the object will do once clicked, if you want it to be a button of course (more on that shortly). If you want the object in the scroller to link to a URL, then enter the full address here, being sure to include the `HTTP://` part. If you decide the object needs to interact with the main movie by controlling some action inside the Flash movie, then simply enter `0`, which nullifies `theUrl` making it non-functional.

Keeping in mind that a flexible component is a friendly component, I wanted to make the next process as intuitive as possible, yet maintain the most flexibility. By setting `theEngine`, the final variable of the `<myItem>` tag, you can choose to have the object 'do something' in your main movie. This may seem a little confusing at first, so it's worth reading carefully. The logic is that we will set `theEngine` to a frame number in a movie clip called `Monnone Engine` that will be dragged onto the main (root) stage from the `Monnone Scroller` folder in the Library of the FLA that contains your component. If you've already dragged the image scroller from the Components panel and onto the stage, open up the Library to see where the `Monnone Engine` movie clip is:

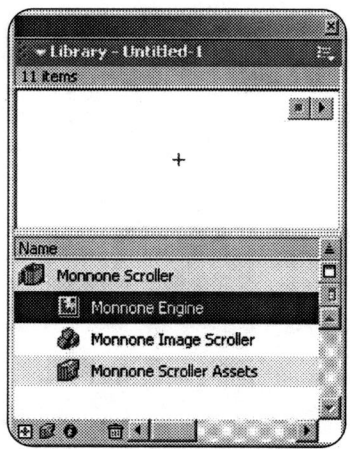

The `Monnone Engine` clip will need to have as many frames as are required, depending on the amount of objects you want in the scroller. It will initially be stopped in the first frame, so frame 1 is taken by default. Once the object in the scroller is clicked, it activates the `theEngine` variable, which assigns the specified frame number to go to in `Monnone Engine`. In the movie clip, on the newly specified frame, will be your code that interacts with the rest of your Flash movie. The following diagram demonstrates this process:

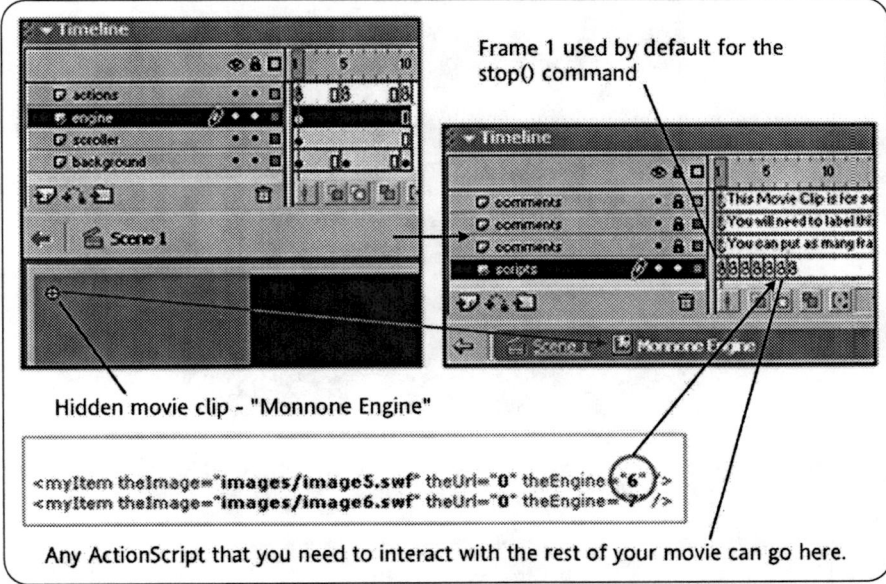

Frame 1 used by default for the stop() command

Hidden movie clip - "Monnone Engine"

```
<myItem theImage="images/image5.swf" theUrl="0" theEngine="6"/>
<myItem theImage="images/image6.swf" theUrl="0" theEngine="7"/>
```

Any ActionScript that you need to interact with the rest of your movie can go here.

Using the image scroller

At this point, you may well be questioning why the structure and workings of this component are so seemingly over-complicated. Well, I decided to handle it this way because it allows for you to have complete control over the actions generated once the object is clicked. You can add as much functionality (code) to each one of those frames as is necessary. The alternative to this method is just to pass the ActionScript commands from the XML file itself to control the movie, but such a technique is limited to simple commands.

Let's take a more detailed look at the process highlighted in the previous section, because without the element of interactivity, this image scroller is nothing more than that – an image scroller! Open up `myImages.xml` once more and refer to the fifth within the `<myMenu>` XML tags:

```
<myItem theImage="images/image5.swf" theUrl="0" theEngine="6"/>
```

Here, `theEngine` is set to 6, meaning when the object is clicked it will go to frame 6 of the `Monnone Engine` and execute any ActionScript that you've inserted there, making the scroller easily interact with the rest of the movie you created. Now open up the example FLA from the download – in `monnone_scroller.fla`. In this sample Flash movie, you can see that the image scroller component has already been dragged onto center stage, the timeline has been given some structure, and also the `Monone Engine` movie clip has been placed in the top left corner of the stage:

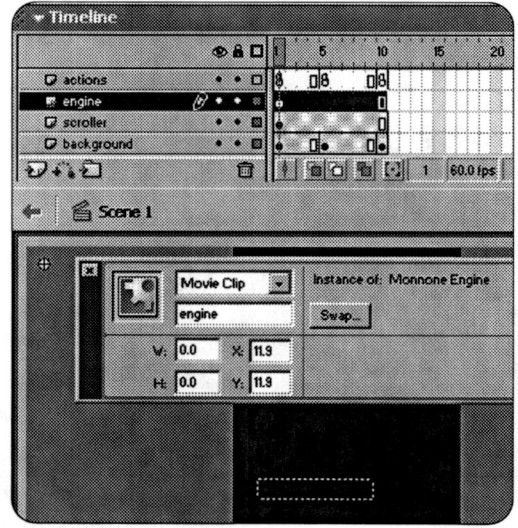

Next, double-click on the Monone Engine clip and take a look at the code attached to frame 6 of its main timeline:

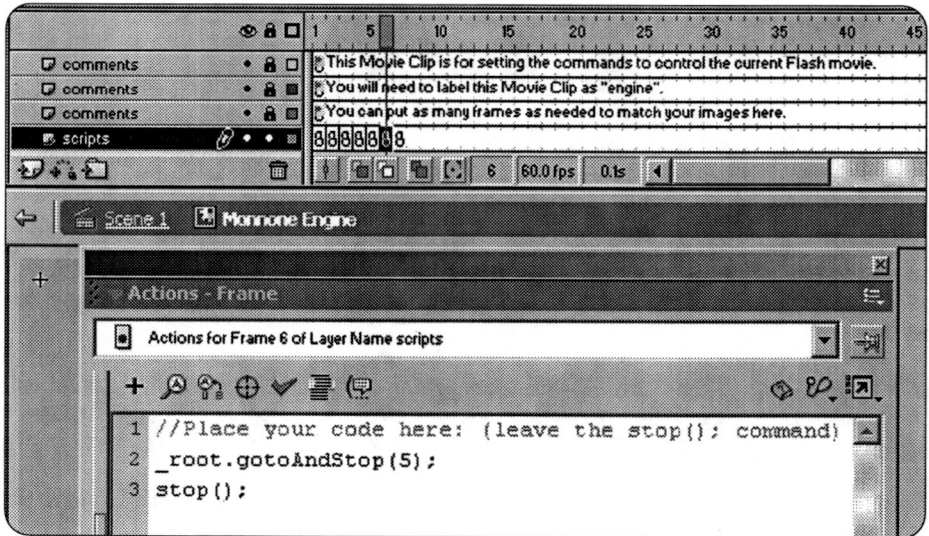

So in this example, the XML file directs the Flash playhead to frame 6 of Monone Engine (via the theEngine variable), which in turn redirects Flash to frame 5 of your main timeline. Test the FLA now to see the finished effect – clicking on the fifth object in the scroller (image5.swf) sends us to frame 5 of the main timeline, which we've filled with some sample content, the text Frame 5, for this demonstration:

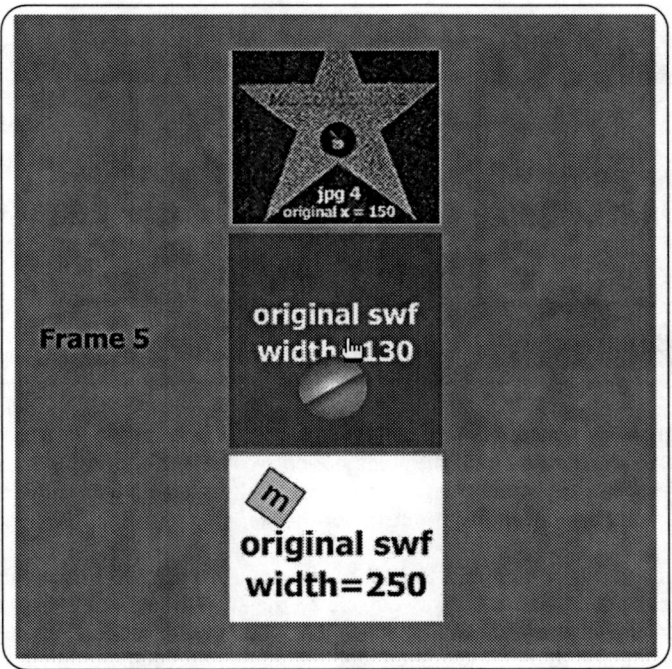

There you have it – a fully interactive and dynamic image scroller!

An additional feature that comes with this image scroller is that it will resize your JPEGs and SWFs to the required height and width of the component, and you can modify these dimensions through the component parameters (discussed in the next section).

There are, however, some limitations when it comes to the SWFs you load in. When using SWFs, it's best to experiment a little while developing that SWF to get the best results. So let me save you some aggravation and tell you what *not* to do while developing the SWFs to load in. Here are a couple of recommendations that should help you to avoid getting any more 'unexpected' results:

- **Including text** – If possible, it's worth breaking apart any text in your Flash movie into vector graphics (select the text and then from the menu choose Modify > Break Apart – do this twice to turn the text in vectors). If you must have text as text, then make sure it is not close to the edge of the stage. Text has a tendency to animate in a slightly different manner to the way graphics do. This could cause the resizing to work unexpectedly. The following images show how the object resizing with text-based objects can produce unexpected results. The image on the left, on the next page, is with the text broken down into vectors and it resizes correctly. The image on the right shows the effect of text that is *not* broken down and you can clearly see how the object is not resizing correctly:

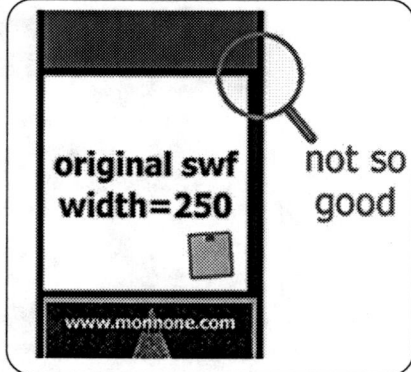

- **Animation** – Try not to animate objects that pass in and out of the stage for that clip. Try to keep all the animations within the stage boundaries of that clip. Again, resizing of this object in the scroller gets hairy when things fly in and out of its stage. What happens is that *everything* in the SWF gets drawn, even if it is outside of the stage.

  In fact, a basic rule of thumb is that when developing these SWFs intended for loading into the scroller, make sure that nothing is outside of the stage boundaries. Flash wants to show every graphic or object in the loaded in movie, and the resizing process might distort these objects slightly, producing strange looking effects.

Now that we've seen exactly what's going on 'behind the scenes' with this component and gained a good understanding of how to use it, let's see exactly how we might customize the look and feel of the image scroller using its parameters.

Customization using the component parameters

In the Flash authoring environment, open up monnone_scroller.fla again (or any other FLA in which you're using the component) and select the image scroller on the stage. Now open up the Component Parameters panel (Window > Component Parameters), and you'll see the parameters listed (you can also view them in the Property inspector):

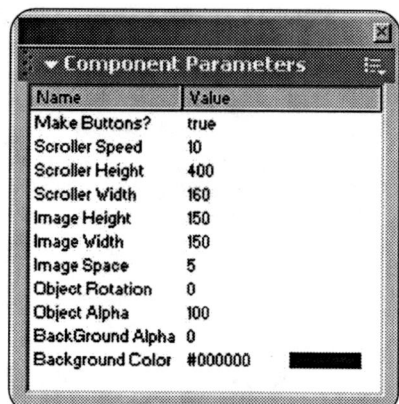

Let's start at the top, and briefly describe what each of these parameters does – try changing the values, and re-testing the Flash movie as you read through:

- **Make Buttons?** – This lets us decide if we want all of the images to be buttons or not. By default it's set to `true`. If this is set to `false`, the objects will not be able to interact with anything or link to URLs.

- **Scroller Speed** – This adjusts the speed at which the images scroll. It's important to note that the movie frame rate will affect this setting as well, so it's best to adjust the main movie's frame rate to your favorite rate and then set this option, adjusting it until you get the desired speed. The default value is `15`.

- **Scroller Height** – With this setting we can determine the height that the scroller will scroll to. It allows us to see more or less of the scroller.

- **Scroller Width** – Here we can set the width of the scroller. This settings does not change the actual width of the images in the scroller, but modifies the viewing size or mask in the scroller. This setting must be set equal to, or higher than, the Image Width setting, or clipping will occur.

- **Image Height** – This is where we set the height of the object in the scroller.

- **Image Width** - This is where we set the width of the object in the scroller. This setting needs to be adjusted along with the Scroller Width – if it's larger, then the object will get cropped.

- **Image Space** – With this setting we can adjust how far apart the loaded in images will be. (Note that it can be set to a negative number, which could produce some interesting effects, combined with the Object Rotation setting).

- **Object Rotation** – Here we can set how the objects will be placed in the scroller. By default, this setting is `0`. Changing this setting to `-45`, for example, produces a diamond shaped scroller.

- Object Alpha – This adjusts the transparency of the loaded objects.

- BackGround Alpha – This adjusts the transparency of the background built into the scroller. If you don't want a background, set this to 0. It's set to 100 by default.

- Background Color – This adjusts the color of the background.

All of these parameters provide a comprehensive set of tools with which you can customize the component to fit into any of your designs. These options can work together to produce some very interesting effects.

Tips and tricks

There are a several things to note regarding the use of these parameters:

1. If you set the image size too small, you will see that objects do not scroll from the top of the Scroller Height to the bottom. You can correct this in one of two ways:

   - Reduce the height of the scroller in the Scroller Height setting. For example, the sample images provided in the download are 150 by 150 pixels square, and that is the default size for the images in the component. If you set the Image Height and Image Width to 50, setting the Scroller Height to 250 works very well.

   - If you want to size the images at, say, 50 pixels in height, but would prefer to maintain a large scroller height, seeing more images at one time, you can make some amendments to the XML file. Just copy all the image elements as a group and paste them right beneath the first set. So, in the example file we'd have a total of 12 elements, doubling the amount that the scroller loads in. This will create a seamless scrolling effect of the images.

2. When changing the Object Rotation be conservative. You will find that if you rotate the objects -90 or 90 degrees the resize will not work. Why? Because the component code bases the resizing on the y-axis rather than the x. Also, if you set the Object Rotation to -180 or 180 degrees, the images will not align in the middle of the scroller.

3. When you create your SWF to be loaded into the scroller, keep in mind that the *entire* animation will show up in the space provided for that object in the scroller. This means that if you create a bouncing ball that comes in from outside the SWFs stage, the ball will show up in the scroller, off the intended stage. The end result will be that the SWF clip distorts to fit everything into the space allotted in the scroller. In other words, try not to animate things outside of the original stage of your loaded SWFs, as noted earlier.

4. You can create a horizontal scroller by selecting the scroller on the stage and rotating it by 90 degrees. However, you will have to do the same thing to each image in a graphics editing program like PhotoShop – rotate each image 90 degrees in the same direction that you rotated the scroller. It might seem like you should be able to rotate each image using Object Rotation, but again it's measured on the y-axis, so image resizing will not work. It is possible to do it this way if all of your objects are the same size to begin with, before they're loaded into the scroller.

So there you have it! Now that you know how to work with this tool, experiment with it and have some fun! You can see the latest improvements to this component, and download future versions, from my site: www.monnone.com.

Paul Prudence

Playing around with computers takes up all of my time —
solid state conspiracies aside, sometimes I'm not sure if
this is a good or bad thing. As an artist I'm always looking
at different media in terms of how i can harness them for
my own peculiar form of creativity. Flash is an awesome
environment for experimental creativity — it permits the
discovery of interesting things through bad code !. Some
of these discoveries can be found at my personal space,
www.transphormetic.com. Commercial application of
some of these experiments can also be viewed at
www.slightspace.com.

Thanks to the friends of ED team for inviting me to get
involved with some cool books in the last year or so. The
concepts for these books have been forward thinking and
beautifully designed. Thanks to warphed, Ash le Catedral,
and most of all the lovely Clo for putting up with me
playing with computers all of the time.

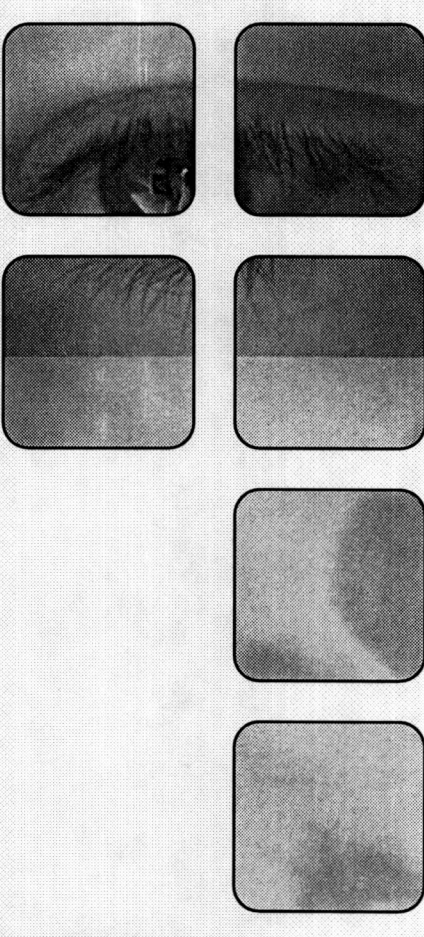

Component 8

Pattern Generators

Pattern generators, interactive mouse toys, and dynamic geometrical designs – three simple post-functional components for amusement and distraction.

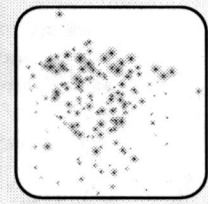

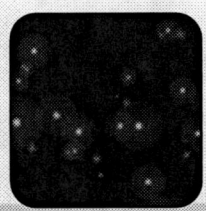

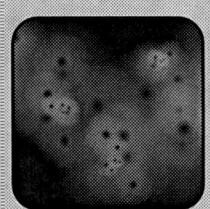

So far in this book you've seen some great examples of highly functional reusable components, extremely inventive OOP classes that can be dragged onto the stage, saving time and making the life of an interface designer so much more easy and efficient. I've deviated slightly from such decidedly practical components to produce a collection of simple but effective *mouse toys* and *pattern makers*. Although the Flash MX environment is obviously ideal for producing such features as autonomous UI components with which we can construct entire web applications, it is equally useful for making useless, beautiful things – and it's this end of the Flash spectrum I've been most interested in.

Look around the web and you'll find loads of very exciting sites also dedicated to pushing Flash designs that are not necessarily functional in nature, so called *Flash experiment* sites. From life generators to particle emitters (see also Component 13 in this book), physics engines to 3D engines; a seemingly endless number of mathematical structures and formulas have been applied within the Flash environment at some point, often ending up with the ubiquitous mouse toy.

In building these experimental Flash art pieces, it's a common occurrence to keep changing, combining, adding, and removing key variables to tweak the look and feel of a final animated system. Components allow the specific variables or parameters of a system to be available and thus allow non-programmers to mess with the inner workings of a programmed system. Of course, for these parameters to be really useful they need to be sufficiently documented, and given suitable property names, such as *rotation rate* or *flicker rate*, so that the non-programmer can quickly grasp what the parameters do to the system.

I'll be honest; I'm no hardcore programmer. I've learned to use ActionScript from a design point of view, and it gives me an extra set of design tools outside of what is normally considered design territory. Many Flash users will refer to this area as the *developer's turf*; to me the boundaries of any project will typically become blurred here – design-development, development-design: but we shouldn't forget that it's what appears on the surface of the monitor that counts!

Another thing to keep in mind is that too much obsessing over correct code and not enough design concept can be a terrible thing. Although the components I've produce are probably not the greatest examples of fine OOP code you'll ever see, or the most functional items in this book for that matter, I hope that some of you will be impressed or intrigued at the combinations, mutations, transformations, and animations that these three pattern generator components can achieve.

Calliscope

Calliscope is actually a word I've just made up! *Calli* as in Calligraphs, pictures or patterns made from writing, specifically the Arabic calligrams, and *scope* as in kaleidoscope. You can see some fine examples of circular calligraphs at www.aramedia.com/sakkal.htm (in particular, see images 1, 2, 19, 23, and 31). .So for me *calliscope* gives the impression of a revolving-transforming calligraphic kaleidoscope – and that's exactly how this mouse toy component appears on the screen. An interesting tangent is that the etymological origin of *calli* is in the Greek *Kallos* meaning beauty, and the origin of *scope* is in the Greek *skopeo* meaning to look at.

The Calliscope component, once installed using the `calliscope.mxp` file, produces a kaleidoscope made of text whose rotation, scaling, and transformation properties are affected by the position of the mouse pointer – this is what makes it a mouse toy!

The animation takes in a number of parameters from the Property inspector or Component Parameters panel, allowing its appearance and movement to be changed as well as a string containing the text to be 'calliscoped'. Its use is fairly intuitive, so just drag the component onto the stage, add in some parameters and have a play!

 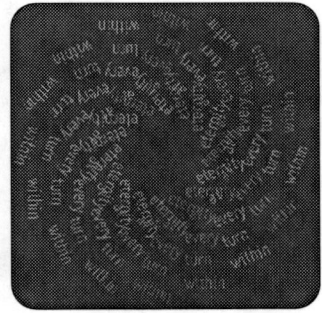 

I'm sure now you can see why I call it a calliscope! Certainly those familiar with Arabic calligraphy will hopefully see some similarities. Try moving the mouse around the screen and see how it effects the rotational movement and scaling of the text causing it to recombine, mutate, and revolve into many textual combinations and patterns. There appears to be rotations contained *within* rotations, and at times you can position the mouse so that some rotations stop while others continue, simple singular properties combining to produce complex end-effects. Personally, I find this kind of design quite satisfying and it surprises me to this day how often I get asked to incorporate simple effects such as these into clients' sites during my day job as a creative developer.

So how does it work? Well it's quite simple, If you look in the `assets` folder, which is inside the main folder of the component in the Library, you'll find three movie clips – `parent`, `child`, and `idea` (each of which is nested inside the other in that order):

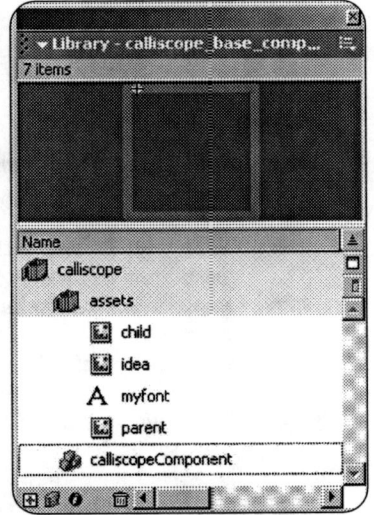

On the timeline of `idea` you will see that the `createTextField()` method is invoked, and a corresponding `TextFormat` object created, to produce a text field called `calliscope` with specific properties. These properties are the parameters that are passed by users into the Property inspector of the component, and include properties like the size and color of the text. The replication and animation of this text field is taken care of in the main timeline of the actual component. The clip is attached to the stage and then duplicated as many times as required always making sure the duplications are evenly distributed and rotated through a circle. Finally, each duplication is given an `onEnterFrame` method to affect its scale and rotation relative to the `_root` mouse position causing the fairly complex final animation.

Another thing you might have noticed if you looked inside the `assets` folder in the Library is a font icon. For those not familiar with this icon, it stores the font properties of a font to be exported – this has to been included to ensure the correct rendering of text field animations. So whenever you change the font name parameter (see below) in the

Property inspector, you also have to remember to change the font from the drop-down box by clicking on the font icon in the assets folder and make them identical. So be aware that if you do change the font from within the component parameters and fail to update the exporting of that font via this icon, you will see nothing on publishing the SWF!

Parameters

With the component selected on the stage, we can study all of its parameters by looking in the Component Parameters panel:

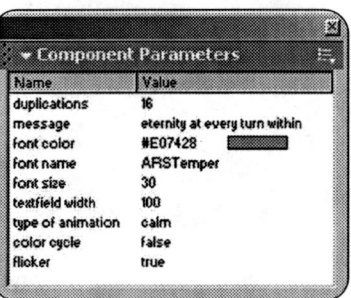

- duplications – Controls number of duplications contained within the calliscope.
- message – Controls the message contained within the calliscope.
- font color – Sets the color of the text message.
- font name – Displays the message with the selected font.
- font size – Sets the size of the selected font.
- textfield width – Sets the width of the textfield for the message – this allows multi-line messages since word-wrap enabled.
- type of animation – Sets the type of animation: `calm`, `moebius`, or `flutter`.
- color cycle – If set to `true`, cycles the color of the text message.
- flicker – If set to `true`, makes the calliscope flicker.

Ideas and inspirations

In the download you'll find a wide range of example files (both FLAs and SWFs) showing this component in action:

- `call_within.swf` – the textfield width is set to `100` here, which causes the message to be placed on multiple lines (because of the word-wrapping). The textfield width and the font size are the two parameters that control formatting of the message. The animation type is set to `calm`, color cycle is turned off, but flicker is set to `true` causing the calliscope to flicker with a subtle strobe effect.

- `cal2_cycle.swf` is similar to the previous example, but this time the color cycle variable has been set to `true` producing text with an array of autumnal hues. The basis for the color variation is derived from the starting selected font color, so there is no accurate means of determining which colors you'll see when you use the color cycle switch – it's all down to experimentation with the starting font color hex value, from which the simple random cycling math is based upon.

- `cal3_abstract.swf` has a change of font, but this time we see an ornate pattern as opposed to lines of text. This is because the message parameter has been set to some rather random characters. I wanted to show how the calliscope component could be used to make kaleidoscopic patterns using such characters. There are no limitations to the type of characters, fonts, or font sizes you can use with this component. Try experimenting with really large abstract fonts to produce some beautiful meshing patterns.

- `cal4_redmoebius.swf` utilizes a different animation type, specifically the moebius selection from the type of animation drop-down list. This causes the message to be convoluted through a spatial aperture – almost as if it's getting stretched through space-time!

- `cal5_spatial.swf` uses the same animation type as the previous example, but this time with an actual text message – an undulating spiral folds in onto itself becoming a vortex of information!

- `cal6_Kalligram.swf` uses an oriental font to great effect; the characters mesh together to form a revolving geometry of signs (see overleaf):

You'll also find some bonus example files of this component in the download – so be sure to check them out too!

TrailerMaker

The TrailerMaker component is used to generate... yes, you guessed it – mouse trails! I think one of the first Flash files I ever saw that really intrigued me was a mouse trailer – that was probably way back when Flash 4 came out. Since then I've seen millions of them and I'm pretty sure that many Flash designers have seen enough to last them a lifetime! But if it wasn't for that early file of a movie clip chasing my cursor around the screen, I may have never bothered to grab a copy of Flash and work out how it was done. Even more so, perhaps if I hadn't seen that mouse trailer at all, I might not be here writing a chapter about them! Actually, some of you may well be wishing I went out for a beer that night... Anyway, out of respect and as a kind of payback, here's my homage to the trailer in the form of the TrailerMaker component.

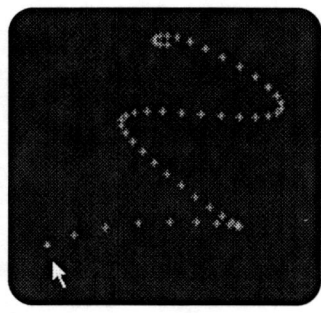

This component is designed to be dragged onto any movie clip on the stage – the component icon will 'magically' snap to the top left hand corner of any symbol it is dragged upon (for those interested, this is achieved by referencing `this._parent[this._targetInstanceName]` from within the component class definition). The mouse trails are then made up of duplications of that chosen movie clip symbol – so it's pretty much as simple as can be!

For the budding ActionScript junkies out there, click on the component icon and have a look at the code contained within the first frame of its timeline. Very simply, this script positions the `trailClip` in the same location as the mouse pointer; however, to give it a nice spring-like feel, I've incorporated some basic elasticity and inertia equations. The strength of elasticity and inertia given to the trailer is passed through to the class from the component parameters, so these properties can be tweaked or even turned off. The `trailClip` is then duplicated a number a times with an `onEnterFrame` function given to each of the duplications. This function defines the properties of each duplication – specifically, its `_x` and `_y` positions, its `_rotation`, and its `_alpha`. There are a number of other variables that obtain their values from the parameters in the Property inspector, and these effect the animation of the trailer in a number of ways to produce a range of effects (see the parameters discussion below, and associated examples for more detail).

Parameters

As usual, you can access the component parameters in either the Property inspector or the Component Parameters panel:

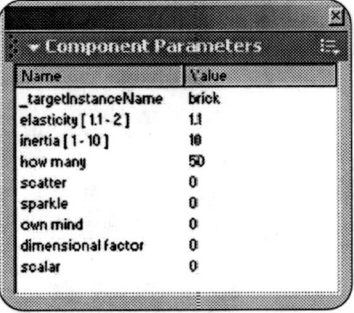

- _targetInstanceName – Name of the movie clip instance to be used in the component. This can be manually changed or will be automatically assigned as the component is dropped onto the specific symbol.
- elasticity (1.1-2) – Controls the elasticity of the trailer.
- inertia (1–10) – Controls the inertia of the trailer.
- how many – Controls the number of duplications for the trailer.
- scatter – Controls the scattering of the trailer.
- sparkle – Controls the sparkle of the trailer.
- own mind – Gives the trailer a 'mind of it own' if set to greater than 1.
- dimensional factor – Produces a pseudo three-dimensional space if set to greater than 1. Note that this parameter will only work in the intended way if the symbol movie clip that the trailer is constructed from is placed off-center from its own central registration point.
- scalar – Defines the progressive scaling of the trail.

Ideas and inspirations

Again, take a look at the sample files in the download:

- `trail1_simple.swf` is a basic trailer with inertia and elasticity, here the elasticity parameter is set to 1.1 and the inertia is set to 1 0. These values give quite pleasant, smooth trailing action with some realistic springiness.

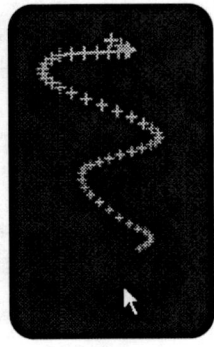

- `trail2_stardust.swf` looks like a trail of stardust! This is accomplished by setting the scatter parameter to 2 and the sparkle parameter to 1 0 0.

- `trail3_swarm.swf` achieves the effect of like a 'swarm' of symbols chasing the mouse pointer. This time scatter is increased to 1 5 and sparkle is reduced to 3 0.

- `trail4_streamer.swf` looks like a paper streamer – almost as if it's floating on air as the pointer pulls it around. It has a distinctively three-dimensional appearance and this is given to the system by setting the dimensional factor parameter to 7. We must note that this affect occurs only if the target instance is placed a little way off of its central registration point. For this version of the trailer we have also set the scatter parameter back to 0.

- `trail5_streamer_coil.swf` looks like a 3D coil as it is pulled around the screen; this file is identical to the previous file except for the dimensional factor which has been increased to 1 0 0.

- `trail6_unruly.swf` is a rather undisciplined trailer – its path has some random elements, while it does its best to acrobatically follow the mouse pointer. This time the own mind parameter is set to 1.

- `trail7_metallicSpring` is like a large metallic spring. This time the scalar parameter makes an appearance, set to 5 0 – it's this parameter that affects the progressive scaling of the trails

So from a simple single-character-based movie clip used as a building block, we can simply tweak the inbuilt component parameters and produce a wide range of different trailer effects.

Radiolaria

I've called this next component *radiolaria* – this name comes from the single celled organisms that live in the ocean in large quantities as part of plankton. The intricate vase-like skeletons of these tiny creatures are extremely beautiful (see www.radiolaria.org/index.htm).

With this in mind, open an example file from the download – `rad1_base.swf`, for example. Here, a single clip is replicated many times to produce a very complex and intricate structure, and at the end of the construction cycle it is rebuilt again with a completely different configuration. Each time it is rebuilt a new variation, or strain, is produced, distinct but similar each time. Changes in the rotation of each clip along with changes to its x and y positions brings this effect about – essentially, it's all about increments applied to some simple geometry:

Just like the previous component example, the Radiolaria component is designed to be dragged onto a movie clip symbol already residing on the stage (or indeed off the stage). It will then use that movie clip as a brick in the construction of something greater than the sum of its parts.

If you're interested in how it works, have a look at the code contained on the first frame of the component's timeline by selecting on the component icon in the Library. The fundamental structure of the code is reminiscent of the TrailerMaker component: the movie clip is duplicated a number of times and plotted on an arc or circle at the center of the stage. Each individual clip is then further rotated by a certain factor. Plotted and rotated duplications continue until a cycle is completed then the plotting begins again, although this time the rotational factor is incremented. There are a number of variables that are embedded into the code, which effect the plotting, scaling, and rotation of the clips and these are passed through from the component parameters that the user sets.

Parameters

Take a look at the parameters available with this component:

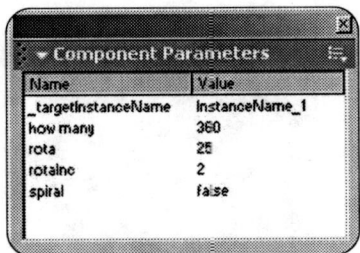

- _targetInstanceName – The movie clip instance to be used in the component. This can be manually changed or will be automatically assigned as the component is dropped onto the specific symbol.
- how many – Defines the number of duplications per construction cycle.
- rota – Defines the initial rotational constant.
- rotaInc – Defines the increment added to the rotation constant per cycle.
- spiral – Boolean value that, if set to `true` makes a spiral configuration, otherwise it's a circle.

Ideas and inspirations

As ever, you should play around with the demonstration files available in the download to familiarize yourself with the use of this component:

- `rad1_base.swf` plots an intricate flower-like shape that mutates into a different configuration for each construction cycle – it just keeps redrawing itself as a new species each time. The movie clip building block plays a large part in the form of the final geometry and shape of the construction. Aligning it off-center from its central registration point also affect the final render. Have a look at how the parameters are set up in Property inspector – the rota parameter is set to 2 5, rotalnc is 2, and there are 3 6 0 duplications of the original movie clip building block.

- `rad2_variation.swf` throws up a completely different sequence of species evolution, even though it uses the same movie clip as the previous example. Check out the changes to the parameters: how many is now set to 1 0 0, rota to 9, and rotalnc to 0.1.

- `rad3_spiral.swf` brings into play the spiral parameter, seting it to true. The result is quite fascinating – a logarithmic spiral shape is formed, and this is particularly evident on the second construction cycle.

- `rad4_spiral_green.swf`, `rad5_spiral_orange.swf`, `rad6_spiral_greenshell2.swf`, and `rad7_spiral_purple.swf` all provide interesting and beautiful examples of this component in action with the spiral switch turned on. What amazes me about these examples is how organic some of them appear; `rad6_spiral_greenshell2.swf` looks like an ammonite to me! It's almost as if we're using the component to draft out the blueprints for some of nature's truly intricate constructions:

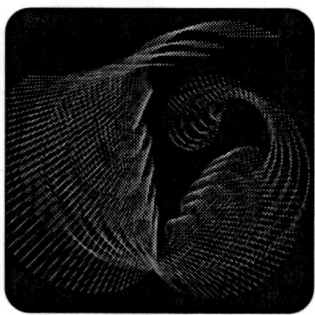 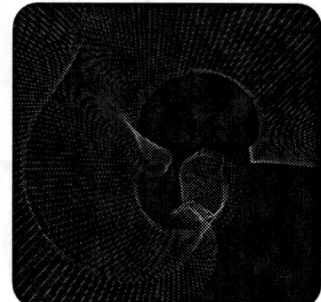 

Fun components in the real world

OK, so like I said in the introduction, these aren't most functional of components, so when would you use them? Well, the short answer is whenever you feel like it! As we've seen in this chapter, just playing around with the parameters in a short amount of time can produce an amazing range of results. I'd imagine an ideal use is that of a preloader, when a large download is necessary to view your site, and there is a little waiting to be done – you can entertain your guests with some simple (and complex!)

geometric animations that are affected by the movement of the user's mouse. Indeed, preloaders are probably the most common uses of mouse toys.

Anyway, more importantly, just have fun playing with them, and let me know if discover any interesting new species!

Jeremy Larkin

Jeremy is educated as a graphic designer but found an aptness for programming while teaching himself Java during his last few years of college. He quickly developed an interest in Flash as a web design tool that could offer the flexibility of traditional print design tools. With further versions he has found Flash to be an ever-stronger development tool and a potentially great medium for merging programming and design. Currently Jeremy is a consultant and developer, and the co-founder of Ricma Studios.

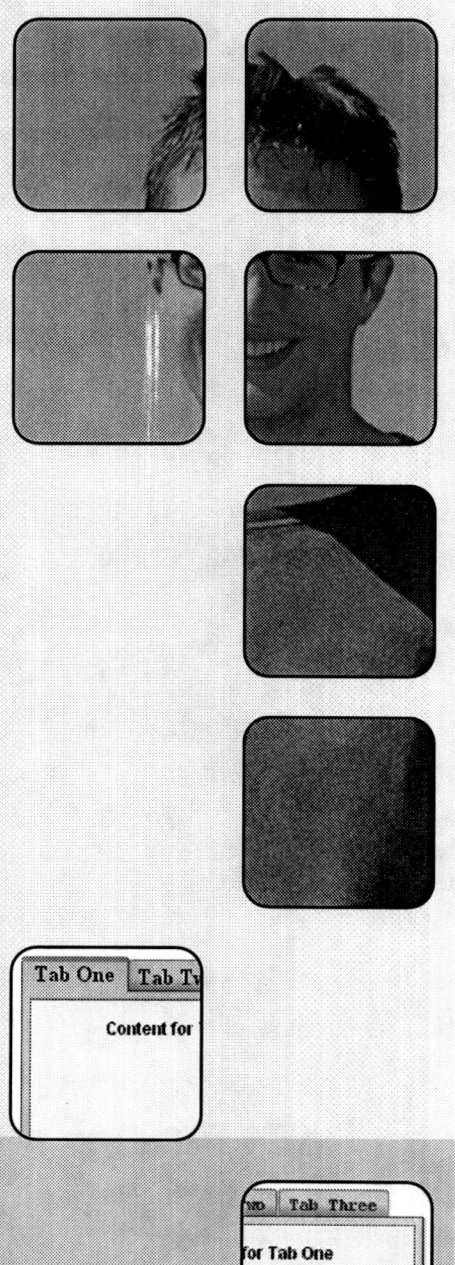

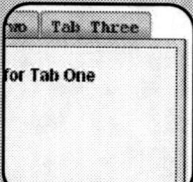

Component 9

TabControl

The TabControl is an easily implemented interface control that give the developer a powerful tool to help manage desktop real estate and give a consistent appearance across multiple projects.

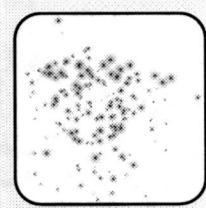

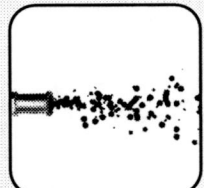
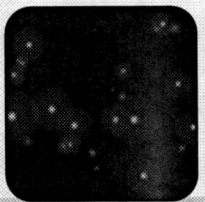

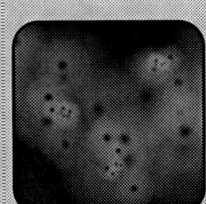

The TabControl component is a graphical user interface element that allows multiple groups of information to be displayed in one area of the screen. This component is quick to implement and is designed to duplicate the tabbed user interface found in all operating systems.

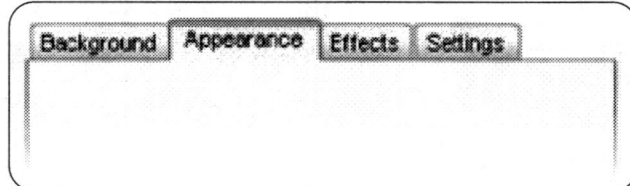

Since the entire TabControl component is constructed using ActionScript, it takes up relatively little file space – it adds less than 4 KB to your Flash movies, regardless of how many instances of the component are added.

Using the TabControl component

Once you have installed the component using the `TabControl.mxp` file from the download, you should find a TabControl component group in your Components panel (Window > Components):

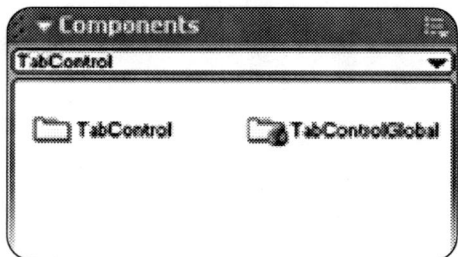

With this group selected, two components will be visible in the panel:

1. **TabControl** - This is the main component that we'll discuss in the bulk of this chapter.

2. **TabControlGlobal** - This is a companion component to the TabControl component. It contains only the color format and font settings used in TabControl, its purpose being to allow these settings to be made globally. Including this component in a project will force all instances of the TabControl component to use the color format and font settings defined in TabControlGlobal. This component is explained further in the section on Customizing the component, towards the end of this chapter.

To add the component to a project, select the TabControl component and drag it into your movie on the desired frame.

Setting the parameters

To adjust the properties of the component you will need to have the component selected and have either the Property inspector (Window > Properties) or the Component Parameters panel (Window > Component Parameters) visible:

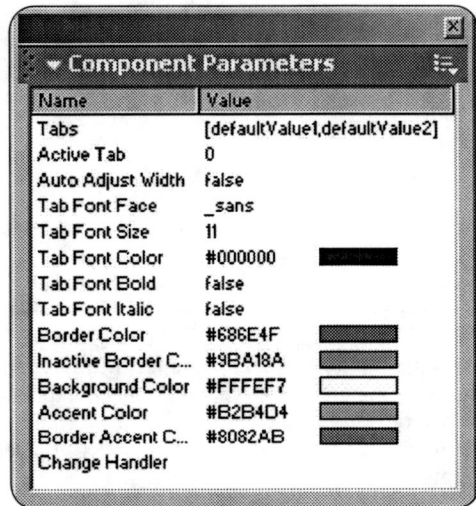

When the component is first added to the project there will be two tabs visible: defaultValue1 and defaultValue2. These values are only for demonstrating the appearance of the component. The Tabs parameter contains the values for the tab labels. To modify them, select this parameter and click on the magnifying glass that appears to the right. In the Values window that subsequently pops up, change these values to the labels that you want displayed in the component and use the + and - buttons to add and remove labels:

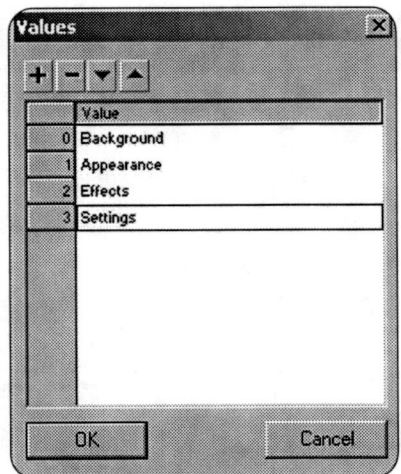

After clicking OK, the component's live preview will now show the tabs that you have added:

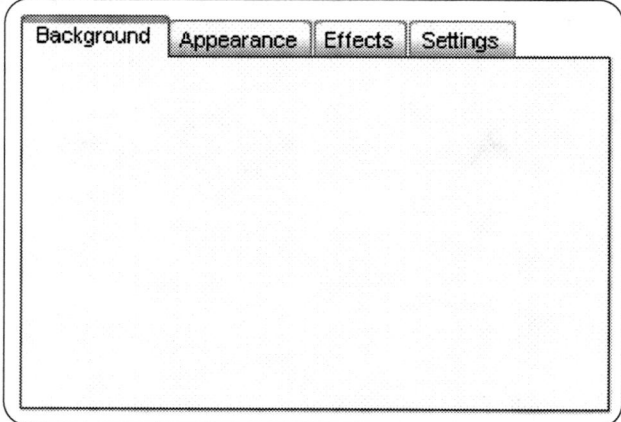

Before we look at controlling this component's appearance with ActionScript, it's worth spending a moment playing with the other parameters – they're all fairly self-explanatory. For instance, the Active Tab parameter is the index of the tab that is initially selected. By default, this value is 0. Note that the tab indices are zero-based, meaning that the first tab has an index of 0. We'll discuss the rest of these parameters later on in this chapter

TabControl methods

Tabs can also be added, removed, and manipulated dynamically using script. In this section, we'll take a quick look at some of the more commonly used methods that are associated with the TabControl component. Further explanations, as well as examples of their usage, can be found in the TabControl entry of the Reference panel (Window > Reference) in the Flash MX authoring environment, after the component has been installed:

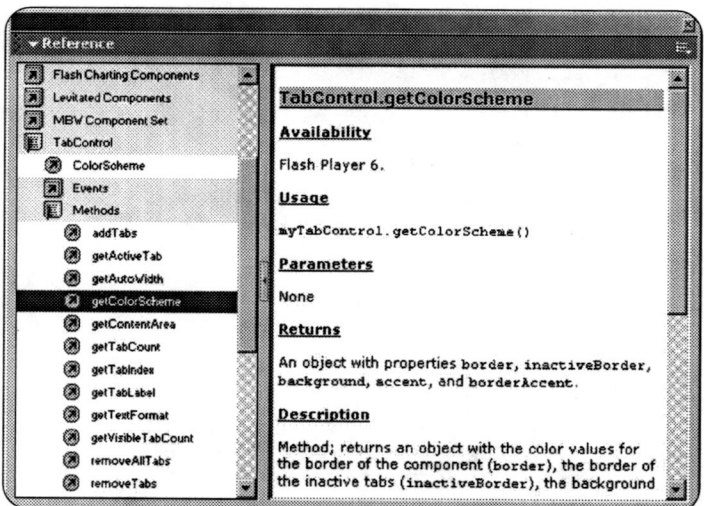

The table below presents some of the highlights of the available methods:

Method	Description
addTabs(tabs, [index])	Adds tabs to the component. The tabs parameter is either a string or an array of strings (if adding multiple tabs) representing the new tab labels. If the optional index parameter is specified, tabs will be inserted starting at the index, otherwise at the end.
getActiveTab()	Returns the index of the selected tab.
getTabCount()	Returns the total number of tabs in the component.
getTabIndex(tabLabel)	Returns the index of the tab with the specified label tabLabel.
getTabLabel(tabIndex)	Returns the label of the tab at the specified index tabIndex.
getVisibleTabCount()	Returns the number of tabs that are visible in the component.
removeAllTabs()	Removes all of the tabs.
removeTabs(tabs)	Removes the tabs specified in tabs. This parameter can be a single tab or an array of tabs.
setActiveTab(tab)	Set the selected tab.
setTabLabel(tab, label)	Sets the label of tab to the new string specified in label.
swapTabs(tab1, tab2)	Swaps the positions of the two tabs.

It's important to note that tabs can be referred to in two ways with these methods:

1. The index of the tab position.
2. The label of the tab.

When using the tab label it will only find exact matches (case-sensitive) and if there are multiple tabs with the same label, the first match will be the one selected.

By default, the Auto Adjust Width parameter is disabled, which means the width of the component is determined by the width set in the authoring environment using the Property inspector, Info panel, or the Free Transform tool. If there are more tabs than will fit in the width of the component, then the right-most tabs will not be displayed. If Auto Adjust Width is enabled, the width of the component will be forced to exactly fill the space needed to display all of the tabs, regardless of the width set in the authoring environment. The component will automatically adjust size if tabs are added via ActionScript as well. The methods getAutoWidth() and setAutoWidth() allow this property to be controlled dynamically.

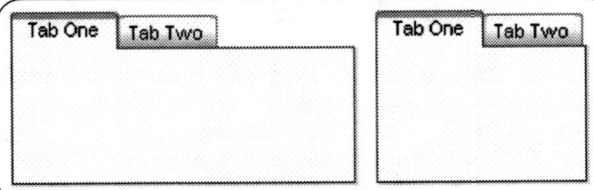

The only difference between these two components is that the second one has the Auto Adjust Width property set to true.

Creating tabbed content

Learning how to use the empty TabControl component is a good starting point, but now we should turn our attention to incorporating content within the component. The TabControl does not inherently modify any content other than the tabs that are displayed. In order to display content specific to the selected tab, we need to create the actual content and add just a little bit of ActionScript. The general technique for displaying the tabbed content is to get the index of the active tab and respond by displaying different content relative to the selected tab. The response to the active tab's index can be to tell a movie clip to go to a certain frame, to attach a certain movie clip, to load an external SWF, to use the drawing API to create new content, or any other response the developer can conjure up.

The following example demonstrates how to use movie clip frames to display different content. For this example, you can either create the file from scratch or, easier still, open the TabControlExample.fla located on this book's accompanying download.

On the root timeline of the movie, we've created three layers labeled, from top to bottom: SCRIPTS, TabContent, and TabControl. Each layer requires only a single frame:

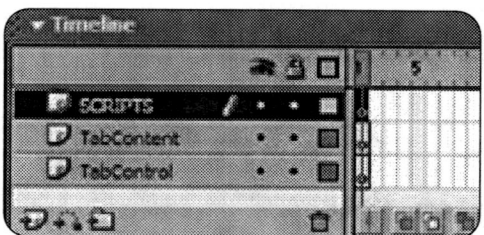

Next, we've dragged the TabControl component onto the TabControl layer and given it an instance name of myTabControl. Using the Property inspector, we gave the component four tab labels (Background, Appearance, Effects, and Settings for this demonstration):

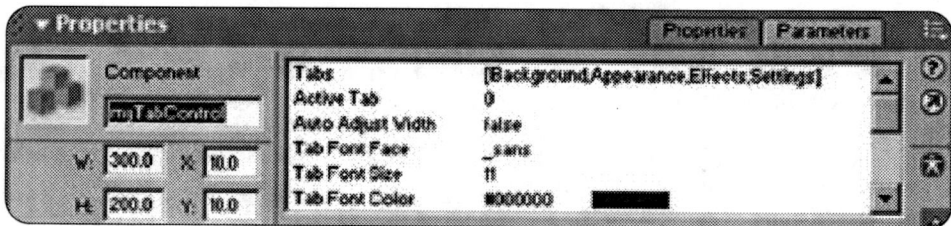

Next, a very simple movie clip was created with a number of frames equal to the number of tabs that were added to the component. For this example, I have created four tabs so this movie clip has four frames. On the first frame, create the content that you want to show when this first tab is selected. I've simply added some text that says: Background Tab. However, you can create something as simple, or as complex as you want. On the second frame, I've created the content for the second tab, and so on for each tab in the component.

After all of the frames have been created, we just add that movie clip to the TabContent layer of the root timeline and give the movie clip an instance name of myContentMovie. I've specifically positioned this movie clip directly over the TabControl component so that it looks like it's inside the tabs.

At this point I needed to do a little bit of coding – don't worry if you're not so used to ActionScript, this should be quite straightforward. On the first frame of the SCRIPTS layer, I added the following code:

```
1  myTabControl.setChangeHandler("tabChange");
2  function tabChange(component) {
3      var activeTab = component.getActiveTab();
4      myContentMovie.gotoAndStop(activeTab+1);
5  }
6
```

Let's break this code down line by line to see exactly how it works:

```
myTabControl.setChangeHandler("tabChange");
```

This first line sets the change handler for the component. The change handler is the function that gets called when the user clicks on a tab, changing which tab is active. The change handler can also be set 'manually' through the component parameters. Setting the Change Handler parameter to tabChange will have the same effect, but there is no option to specify the location of the change handler function, so when defining the change handler through the component parameter, the function must be defined on the same timeline that the component is put on.

```
function tabChange(component) {
```

This next line is where the function tabChange is defined. The parameter component is set because when the change handler is called, it is automatically passed a reference to the component as an argument. This means that whatever is put as the argument (in this case component) becomes a pointer to the component itself, and we can treat it exactly as if it were the component. For example, the code component._x refers to the current x position of the component.

```
var activeTab = component.getActiveTab();
```

Next, getActiveTab() is a method of the TabControl component that will return the index value of the currently selected tab.

```
myContentMovie.gotoAndStop(activeTab+1);
}
```

111

Finally, the movie clip myContentMovie is sent to a frame based on the active tab's index. The index value is increased by one because the tab indices are zero-based (the first tab has an index of 0, the second tab has an index of 1, and so on), whereas the movie clip frame numbers are one-based.

There is a second way to capture the event of the user changing the tabs: assigning an onChange() event function to the component. The difference with this approach is that a function is created in the component itself which means that the keyword this is a reference to the component, instead of requiring the component parameter:

```
myTabControl.onChange = function() {
    var activeTab = this.getActiveTab();
    myContentMovie.gotoAndStop(activeTab + 1);
};
```

If a change handler is set, defining the onChange() event will cause the change handler to be ignored. However, if an onChange() event is defined, setting the change handler will remove the function defined to capture the onChange() event – the change handler and onChange() event are not allowed to co-exist. For a more in depth explanation of the setChangeHandler() method and the onChange() event, see their relevant entries in the TabControl section of the Reference panel (Window > Reference)in the Flash MX authoring environment.

Customizing the component

The TabControl component exposes its tab label text format and color scheme as customizable parameters. These allow the developer to match the text formatting and color scheme of the component to the text and colors used in the design of the Flash project where the component will reside. Remember, you can modify these component parameters using the Property inspector (Window > Properties).

There are five text format parameters available to customize the component's properties:

- Tab Font Face
- Tab Font Size
- Tab Font Color
- Tab Font Bold
- Tab Font Italic

These will adjust their respective properties of the text formatting used in the tab labels, and will be represented in the live preview of the component. Note that some of these properties will require a change in the width of the tabs. If Auto Adjust Width is enabled, the width of the component will automatically be changed. If not, a change to the font properties may cause a tab to not display and require a change in the width of the component.

Next, there are five color properties of the component that can be changed:

- Border Color
- Inactive Border Color
- Background Color

- Accent Color
- Border Accent Color

The following diagram shows the parts of the component that each color corresponds to:

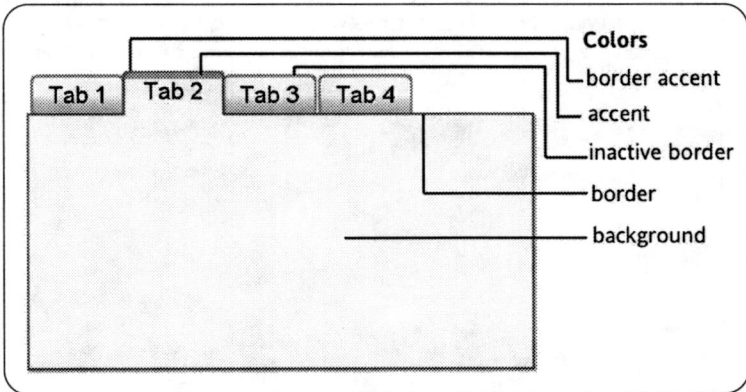

Referring back to the `TabControlExample.fla` that was created previously, we can modify these properties and see how they affect the component. Notice that there's a second copy of the component below the first one – this is the same as the first component except that the font settings and colors have been changed. Note that the tabs change size (vertically and horizontally) to compensate for the font settings:

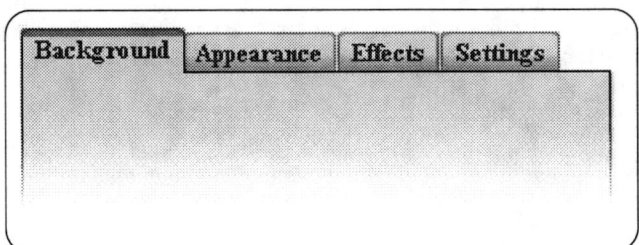

Modifying these properties will only affect the one instance of the component; therefore, it can be difficult to make sure that all instances of the component have the same appearance. However, remember the companion component to the TabControl that was mentioned at the start of this chapter? TabControlGlobal is designed to simplify the process of unifying the appearance of every instance of the components that you use in a Flash movie. When included in a project, the TabControlGlobal component will set all of the current and succeeding TabControl components to the font and color settings defined within it (its 'global' icon is only displayed within the authoring environment for a visual reference; it will not be visible in the published movie).

A convenient way to make sure that all TabControl components in multiple Flash files adhere to the same appearance is to create a SWF that contains only the TabControlGlobal component and load it into a movie using the `loadMovie()` method. This technique can also be employed to dynamically load different styles by utilizing multiple TabControlGlobal components in multiple SWFs.

For a demonstration of the real power of this component, take a look at `LoadStyle.fla` from the download. Running this example will initiate the TabControl component using the default style settings. Clicking on the Load Style 1 and Load Style 2 buttons will then load the respective styles. These styles are defined in the files `Style1.fla` and `Style2.fla` that are also included in the download:

It's worth spending some time studying the code on frame 1 of the SCRIPTS layer of `LoadStyle.fla` to see how this effect was achieved.

Finally, the font and color properties of a component instance can also be set at runtime with ActionScript by using the `setTextFormat()` and `setColorScheme()` methods of the TabControl component. These also have the ability to change the component settings globally for all currently and subsequently displayed instances. Again, for more information about these methods and examples of their use, refer to their entries in the ActionScript Reference panel of Flash MX.

Todd Marks

Todd is a developer, designer, instructor, and author, not to mention President of MindGrub Technologies, LLC (www.mindgrub.com). He graduated from Loyola College with a Bachelors of Science in Mathematics, and then entered the public realm teaching Mathematics and Computer Science in Columbia, Maryland, continuing his studies with a Masters of Technology at Johns Hopkins University. In 2000 Todd became Vice President of R&D at digitalorganism (www.digitalorganism.com), and since then he's worked extensively with ActionScript, PHP, ASP, Lingo, and many other development languages, working on numerous cutting edge projects. Todd's efforts have earned three Flash Film Festival nominations, Macromedia Site of the Day, two Addy Awards, and several educational partnerships, and now he's a Macromedia Certified Developer, Designer, and Subject Matter Expert. He has been a technical editor for an array of books, and a contributing and lead author to several more – including Beginning Dreamweaver MX, Foundation Dreamweaver MX, Flash MX Video, and Advanced PHP for Flash MX.

Bill Spencer

Bill is the founder and CEO of Popedeflash.com, and a well known speaker, author, and artist, having spoken at many new media conferences in Australia and the US, including FlashForward and FlashKit. Bill has served as an author and technical reviewer for both New Riders and friends of ED, and has appeared in a number of professional journals and periodicals. Some of his work has also featured as a finalist in the Flash Film Festival. He has served as a beta tester for Macromedia, Electric Rain, and Discreet, and a technical advisor for Electric image in the development of Amorphium Pro. Bill is a moderator at FlashKit.com and UltraShock.com, and is a staff member of Flashdevils.com.

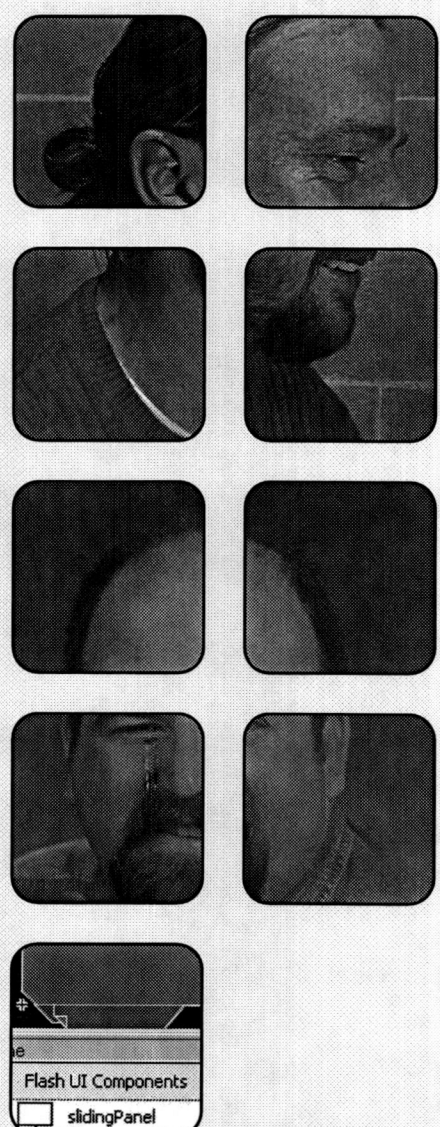

Component 10

Sliding Panel

Panels provide a means to tuck content away and keep a viewing area uncluttered, while providing a one-click method of exposing the hidden content. The sliding panel component maintains this ability to economize on your visible content, but adds an element of pizzazz by sliding on and off stage. In addition, with this component you can choose from a few pre-built panel appearances, or design your own from scratch.

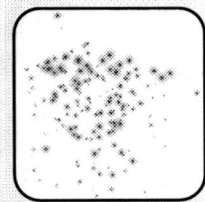

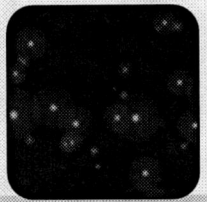

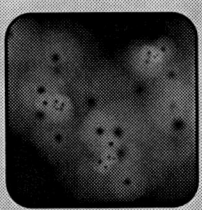

The sliding panel is a highly flexible and robust component that works like the information panels found on many applications, like Macromedia Flash MX. With this component, the sliding panels typically slide from offstage to onstage, and you can use it to display numerous different elements or sections of information that are not continuously required on stage. Ideas for its use include:

- News Bloggers
- MP3 Players
- Client Login
- File Directories
- Media Lists

You can designate the panel orientation as a left, right, top, or bottom. For instance, the sliding panel in the images below is bottom-oriented such that it is located just off the bottom of the screen and when activated it slides into the center of the stage:

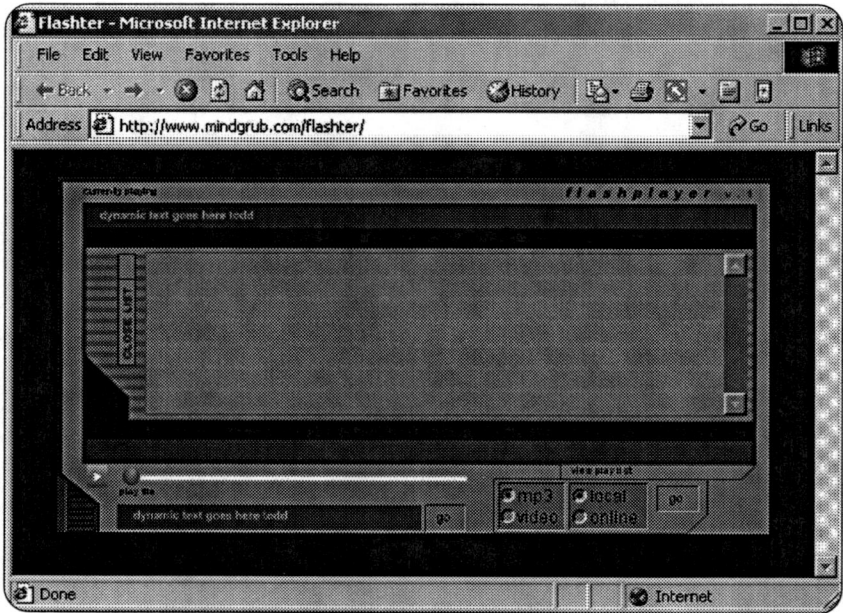

You can place the sliding panel anywhere on the stage, and within any timeline, and you can set the panel to activate at the click of the mouse, or on rollover and roll off. You have the ability to make the tab visible or not visible – the tab acts as either the button that triggers the panel, or the hit area for the rollover action. You can also choose to have the mouse pointer visible or not visible, and you can set the speed in which the panel moves. Lastly, you can have multiple instances of the panel object work in conjunction with each other – just like CheckBoxes and RadioButtons.

Perhaps the most important aspect of the sliding panel component is that you can specify the graphics or movie clips that you want displayed for the panel and tab, and you can give them any dimensions. In addition, there are four different default panel sets that ship with the component, if you do not feel like creating your own. As a teaser of what's to come in this chapter, and to see the all four default panel sets in action, check out `slidingPanel_Examples.swf.` from the download – in this file, we've gone panel-crazy and added sliding panels all over the movie!

The first sliding panels that I coded were for the digitalorganism Genesis website at www.digitalorganism .com/genesis. Back then I was using Flash 4 ActionScript, but still managed to code the panels in such a way that they were reusable and functioned as a group. At the time this was cutting edge, though I cringe at the appearance of that code now, compared to what's possible with Flash MX!

Recently, I teamed up with Bill Spencer to make an MP3 and video player in Flash called *Flashster* – www.mindgrub.com/flashter (the previous image is taken from this application), and was once again asked if I could code a sliding panel. This time, using Flash MX, I developed a solution that not only allows complete customization, but also has two beautifully written classes (if I do say so myself!). So, for those who are on the verge of writing their own classes, and for those that already have, I recommend you take a peak under the hood of this component and check out the `CTabbedPanel` and `CEventManager` classes. But first, let's learn the basics of how we can make the most out of our sliding panels.

Using the sliding panel component

For those that choose to install the component using the `slidingPanel.mxp` extension file using the Macromedia Extension Manager, the sliding panel component will be found in the Components panel. (Window > Components). You can simply drag the component out of that panel and on to the stage of your movie. Otherwise, you can just drag the `slidingPanel` out of the Library of the `slidingPanel.fla` file. As usual, all installation and example files can be found in the download.

Setting the parameters

In the following sections, we'll describe each of the parameters available with the sliding panel component to demonstrate the level of customization that is possible. After dragging an instance of the sliding panel to the stage, you can view all of the parameters in the Property inspector or the Component Parameters panel:

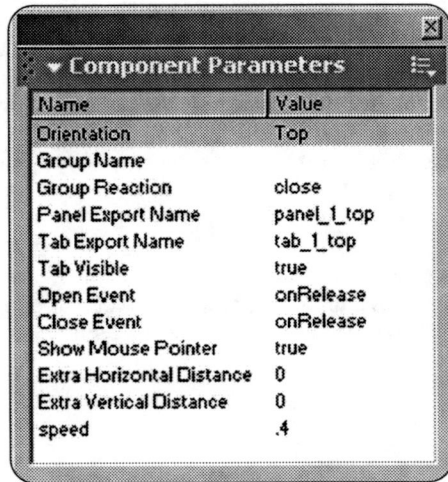

Orientation

The sliding panel can function such that it slides from the top into position, from the bottom, the right, or the left:

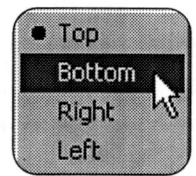

If the panel is top-oriented, for instance, it will slide from its starting y position, down to a y value equal to its starting position plus the height of the panel. If the Extra Vertical Distance parameter (discussed later in this chapter) is set, then it will include this distance in its movement.

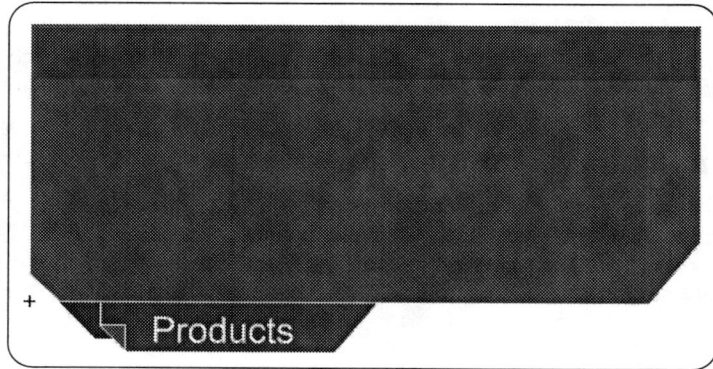

The sliding panel moves similarly to the top orientation when the orientation is set to bottom. The difference is that the panel will move from its starting y position, to a position equal to its starting y position *minus* the height of the panel.

Note that if the panel is bottom-oriented, then you will want to have a *negative* value set for the Extra Vertical Distance to get the panel to move that additional distance upwards.

One additional feature of the orientation of the panel that is nice is that you don't need to worry about the positioning of the tab in relation to the panel. The tab's x position will line up with the x position of the panel when oriented to the top or bottom, and will line up left, or right accordingly.

An important tip here is that you should create your panel and tab graphics such that the top left corner of each sits at (0,0) within the movie clip that contains it. You can, however, offset the tab within the movie clip (as seen above).

A side-orientated panel moves similarly to the top or bottom orientation except that it moves from its starting x, as opposed to y, and moves a distance equal to its width, as opposed to its height. You can also get the panel to move an extra distance specified in the Extra Horizontal Distance parameter.

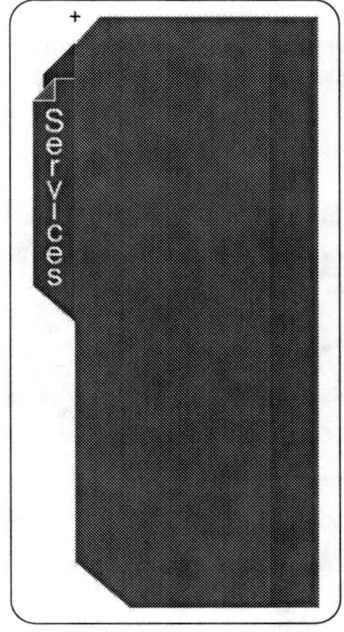

Remember, if the panel is right-oriented then you will want to have a negative value set for the Extra Horizontal Distance to get the panel to move that additional distance left.

Group Name

One of the neat features of the RadioButton component that has always impressed me is that they can work in a group. When you click on one radio button, it makes any other radio button that was previously selected, unselected.

This component, similarly, has the ability to work in groups – you can view the sliding panels working in groups in `slidingPanel_Examples.swf`. All you need to do is to enter the same name for multiple panels in the Group Name parameter in the Property inspector:

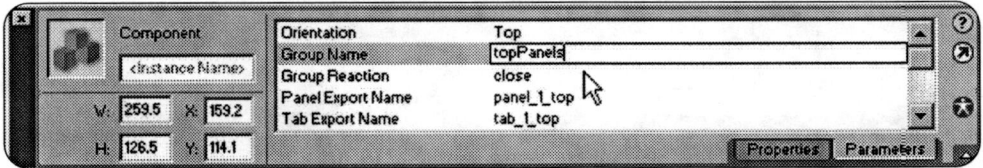

So, for instance, if Group Reaction (described next) is set to close, and you open any panel in the group, any previously opened panel will close. For aspiring class programmers, check out the `CEventManager` class inside the sliding panel component that manages this activity.

Group Reaction

You have the option to have any panel open or close when another is selected, depending on the value of the Group Reaction parameter, and as long as the two panels have the same Group Name.

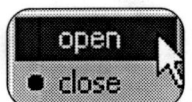

Note that group reactions work best when the Open Event and Close Event parameters are either both set to onRelease, or are onRollOut and onRollOver accordingly. Group reactions become unpredictable when a combination of these is used.

Panel Export Name

Before looking specifically at this parameter, check out the four panel sets that are included with this component – open up the Library of your Flash movie by hitting F11 and look inside the slidingPanelSkins folder:

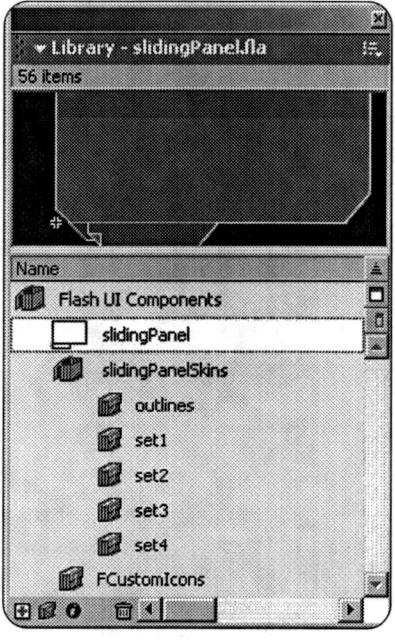

Each of these panel sets contains eight movie clips, all reusing the same graphics for the panel and tab. The possible default panel designs are as shown below:

Set 1

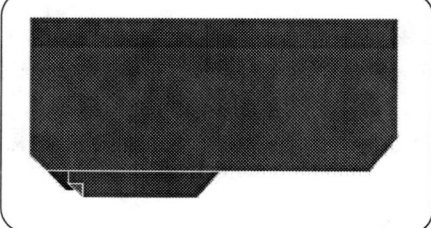

Set 2

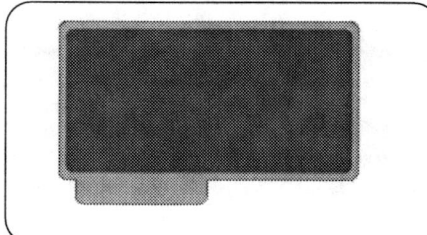

Set 3

Set 4

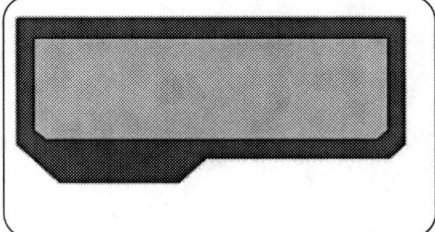

Now, in the Property inspector you will notice the Panel Export Name parameter gives you 16 different choices from the default panels list:

| panel_1_top |
| panel_1_right |
| panel_1_left |
| panel_1_bottom |
| panel_2_top |
| panel_2_right |
| panel_2_left |
| panel_2_bottom |
| panel_3_top |
| panel_3_right |
| panel_3_left |
| panel_3_bottom |
| panel_4_top |
| panel_4_right |
| panel_4_left |
| panel_4_bottom |

You will need to select the panel that corresponds to whatever Orientation you have specified for your sliding panel. Select the panel style of your preference, from 1 to 4 as we saw above, and the direction that coincides with the orientation of your panel. If, for instance, you want to use default panel 1 and have selected an orientation of top, then you should select panel_1_top.

In addition, you can edit any of the default panels in the Library, or create your own panels and add their names to the component definition by right-clicking (PC), or control-clicking (Mac), selecting Components Definition…, and adding the name of your panel to the drop-down menu of the component.

Both the Panel and the Tab graphics or movie clips must reside in the Library and have a linkage identifier. You can have any number of appearances for each of your different panels - you must simply create a graphic or movie clip for each panel, give it a linkage identifier, and enter that name for the Panel Export Name value in the Component Definition panel. Then simply select that panel in the Property inspector when you use the component. You can, in addition, simply edit one of the default panels (described below) that already reside, in the Library.

One of the main drawbacks of Macromedia's built-in components is that you are pretty limited in the number of ways you can customize the appearance of the components. For that reason, the sliding panel component has not relied on using built-in visual settings, giving you extreme freedom in the appearance of the sliding panels. You should physically add tab names, and so on, by editing or creating graphics, and then exporting them in the Library.

To give a panel or tab a linkage identifier, simply right-click (or CONTROL-click on a Mac) the graphic or movie clip in the library and select linkage. Then, give the panel or tab an Identifier, and remember to enter the same name in the Component Parameters panel:

123

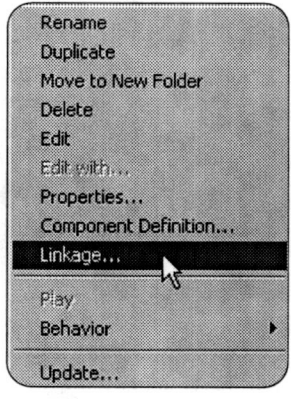
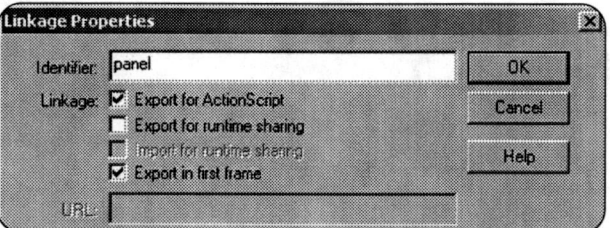

The classes that form the sliding panel are contained within `#initclip` tags of the component's code. You must have Export in first frame checked off to insure that the sliding panel builds properly. If you don't want to use the panel at the start of the movie, then simply house the panel in an additional SWF and load that file in when you want to use it.

As mentioned earlier, the tab positions itself in relation to the panel based on height and width. The panel, in addition, slides accordingly to its height and width. Therefore, make sure to position the panel and tab graphics such that they line up at the registration point (0,0) within the graphic or movie clip:

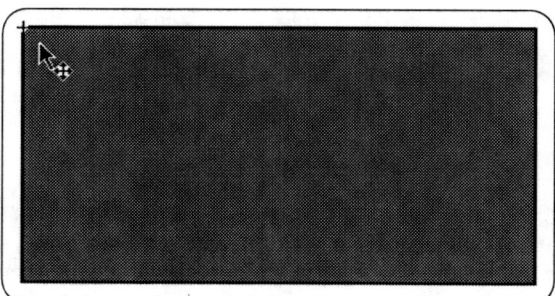

Tab Export Name

The Tab Export Name parameter functions in a similar way to Panel Export Name. You can have different tab appearances for each of your panels by either using one of the four default panels that ship with this component, or by creating your own panels and tabs.

Tab Visible

Setting the tab visibility to `false` is used exclusively when you set the Open Event and the Close Event to `onRollOver` and `onRollOut`, respectively. In this case, the tab, as well as the panel itself, is used as a drop target to register when the panel needs to open or close. Essentially, when you mouse is over the panel or tab it will register the panel to open, and when you roll off the panel and tab, it will register the panel to close.

Note that when you turn the visibility of the tab to `false`, you should also make sure that you have Show Mouse Pointer parameter set to `false` as well. Otherwise you will have the mouse changing to the 'mouse over' graphic when there is nothing visible to constitute doing so.

Open Event

You can have the panel triggered to open either `onRelease` of the mouse when you click on the tab, or `onRollOver` when the mouse is positioned over the tab or panel:

Remember to set the visibility of the mouse to `false` when you use the `onRollOver` option. Also, note that unexpected results can occur when Open Event is set to `onRelease`, but the Close Event is set to `onRollOut` when having multiple panels set to work as a group.

Close Event

You can have the panel triggered to close either `onRelease` of the mouse when you click on the tab, or `onRollOut` when the mouse moves off of the tab and panel. Remember to set the visibility of the mouse to `false` when you use the `onRollOut` option.

Show Mouse Pointer

Set Show Mouse Pointer to false when you have either the *closeEvent* set to onRollOut, or the *openEvent* set to onRollOver and the Tab Visibility is false. This will ensure that the mouse does not change its appearance to the mouse hand when you are over top of the non-visible tab and panel.

Extra Horizontal Distance

Use this setting to have the panel move an extra distance right or left when the Orientation is set to right or left. Remember to use a negative number when you want the panel to move a greater distance toward the left side of the stage, and a positive number when you want the panel to move a greater distance toward the right side of the stage.

Extra Vertical Distance

Use this setting to have the panel move an extra distance down or up when the Orientation is set to top or bottom. Remember to use a negative number when you want the panel to move a greater distance toward the top of the stage, and a positive number when you want the panel to move a greater distance toward the bottom of the stage.

Speed

The Speed parameter refers to damped rate at which the panel slides from it's starting position to the finishing position, and it's value must be specified between zero (infinitely slow) and one (instant).

Public Methods

The final feature to mention is that the sliding panel component also comes complete with two public methods – `open()` and `close()`. In the case of Flashster (www.mindgrub.com/flashter), the panel is triggered not by the tab (whose visibility is set to `false`), but by selecting the View Playlist button in the bottom right hand corner of the interface.

To utilize these methods, you simply need to give your panel an instance name, such as `myPanel`, and then add the code `myPanel.Open()` and `myPanel.Close()` anywhere in the timeline, or on a button within your project. If you want to open or close the panel from within the panel itself, then you could simply use `this.Open()` and `this.Close()`.

With all of these component parameters at our disposal, as well as the two associated ActionScript methods, you should find that the sliding panel component is flexible enough to be easily incorporated within many of your designs, with the ultimate benefit of streamlining your content presentation.

For an example of how to incorporate content within the sliding panels of this component, take a look at the sample files `slidingPanel_content.fla` and `slidingPanel_content.swf` – be sure to check out the customized panel sets in the Library.

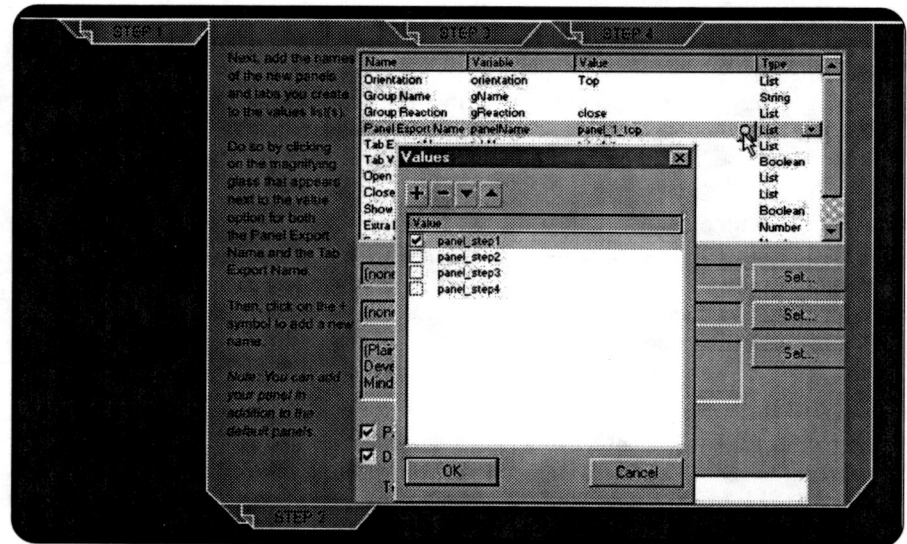

Jeremy Larkin

Jeremy's bio can be found at the start of component 9

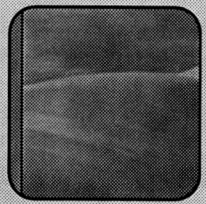

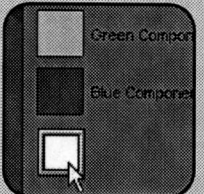

Component 11

ColorPicker

The ColorPicker component gives developers a quick way to allow the user to control the color of any element of a design This color picker is extremely flexible because it allows colors to be selected from a hexadecimal color palette as well as the more logical Hue, Saturation, and Brightness selections.

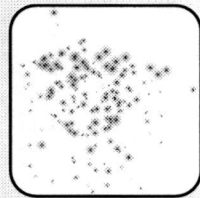

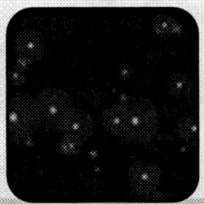

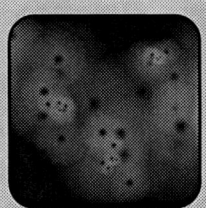

This component is designed to allow a developer to quickly and easily integrate into a project the ability for users to select colors and customize their UI experience. As you will soon see when you come to test the component, the ColorPicker starts as colored swatch:

Clicking on this swatch will expand it to reveal the ColorPicker options:

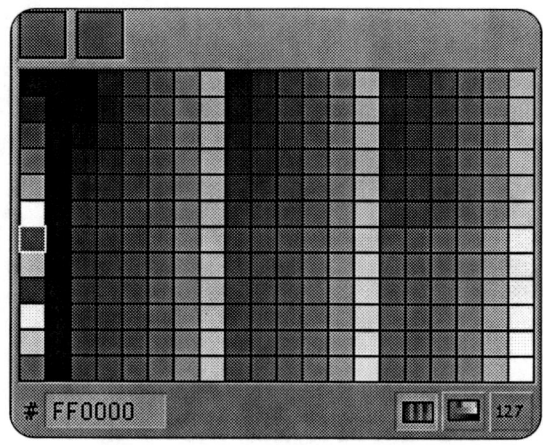

There are in fact three modes that the ColorPicker functions in:

- **Web-safe hexadecimal color palette** (seen above)
- **HSB slider controls**
- **Numerical entry field for RGB, HEX, and HSB**

Before we start to actually use the ColorPicker, it's worth taking a moment to describe these three modes so we understand how to get the best use out of them later. When opened, the ColorPicker has three toggled buttons in the bottom right corner that allow the user to move between the different selecting modes while the component is opened. In the bottom left corner there is also a field for manually entering hexadecimal colors – this option is present in of all the color editing modes. The ColorPicker can also intelligently react to its selection – when opened, if the selected color is web-safe, the ColorPicker will be opened to the hexadecimal palette. Otherwise, it will be opened to the HSB (Hue, Saturation, and Brightness) sliders.

The hexadecimal palette includes all 216 colors that are designated as web-safe: that is, they will look the same in all browsers. This selection mode also works to translate any non-web-safe colors to the nearest web-safe equivalent. For example, if a color is selected using the HSB sliders, and then the user switches the ColorPicker to the hexadecimal palette, the preview color will be changed to the nearest web-safe color.

Editing colors in HSB is a more intuitive method of selecting colors than RGB (red, green, and blue) sliders because users select colors based on a more commonly accepted concept:

Hue is the base color and can be described in specific color names such as red or violet. **Saturation** is the grayness of the color – a fully saturated color is when the base hue has none of its complementary (opposite) color added. For example, the more cyan (the opposite of red) that is added to our base hue of red, less saturated (or grayer) the color becomes. A fully de-saturated color is always a shade of gray, the shade being determined by the brightness. **Brightness** describes how light or dark the color is. Decreasing brightness will make the color appear blacker. Any color with a brightness of 0, regardless of hue or saturation, will be black.

HSB is not, however, a mathematical color value; it is only a way of describing a color. This means that to be usable in print or the web, HSB values must be interpreted into RGB values. This is where HSB color pickers can differentiate slightly. Photoshop, for example, converts HSB to RGB in a slightly different way than this ColorPicker.

In color theory, particularly when associated with printed color, brightness is not considered accurate nomenclature because technically it describes the intensity of a light-emitting object. Lightness is the correct descriptor for a printed color. It is arguable though that describing color in the capacity used here *can* be referred to as brightness because it is not in print form. In any case, we'll stick with brightness here for the simple reason that it's the more commonly accepted non-technical name

The numerical entry fields allow the user to input individual values of red, green, blue, or hue, saturation, and brightness into the ColorPicker and have them represented by a color:

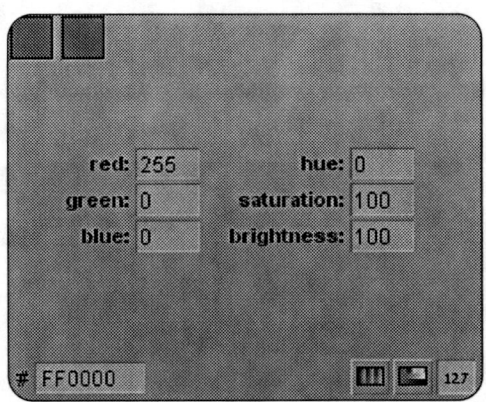

When the ColorPicker is closed, there is one color swatch that visually represents the currently selected color. When the ColorPicker is opened, a second color swatch is visible. This second swatch is a preview of the color that is being picked. If this second swatch is clicked (or a color is selected from the web-safe palette) the ColorPicker is closed and that color becomes the selected color.

Using the component

If you haven't done so already, use the `ColorPicker.mx` file from the download included with this book to install the ColorPicker component. After restarting Flash, you'll find that the ColorPicker group has been added to the drop-down list in the Components panel (Window > Components):

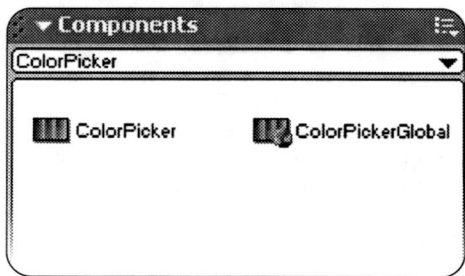

This ColorPicker group contains two components (those of you who have already looked at my TabControl component a couple of chapters back will be familiar with this setup):

1. **ColorPicker** – This is the main component.

2. **ColorPickerGlobal** – This is a companion component to the ColorPicker component containing only the color format settings used in the ColorPicker. The purpose of this component is to allow these settings to be made globally. Including this component in the project will force all instances of the ColorPicker component to use the color format settings defined in the ColorPickerGlobal component. This component is explained in more detail later in this chapter.

The following example creates a simple implementation of the ColorPicker component that will change the color of a movie clip based on the selected color. For this example, you can either follow the steps and create the file from scratch, or just open up `ColorPickerExample.fla` found in the download and read along to learn how it was created.

When constructing `ColorPickerExample.fla` I began by opening a new file and setting the stage dimensions to 300 x 250 pixels. Next, I created three layers on the root timeline and labeled them as shown below:

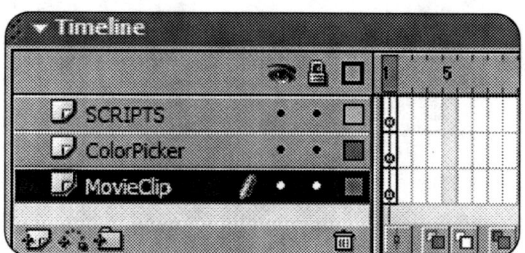

After dragging the ColorPicker component from the Components panel and onto the stage, on the ColorPicker layer, I gave it the instance name `myColorPicker`. Note that at this point the default appearance of the component can be modified. For instance, the swatch color values can all be changed using the Properties tab of the Property inspector. The size of the component is mostly important for design considerations, but note that the size, in part, determines the size of the colored swatches indicating the selected and preview colors. To adjust the size, change the width and height properties of the Info panel or Property inspector, or just use the Free Transform tool and drag the handles.

The position of the ColorPicker on the stage also has some significance. As part of its functionality, the component attempts to 'figure out' its global position on the stage using the width and height properties of the `Stage` object. It will attempt to open in a direction that assures none of the component will be cut off by the stage boundaries. This is most accurate when the `Stage.align` property is set to `TL` (aligning the stage to the top-left). We'll learn more about the modifications that are possible with this component in the next section.

If you position the ColorPicker in the top-left corner of the stage and test the movie in a browser (CTRL/COMMAND+F12), you should notice that the ColorPicker opens down and to the right from the position of the swatch:

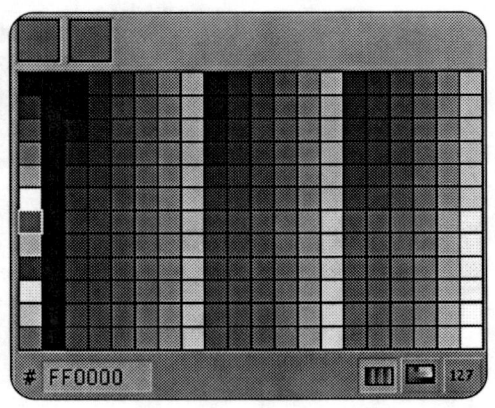

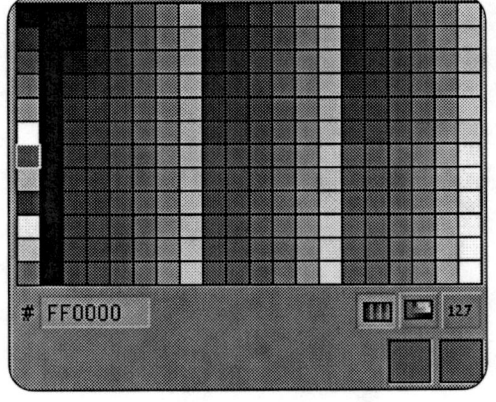

Next, try moving the ColorPicker to the bottom-right corner and notice how it opens up to the left:

Before continuing with our example and learning how to link the ColorPicker to a movie clip to be able to change its color, we'll take a quick look at the parameters of ColorPicker.

Customization using the component parameters

To adjust the appearance of the component you will need to have the component selected and have either the Parameters tab of the Property inspector (Window > Properties) open or the Component Parameters panel (Window > Component Parameters) visible at hand:

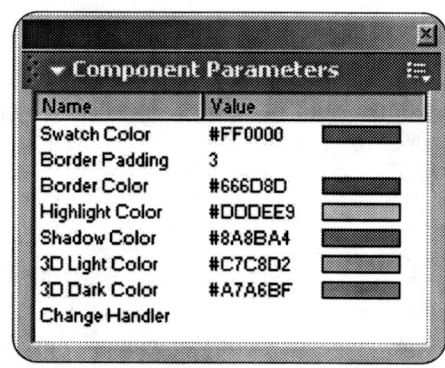

The Swatch Color property determines the initial selected color of the ColorPicker. This value is not stored by the component, so it will only be the selected color until the user changes it.

The Border Padding property indicates how much space is put between the color swatches and the other parts of the component. Remember, this value will obviously affect the size of the color swatches: the swatch width and height is the respective width and height of the component, less the padding, as shown in the diagram below. The minimum padding is 2 and the maximum is 10. This value can be controlled with ActionScript using the getPadding() and setPadding() public methods of the component.

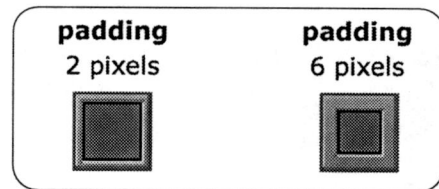

There are five colors that control the appearance of the ColorPicker user interface:

- Border Color
- Highlight Color
- Shadow Color
- 3D Light Color
- 3D Dark Color

The following image shows the parts of the component that each color corresponds to:

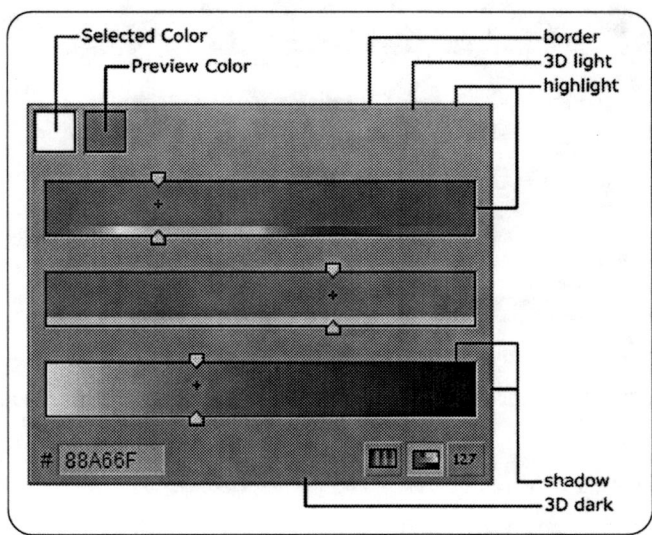

All of these settings are instance properties, meaning that modifications to them only affect the one component and not any of the others. This is convenient if there is only one component in the movie or it is intended that each one is to have its own appearance. However, this can make it difficult to assure uniformity when multiple components are used. This can be especially difficult when changing the color scheme after they have been implemented. The ColorPickerGlobal component is a companion to the ColorPicker that allows a developer to easily overcome this issue.

As mentioned at the start of this chapter, when ColorPickerGlobal is included in a project it will set all of the current and succeeding ColorPicker instances to its own color settings. To implement this, simply drag it onto the stage of your project. The icon that is displayed is there only to give a visual reference for the component in the authoring environment; it will not be visible on the published movie. The ColorPickerGlobal has the same color appearance properties found in the ColorPicker component, but not the Swatch Color or Border Padding properties.

The color properties of a component instance can also be checked and set at runtime through ActionScript using the `getColorScheme()` and `setColorScheme()` methods of the ColorPicker component. This method also has the ability to change the components properties globally for all currently and subsequently displayed instances. For more information and an example of this method, see the ColorPicker entry of the Reference panel (Window > Reference) in the Flash MX authoring environment:

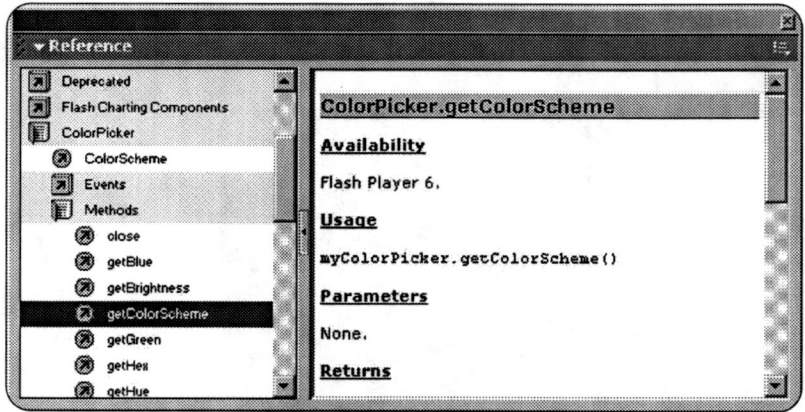

Setting the Change Handler

Now we'll turn our attention to the ColorPicker's final parameter – defining the Change Handler for this component allows code to be executed after a new color has been selected from the component. All that is needed to define the change handler is the name of a function to call. In fact, there are two ways to define the change handler:

- Enter the name of the relevant function as the Change Handler component parameter. This method *requires that the function be in the same movie clip timeline that the component is in.* However, the function does not need to exist prior to the change handler being defined and it can be changed without affecting the Change Handler definition.

- Use the `setChangeHandler()` method of the component to set the change handler through ActionScript. This offers the option to specify a function location other than the movie clip of the component. This means that the function can exist on other timelines and inside data objects. Like with the Change Handler parameter, the function does not need to exist prior to it being defined in the component. Although if the location is specified then that location does need to exist prior to defining it. For more information, see the explanation for `setChangeHandler()` in the ColorPicker > Methods section of the Reference panel (SHIFT+F1).

Let's refer back to the to the `ColorPickerExample.fla` file that we were studying earlier. With the ColorPicker on the stage, we need an object that will change as a result of the ColorPicker before we can apply actions to it. Accordingly, on the MovieClip layer, I've added a black square that is approximately 200 x 200 pixels and turned it into a movie clip (by hitting F8) with an instance name of myMovie. The stage looks like this:

Now that we have a movie clip to change, we can begin doing a little coding to make it change color, based on the selection in the ColorPicker. With frame 1 of the SCRIPTS layer selected I've added the following code to the Actions panel:

```
1  myColorPicker.setChangeHandler("colorChange");
2  function colorChange(component) {
3      var rgb = component.getRGB();
4      var myColor = new Color(myMovie);
5      myColor.setRGB(rgb);
6  }
7
```

The code is an example of how to create and set a change handler function that will change the color of the movie clip myMovie to the color selected in the component myColorPicker. Let's analyze the code line by line make sure it's clear:

```
myColorPicker.setChangeHandler("colorChange");
```

This first line sets the change handler for the component. Setting the Change Handler in the Property inspector to colorChange will have the same effect. However, there is no option to specify the location of the change handler function, so when defining the change handler through the parameter, the function must be defined in the same timeline that the component is put on.

```
function colorChange(component) {
```

The next line is where the colorChange function is defined. The parameter component is set because when the change handler is called, it is automatically passed a reference to the component as an argument.

```
var rgb = component.getRGB();
```

The getRGB() is a method of the ColorPicker component that will return the numerical RGB value that is currently selected; component is direct reference to the ColorPicker instance that evoked the change handler.

```
var myColor = new Color(myMovie);
```

Here, an instance of the Color class is created with myMovie as the movie clip to control.

```
myColor.setRGB(rgb);
}
```

Finally, calling the setRGB() method of the Color object will set the movie clip myMovie to the RGB value of the ColorPicker.

Go ahead and test this example file – there's now a link between the ColorPicker and the object within the movie (the square movie clip, in this case). The color that is initially set in the ColorPicker (through the Swatch Color property) is the color that the movie clip will automatically be set to. Of course, you can change this color to whatever color you would like to have as the default, and anytime that the color is changed in the ColorPicker, the movie clip color will update. This includes changing the color using ActionScript.

For reference, the following table describes the methods that are available for dynamically changing the colors:

Method	Description
setRGB(numericRGB)	This will set the color of the ColorPicker to a numeric color value (for example, 0xFF0000 in hex or 16711680 in decimal).
setRGB(red, green, blue)	This will set the color of the ColorPicker using elemental values for red, green, and blue. Each value can be between 0 and 255.
setRGB(hexString)	This will set the color using an RGB hex string, such as "0xFF0000", "#FF0000", or "FF0000" (note that this differs from the numeric RGB value because it is a string).
setHSB(hue, saturation, brightness)	This will set the color using the HSB color model. The value will be converted to RGB and that value will be used to set the swatch.

These values can also be retrieved from the component in all of the same formats using the following methods:

Method	Description
getRGB()	Returns the numeric RGB value.
getRed()	Return the numeric value for the red component (0-255).
getGreen()	Return the numeric value for the green component (0-255).
getBlue()	Return the numeric value for the blue component (0-255).
getHEX()	Returns the RGB hex string in the format "FF0000".
getHue()	Return the numeric value for the hue of the color (0-359).
getSaturation()	Return the numeric value for the saturation of the color (0-100).
getBrightness()	Return the numeric value for the brightness of the color (0-100).

Note that each of the methods in the previous table will accept an optional argument of either 1 or 0, where 1 returns the value for the preview color and 0 (or no argument) will return the selected color.

Now you should have a functional implementation of the ColorPicker component, however basic. There are two more bonus example files included in the download that demonstrate further implementations of this component. MultipleMCs.fla uses one ColorPicker to change the color of eight movie clips, and ApplyTint.fla demonstrates how to use the ColorPicker to apply a tint to a photograph. The ActionScript in both files are well commented and use some of the events that are explained in the next section, so don't be afraid to have a poke around!

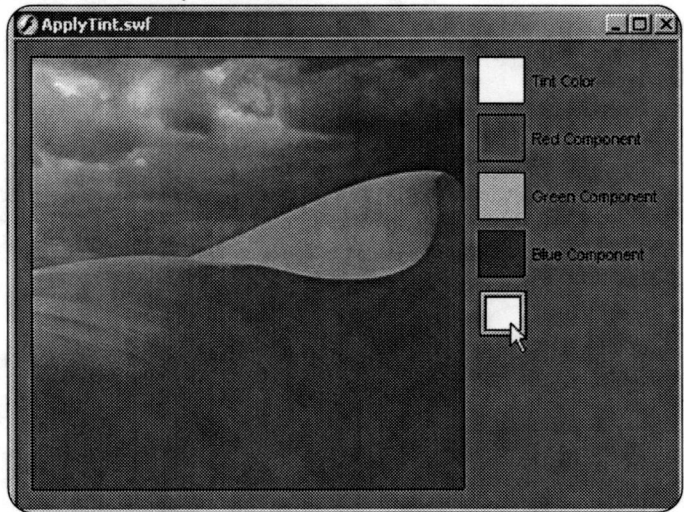

Capturing the user events

Like the change handler, events allow for code to be executed as a result of user interaction with the component. However, creating the code to capture the events differs subtly from how we did it with the change handler. Capturing events involve creating a specifically named function inside of the component, like this:

```
myColorPicker.onChange = function() {
      // Code to be executed
};
```

The ColorPicker component has four events that can be captured and reacted to. These allow more options than using the change handler alone:

- onChange – when the color of the component is changed. This is same as the change handler, but note that only one will execute. The change handler will not interfere with the other events. Changing the color through the setRGB() and setHSB() methods will also cause this event to register.

- onChangePreview – when the preview color of the component is changed. This event will fire continuously while the preview color is changed.
- onOpen – when the ColorPicker is opened.
- onClose – when the ColorPicker is closed.

The following code demonstrates how to capture an onChange event. Except for the first line, this example is almost identical to our earlier demonstration of the change handler. The difference with the event is that instead of specifying the component parameter, the keyword ~~this~~ refers to the component. This general technique is the same for all of the events:

```
myColorPicker.onChange = function() {
        var rgb = this.getRGB();
        var myColor = new Color(myMovie);
        myColor.setRGB(rgb);
};
```

You can see some of these events in action in the MultipleMCs.fla and ApplyTint.fla example files from the download. For a more in depth explanation of the setChangeHandler() method and the onChange, onChangePreview, onOpen, and onClose events, see the ColorPicker section of the Reference panel in Flash MX.

Todd Coulson

Todd joined Haley Productions (www.haleypro.com), a company specializing in multimedia, website design, and video, in late 1999. Todd earned his Associate Degree in Multimedia and Web Design from the Art Institute of Philadelphia in 1999. Prior to attending the Art Institute Todd got his Bachelor of Science in Business Administration from Marist College.

Todd would like to thank most of all his family, including his mother Hilary, his father D. Robert, his sister Ann, and his grandmother Dorothy, for always encouraging him to outdo himself. He would like to thank the staff at Haley Productions, including most of all Bill Haley, Luke Krill, Pete Bretz, Meei Ling Ng, Lisa Kruczek, Brennan Lindeen, and countless other interns who have allowed him to write the book and for giving him the opportunity to grow as a person and as a multimedia developer. Also, he would like to thank all his friends, too numerous to mention by name, but who have stuck with him through the years of endless work. They have been there at every turn of his career, and he wouldn't have survived without them! He thanks the entire Flash community, most of all Linda.com for putting on the Flash Forward conference each year and David Vogeleer for working through this component's bug testing. Finally, he would like to thank the staff of friends of ED and the crew who collaborated to make this book possible.

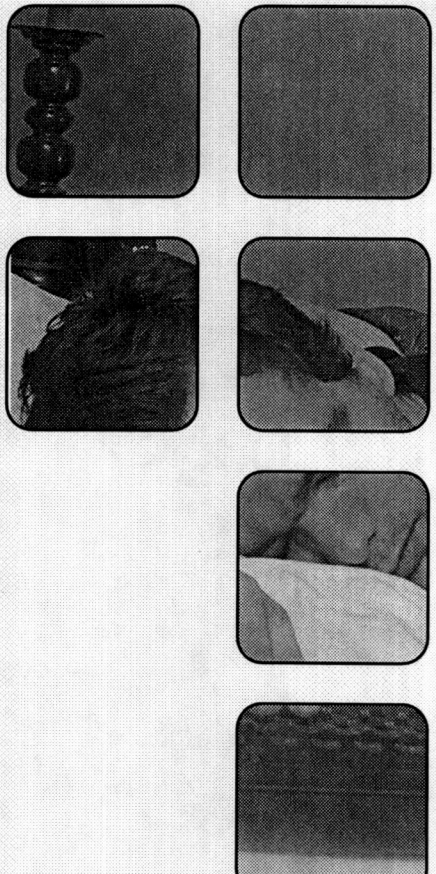

Component 12
Game Player
Selector

Build your games in half the time using this Game Player Selector component. The Game Player Selector gives you the versatility to select either players or skill level, keep score, and maintain graphical continuity within your game.

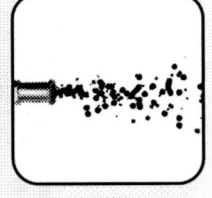
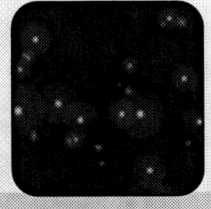

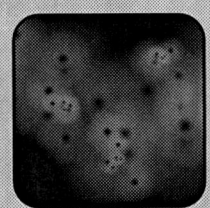

This component allows you to quickly and easily incorporate game-time decision functionality within your projects. But first, let's take a trip down memory lane...

Back when Macromedia Flash 5 was only an infant, I created an experimental dart game. For me, the construction of this game served as my introduction to ActionScript, and during the project I went through all the natural steps in creating a game: first, I created numerous variables – for the number of players in the game, the number of throws per round, the skill level, and so on. After I finished creating this kind of essential 'behind the scenes' foundation to the game, my work wasn't yet complete. I still had to create an interface to assist the end user in making choices within the game. It would certainly frustrate any users if they could only choose a two-player game with a skill level of 3.

Back then, the problem was that creating the user interface (UI) was just as complex as building the game itself. I had to have slider bars to assist the end user visually, giving them prompts to select what level or player they were choosing. Obviously, the interface of this player selector had to be very clear and easy to understand.

After what seemed like a lot of hard work, the end result was pretty neat, at least functionally and aesthetically speaking. However, the big problem was that it wasn't very flexible – my original selector wasn't reusable or easy to change. If, for instance, I chose to have five players as a maximum number of players instead of four, it presented a few problems to my game. In fact, to do that, I would have needed to add new graphics, change a variable in my code, and so on. In the end, any small change in the game would have a knock-on effect to various other areas. In addition, I had so many items on the stage when creating individual slider bars that it just looked a mess. Ultimately, it took me almost as long to build the front end of the game as it did to build the back end!

Fast forward to Flash MX, where components are starting to rule the ActionScript world. With the game selector component that I'll be discussing in this chapter, you no longer need to worry about creating the code behind the player or skill-level selector in your games. Now you can completely focus on the all-important game code, rather than the less interesting UI constructions that have been created a thousand times before. Plus your selection functionality is easily changed if you decide to change the rules of your game.

Using the Game Player Selector component

Install your component through the Macromedia Extension Manager by double-clicking the FoED-GameSelector.mxp file from the download. Once the component is loaded you should notice it in the Components panel, like the other components in this book, ready to be dragged into your Flash games and movies.

Setting the parameters

To view the parameters assigned to this component, select the component on the stage and open up the Property inspector (Window > Properties) or the Component Parameters panel (Window > Component Parameters):

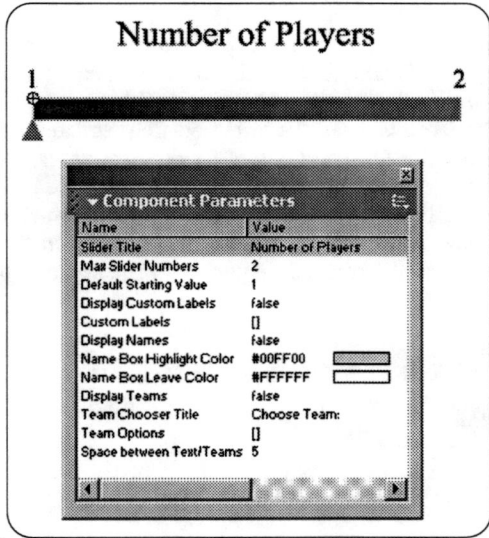

For reference, let's briefly highlight the properties that these parameters control (we'll see examples of their use throughout this chapter):

- Slider Title – Change the title at the top of the component.
- Max Slider Numbers – The maximum choices along the slider bar that will be used for the component.
- Default Starting Value – This is the starting value for the component's slider marker at the beginning of your movie.
- Display Custom Labels – This Boolean value, when set to `true`, allows you to have custom labels for each iteration along the slider bar. These labels appear above the slider bar. Defaults to numbers if this property remains `false`.
- Custom Labels – An array that represents the labels you want displayed when the Display Custom Labels parameter is `true`.
- Display Names – Boolean, when `true` the text boxes will display as the slider marker moves in real time.
- Name Box Highlight Color – When the end user selects a text box, this is the color you want that box to highlight.
- Name Box Leave Color – Keep this color the same as the original background of your text boxes.
- Display Teams – A Boolean that allows you to display a team logo to represent that particular team. When `true` the logos will appear to the left of the text boxes and allow the end user to choose between an array of values (see Team Options parameter, below).
- Team Chooser Title – This is a title that will appear directly next to each text box as they are selected. This provides instructions for the end user to choose a team.
- Team Options – An array containing the instance names of the movie clips that represent the logos of each team. The movie clips used for this property must reside on the `_root` level timeline.
- Space between Text/Teams – This represents the space between text boxes and team logo choices.

Now look at the component on the stage as we delve into these parameters a little deeper. Notice the default values in the Component Parameters panel – these correspond to the selected component, on the stage. If your Live Preview is enabled (**select** Control > Enable Live Preview) you can change the values of any of these properties and you will see them immediately updated on your stage. For instance, try changing the default value for the Display Custom Labels parameter to `true`. This should cause the numbers above the slider bar to disappear. Next, click on the square brackets ([]) next to the Custom Labels parameter – this should bring up the Values dialog box in which you can enter values into the array. To enter values into this array simply press the plus sign (+) in the top left hand corner of the window, and click OK to return to the stage. Sure enough, you should notice that it now has new labels above the slider bar:

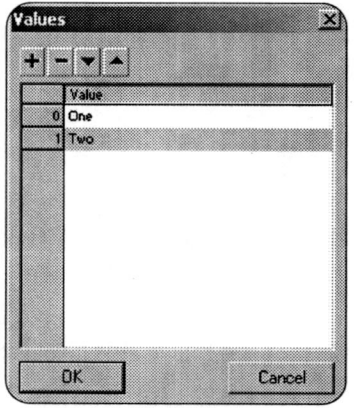
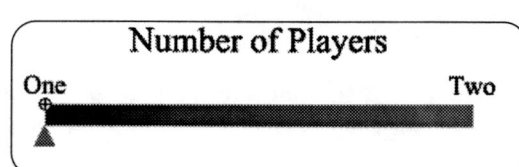

Note that, for this component to look correct, you must be sure to enter as many array elements as are specified in the Max Slider Numbers parameter.

Next, change the value of the Display Names parameter to `true`. In our live preview we should now see a text box appear below the slider bar of our component – this allows the end user to input their names into a game. The two parameters that follow Display Names have to do with the color of the text boxes once the end user clicks their mouse into any of the team name text boxes that just appeared, so just leave them both as their default values and go ahead and test your movie with CTRL/COMMAND+ENTER (PC/Mac). Click inside the text box to see the box highlight green, as specified in the Name Box Highlight Color parameter:

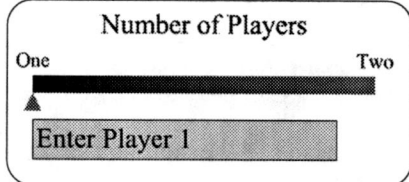
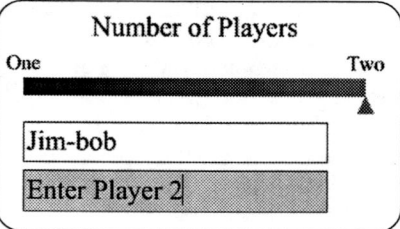

The Name Box Highlight Color and Name Box Leave Color parameters will not appear in the Live Preview because they are runtime parameters. Likewise, the next three Team parameters are also runtime parameters. The Display Teams Boolean (true/false) will allow the end user to choose teams. The Team Chooser Title option will allow you to choose a title that will appear next to the selected text box. This will allow your end user to choose a team anytime they click in a particular text box. The team icons displayed will be reliant on movie clips you create and place on the root level of the timeline. You then must name each team you want displayed in the array corresponding to Team Options parameter. Make sure the name in the array is exactly the same as the instance name of the designated movie clip that you placed on the _root level of the timeline.

Let's look at the use of some of these other component parameters an example – open up selector1.fla from the download and examine the stage:

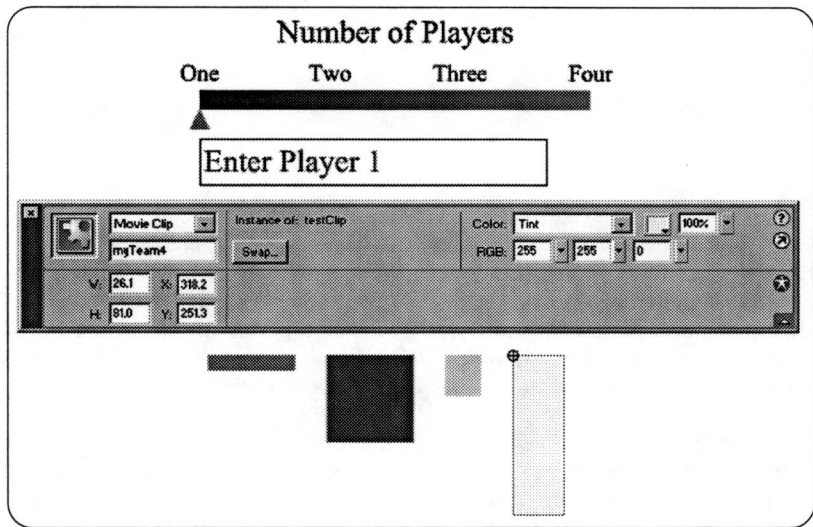

This time, the game selector component has been given four Custom Labels. You'll also notice that below the component we've got four instances of a rectangular movie clip (called testClip), each of which has had its color and size modified through the Property inspector. These movie clips have been given instance names: myTeam1 to myTeam4. Now, select the game component and divert your attention to setting of the Component Parameters panel:

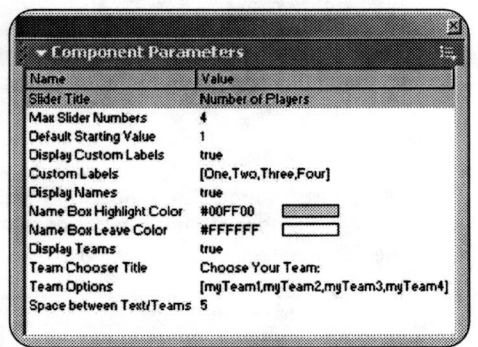

Notice here that the Display Teams parameter is set to true, and we've got the message "Choose Your Team" in the Team Chooser Title parameter. The most important step in setting up this particular use of the component is to give suitable values to the Team Options - here we've added each instance name of our movie clips (myTeam1, myTeam2, and so on) as items in the array

.

On testing the movie, you'll be able to enter your player name, as before, and now you can also select your team affiliation, as denoted in this case by the colored rectangles of our simple demonstration:

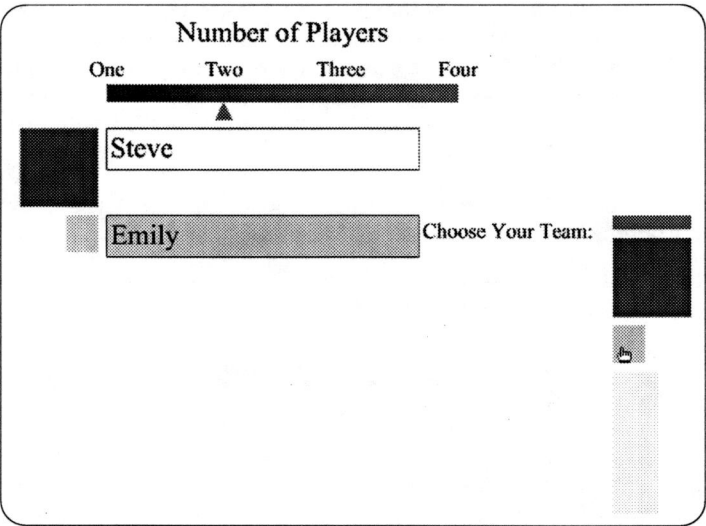

There are a couple of subtleties worth highlighting at this point. The first thing you might notice is that each player is automatically assigned a team 'logo' based on the order of the array that you set up in the Team Options parameter. Also, the positioning of these logos is automatic – you simply have to place the movie clips on the stage and the component will align the movie clips for you.

Secondly, note the placement of the Team Chooser Title value located next to the selected box – this is there to give the end user some instruction to choose a team logo. Logically, next to the Team Chooser Title we have all of the possible team values from our Team Options parameter that the end user can choose from. If the end user chooses different sized values for their team, it will automatically realign all following text boxes and logo items.

Go ahead and play around with some of these parameters and values to learn how you could make the best use of this component in your games and applications.

Using the Results

At this point, you may be wondering, "Well that's great, but how do I actually *use* these results?" In fact, there are a number of public methods that I've created to assist you in that very action. These are all used in the form *componentInstanceName.methodName()*, and are described in the following table:

Method	Description
returnPicked()	**Method**; returns the resting position of the marker at that moment in time. **Parameters**: none **Returns**: value

Method	Description
returnNames()	**Method**; returns names of players taken from the text boxes. Player 1 is the first name in the array. **Parameters**: none **Returns**: array
returnTeams()	**Method**; returns movie clip names in an array. The first team in the array is Player 1. **Parameters**: none **Returns**: array
changeMarker(temp)	**Method**; allows control over the marker position. **Parameters**: a variable representing the new location of marker **Returns**: nothing
changeTitle(temp)	**Method**; allows control over the Title entry. **Parameters**: a variable representing the new title of the component in question. **Returns**: nothing
removeChoices()	**Method**; removes movie clip team choices if you decide to use different graphics. **Parameters**: none **Returns**: none

Now that we know which methods are available to us, we can begin to use them in our games. Let's look at another sample file that demonstrates some of these powerful new methods – open up selector2.fla. This is basically just an extension of the previous example, which now includes some of the ActionScript methods mentioned above.

One of the most important points to remember when you want to access your components' properties through ActionScript is to give them instance names. Note that in selector2.fla we have two instances of the game selector component on the stage, with instance names myComponent and skillLevel. These two component instances will both work independently of each other, returning different values for each method called. Additionally, in the lower corner of the stage, we have a PushButton component, with instance name testButton, that will serve to test the return values from our two components.

Now open your Actions panel on frame 1 of the actions layer, where you'll find the following code:

```
testButton.onPress = function() {
    trace("Skill Level chosen:"+skillLevel.returnPicked());
    trace("Players in Game:"+myComponent.returnNames());
    trace("Teams associated with Players:"+ myComponent.returnTeams());
};
```

Test the movie: move the slider bar of each component, change the team logos, and enter names in the myComponent instance, and then test button - in the Output window you should see values associated with what you've entered, as accessed through the above ActionScript:

149

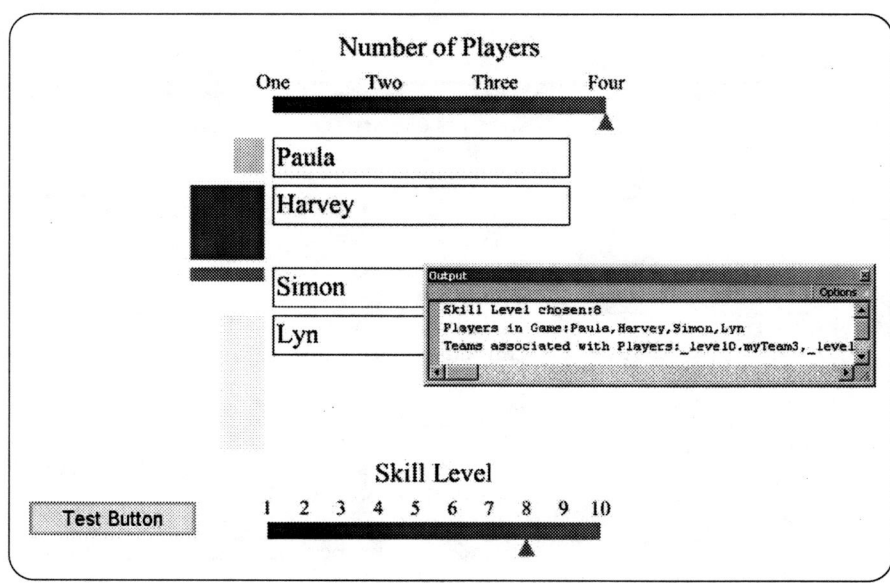

The more you play with the values of this component, the more you can see its flexibility – we can place as many slider bars as we like in our movies, with custom labels, team and name selectors, and so on. Furthermore, we've just seen how easy it is to extract values from the components and return them as variables that specify how our game will actually be played.

In the download I've included a folder called `sports_trivia` – this contains a fully functional game, `trivia.swf`, which incorporates the game selector component and utilizes it with ActionScript to great effect. If you're interested in how this game was constructed, just open up `trivia.fla` and check it out!

It's worth keeping in mind the fact that placing extra components on the stage takes up little extra file space. So when you include the component at the start of your game and use it as a scoring device like this, you get more mileage out of it. Also, you can see how flexible the game is – if my client decided they wanted to have this be a four-player game, it would be easy to make that change just by modifying the characteristics of my component.

Next, we'll learn how to change the appearance of the component to give it a unique look and feel for any given project, by modifying the 'skins'.

Skinning the component

As always, your components are going to need some tweaking to change the graphics to match with your particular game, application, movie, or design. Drag an instance of the game selector component into a new Flash movie and open up the Library. Here you'll see how its graphics are set up – of particular interest to us are the symbols within the Skins folder, as detailed below:

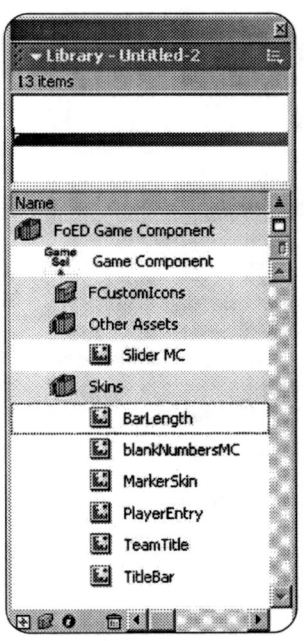

- **BarLength** – This is the graphic used to create the length of the bar for the slider. Open this movie clip to change the appearance of the bar, but you can change the height and width for each instance of the component on the stage.
- **BlankNumbersMC** – Text box used to place the labels above the slider bar.
- **MarkerSkin** – Graphic for the marker – you can change the look to this pointer to suit your designs.
- **PlayerEntry** – Text box used to house the player names. These items appear when the Display Names parameter is chosen to be true.
- **TeamTitle** – Text box used to house the Team Chooser Title value chosen from the parameters list.
- **TitleBar** – Text box that houses the title bar of the component.

In addition, inside the Other Assets folder you'll find the Slider MC movie clip – this is attached to form the marker for the component. However, only change the rollover color here – changes to the marker graphic should be made to the MarkerSkin movie clip.

Now that we have been introduced to the graphical elements of our component, it's fairly straightforward to change the properties of the movie clips in the Skins folder – simply double-click on the movie clip that you want to modify to edit its properties. Note that this will change the look and feel of every component in your movie. If you want the appearance of individual components to be different, then you must change the instance properties of that particular component, through the Property inspector.

Open up `selector3_skin.swf` to see the effect of some simple graphical customizations (and look in `selector3_skin.fla` to see how I accomplished these changes):

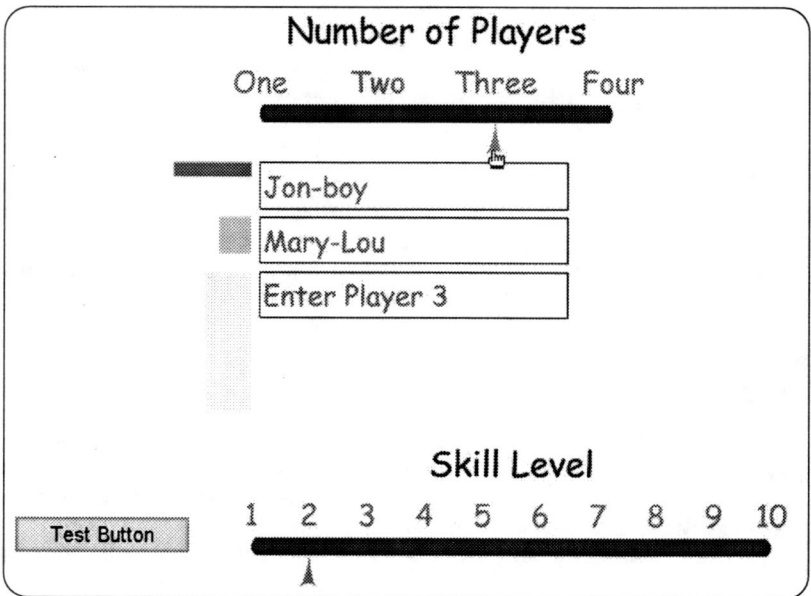

Remember that you can also change textual properties to alter the component in a way that is appealing for the overall design. And don't be afraid to change the size of the text box to fit whatever text you want placed in these text boxes. You may have also noticed that the graphics on the stage still contain the red and black colors of the original component in the Live Preview. This is because components do not update changes to the skins in the authoring environment. You will see the changes to the graphics once you test your movie. So what are you waiting for? Go on and change the graphics however you see fit!

Making games is hard enough when you are just starting out in the world of ActionScript – the game selector component would have given me far less to worry about if it existed when I was Flash novice. This component allows you to concentrate on developing the code for your games and applications, rather than getting sidetracked into re-creating the kind of selector functionality that developers have already built a thousand times over.

Jared Tarbell

When I was eighteen, I decided to buy a computer instead of a car. That was back in 1991. I did this also in 1993, 1995, and again last year. To me, this is an absolutely brilliant thing to do – at least until cars can fly.

Even before I owned a computer, in some form or another, I have been borrowing CPU time on other people's computers. I was initially motivated to use the computer through the text-based adventure games my father would write while I was asleep. It became clear to me that a programmer truly could create something from nothing, and this idea intrigued me.

I completed the ten year program at New Mexico State University and was rewarded a Bachelor of Science in Computer Science for my participation in their experiment. During this time I learned the value of abstracted programming and why I never want to program at a micro level.

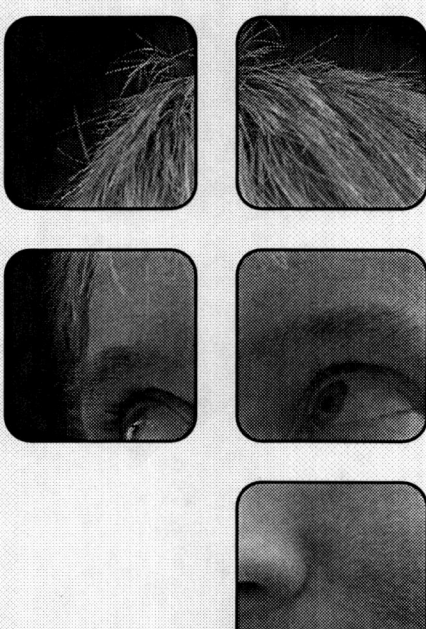

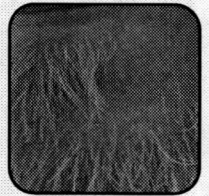

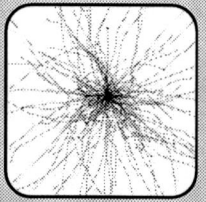

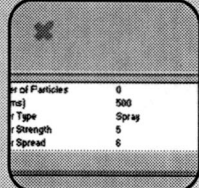

Component 13
Particle Emitter

The Particle Emitter Component is a great tool for creating fields of self-similar, moving, shrinking, growing, and fading objects. In its completely unmodified form, there are thousands of possible variations but by modifying the Particle movie clip only slightly, millions of totally unique effects can be achieved. Particle fields are good at providing computational environments of depth and complexity, adding a special decorative touch, to your design.

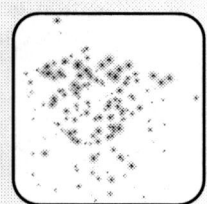

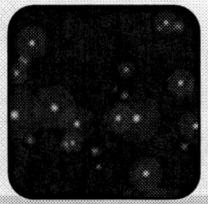

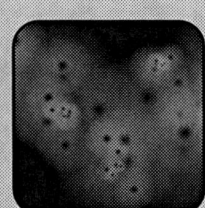

The particle emitter component generates an easily adaptable field of dynamic particles. Each particle is an autonomous object, optimized to move about, change size, fade, and self-destruct under a collection of attributes given to them at creation time.

Perhaps the coolest thing about the particle is that it doesn't necessarily have to be a simple graphic symbol. It can be any asset you've already developed – even something highly complex, such as an animation or scripted movie clip. The particle could even be something as abstract as a sound object. The particle emitter component provides a novel way to instantiate collections of your movie clips with extended movement and lifetime functionality.

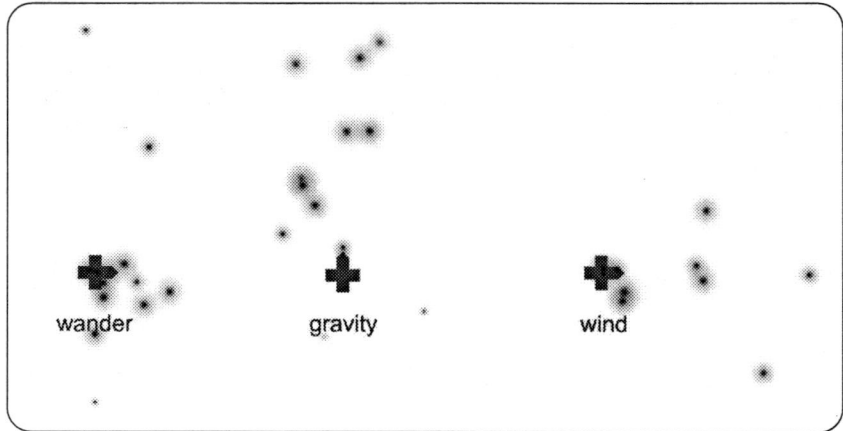

Particle emitters can be as fun as a garden hose on a hot summer day – just point the thing in some direction, turn it on, and enjoy the chaos that spills out. Experimenting with particle systems is like watching the seeds of a dandelion blowing in the wind, or a collection of marbles rolling down stairs – the result is different every time!

Particle systems are also regarded as an essential in the study of many natural phenomena. They can be used for any number of purposes, from simulating disturbances in a field of suspended oil bubbles, to something like modeling the dangers that huge piles of potatoes present to humans working on potato farms. Learning about chaotic situations in a controlled environment has many obvious benefits, and, while Flash is not necessarily the most efficient platform from which to study these phenomena, it is still an enjoyable pursuit to model and visualize these types of systems. Through quantity alone, particles are a good method of creating computational systems that exhibit emergent behavior. They're also great for special effects!

One important thing to note about the particle is that it has been computationally abstracted so that it can be just about anything. For generalized purposes, the particle is a simple graphic. Later in this chapter we'll learn some ways in which to modify the particle.

How it works

The Particle Emitter is actually a system of two components, one nested within the other. First, the ParticleEmitterComponent is what we place on stage to generate objects. Nested inside of this component, is the ParticleComponent. It is likely that you will never need to directly instantiate the ParticleComponent, only the ParticleEmitterComponent.

All particle emitters begin emitting particles immediately after their position on the movie's timeline has been reached. Particles are emitted until the maximum number of particles has been reached, or the particle emitter is removed from the stage. The behavior of the particle emitter is highly modifiable; each instance of the emitter can have a unique set of values that control how particles are emitted, what size they are, their behavior, and their expected lifetime. Changing these values produces drastically different particle effects.

It is important to note that, due to their nested design, all generated particles are attached to the emitter from which they came. This means that transformations (such as color and scale) applied to the emitter will also apply to the particles contained within it. The alternative to this implementation is attaching the particles at the same level as the emitter, or to some predefined stage. When considering the two implementations, I've opted for the former as I believe it provides advantages and an ease of use that the other does not.

One advantage of attaching the particles to the emitter is that it is quick and easy to make changes to the color or general size of the particle system.

Since all particles are contained within the emitter, we need not concern ourselves with attached particles overwriting the depth of other movie clips on stage. Because of this nested design, multiple particle emitters with unique value sets can be used on stage together without fear of interference.

Another advantage worth mentioning is the ease with which particles can be destroyed. If you find the need to get rid of some particles, perhaps during a scene transition, or to alleviate CPU burden, simply removing the emitter will automatically destroy all particles that came from it. The one potential drawback to attaching particles within the emitter is that the emitter cannot be moved without all the particles attached to it also moving.

Setting up and using the particle emitter

To use the ParticleEmitterComponent, simply select and drag an instance of it from the Components panel onto the stage of your Flash movie. The particle emitter and all its dependencies and assets will now automatically be added to your movie's Library, including the ParticleComponent. For this reason, it is not necessary to also drag in an instance of the ParticleComponent.

While it is possible to use the ParticleComponent on its own (in such a scenario, a single instance of the particle component would grow once the movie begins and then simply float away), without the emitter, it is not recommended. The particle is specially designed to be instantiated and initialized by the emitter. Using the particle on its own is difficult because each of its ten parameters must be explicitly defined in your movie. Using the emitter eliminates these problems by automatically setting each particle's parameters and checking those values. Ultimately, if you really want to use a single particle in your project, it'd probably be best to use an emitter, and set its Number of Particles parameter to 1 (discussed below).

The emitter has a long list of properties that determine the duration, speed, and behavior of emitted particles. These properties have default values that will produce a simple particle field. Most likely, however, you'll want to modify these settings in the component parameters to get the kind of behavior and appearance that you desire.

Component parameters

The best way to describe the settings is to go through them one by one. They are presented here in the same order that they appear in the Property inspector or the Component Parameters panel with the component selected. Some settings have restrictions on the range of valid values. By modifying these properties, hundreds of different particle effects can be produced:

Note that, after installing the component, details of these parameters can also be found in the Levitated Components > Particle Emitter section of the Reference panel (SHIFT+F1) in Flash MX.

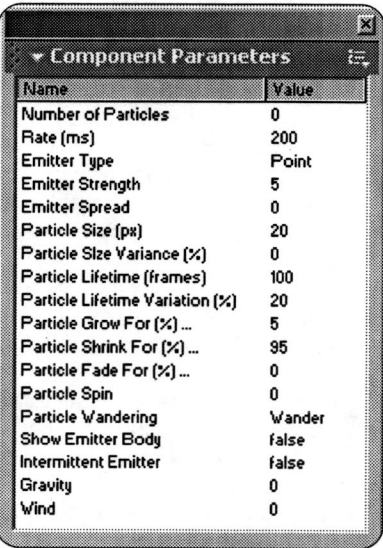

Number of Particles

The total number of particles emitted over the lifetime of the particle emitter: if this value is 0, the particle emitter emits particles indefinitely.

- Type: number
- Units: integer count
- Range: 1 (infinite)
- Default: 0 (infinite)

Rate (ms)

The rate at which particles are emitted. Every *n* milliseconds, a new particle is emitted. The default value of 250 milliseconds emits four particles every second.

- Type: number
- Units: milliseconds
- Range: 5 - `maxinteger`
- Default: 250

Emitter Type

Sets the way in which particles are ejected from the emitter. There are two types: Point creates all particles at the same point, letting the particles diffuse away from the emitter 'naturally', under their own guidance, while Spray emits particles in a powerful stream within a directional range. A powerful omni-directional point emitter can be simulated using the Spray type with an Emitter Spread value of 360 degrees and some non-zero value for Emitter Strength.

- Type: list
- Range: Point, Spray
- Default: Point

Emitter Strength

Determines the maximum initial velocity of particles emitted (for sprays only). The higher the number, the faster the particles will move after being emitted. Negative values will emit particles in the exact opposite direction of the emitter. This value is ignored for emitters of type Point.

- Type: number
- Units: pixels/frame
- Range: any number
- Default: 5

Emitter Spread

Determines the angle of the arc in which particles are emitted (for sprays only) – the higher the number, the larger the sweep of the arc. A value of 360 will cause a Spray emitter type to behavior much like a Point emitter type but with some degree of initial velocity as defined by Emitter Strength. This value is ignored in for emitters of type Point.

- Type: number
- Units: angular degrees
- Range: 0 - 360
- Default: 0

Particle Size (px)

The size of the each particle after it has fully grown and before it begins to shrink. This value assumes that the total width of the particle graphic is 100 pixels. The size of a particle can be randomly modified by the Particle Size Variance parameter (see below).

- Type: number
- Units: pixels
- Range: 1 - maxinteger
- Default: 20

Particle Size Variance (%)

The random variation in size between emitted particles. The larger the percentage, the greater the variation of size within the emitted particles. A Particle Size of 10 with a Particle Size Variance of 50 will produce particles from size 5 to size 15.

- Type: number
- Units: percentage
- Range: 0 - 100
- Default: 0

Particle Lifetime (frames)

The total number of frames that a particle exists for before self-destructing. The lifetime of a particle can be randomly modified with the Particle Lifetime Variation parameter.

- Type: number
- Units: frames
- Range: 1 - maxinteger
- Default: 100

Particle Lifetime Variation (%)

The variation in the lifetime of each component. The larger the percentage, the greater the range of expected lifetimes for particles. The lifetime of a particle is measured in frames, and set with Particle Lifetime.

- Type: number
- Units: percentage
- Range: 0 - 100
- Default: 0

Particle Grow For (%)

The percentage of time the particle will spend growing from nothing to its Particle Size. A value of 0 emits particles that instantaneously grow to their specified Particle Size. A value of 100 will emit a particle that gradually grows to its Particle Size over the course of its entire lifetime. Note that the Particle Grow For and Particle Shrink For values should not sum greater than 100.

- Type: number
- Units: percentage
- Range: 0 - 100
- Default: 5

Particle Shrink For (%)

The percentage of time the particle will spend shrinking from its Particle Size to nothing. A value of 0 emits particles that never shrink in size. A value of 100 emits particles that begin full size and gradually shrink to nothing over the course of their lifetime. The Particle Grow For and Particle Shrink For values should not sum greater than 100.

- Type: number
- Units: percentage
- Range: 0 - 100
- Default: 95

Particle Fade For (%)
The percentage of time the particle will spend fading into complete transparency. A value of 0 will emit a particle that never fades. A value of 50 will emit a particle that begins to fade in the middle of its lifetime and continues to fade until it disappears completely and self-destructs.

- Type: number
- Units: percentage
- Range: 0 - 100
- Default: 0

Particle Spin
The range of angles that particles rotate each frame. A value of 0 emits particles that do not rotate.

- Type: number
- Units: angles per frame
- Range: -360 - 360
- Default: 0

Particle Wandering
The degree to which particles wander after being emitted. The default setting of wander produces some degree of random motion. As their names suggest, Wander Far and Wander Further produce more intense random motion.

- Type: list
- Range: None, Wander, Wander Far, Wander Further
- Default: Wander

Show Emitter Body
A Boolean value specifying whether or not the particle emitter body should be shown.

- Type: Boolean
- Range: true or false
- Default: false

Intermittent Emitter
A Boolean value allowing the emitter to occasionally skip the emission of a particle. When set to true, the particle emitter produces approximately 80% of its normal rate, at varying intervals.

- Type: Boolean
- Range: true or false
- Default: false

Gravity
A constant affecting the vertical velocity of all particles. Positive values for gravity will pull particles down towards the bottom of the screen, while negative values will do the opposite (negative gravity can be thought of as *levitation*). The higher the number, the stronger the displacement. It is important to note that with both Gravity and Wind, any rotation of the emitter will also effect the directions in which these

forces apply to the particle. For example, rotating the emitter clockwise 90 degrees will, in effect, turn wind into gravity and gravity into wind.

- Type: number
- Units: pixels/second
- Range: -maxinteger - maxinteger
- Default: 0

Wind

A constant affecting the horizontal velocity of all particles. Positive values of wind will push particles to the right, while negative values will do the opposite. The higher the number, the stronger the displacement.

- Type: number
- Units: pixels/second
- Range: -maxinteger - maxinteger
- Default: 0

Dynamic creation of emitters

Beyond residing on the stage within a specific frame in the movie timeline, emitters can also be dynamically instantiated. That is, using ActionScript, you can create and destroy as many particle emitters as you desire, at any time, at any place. We'll see a detailed example of this when we come to study particle emitters in action – the convention that we'll be using to dynamically attach components can be generalized as follows:

```
// Dynamically attach a particle emitter component
// each time the mouse button is pressed
this.onMouseDown = function() {
    // Explicitly define all the emitter's parameters
    var initialization = {    dustType:"Spray",
                              dustStrength:5,
                              dustSpread:360,
                              dustRate:5,
                              // and so on...
                              };
    // Physically attach the emitter movie clip
    neoObject = this.attachMovie("particleEmitterComp", "neo", 1,
    ➥initialization);
    // Position the emitter under the mouse's location
    neoObject._x = this._xmouse;
    neoObject._y = this._ymouse;
};
```

The code example above would create a new particle emitter called neoObject. First, we've defined an array of values to be passed to the component, and then we need to 'physically' attach the component. The final two statements position this component at the current location of the mouse. It is important to note that when creating components dynamically, all emitter parameters must be well defined within the initialization. Otherwise, some emitter values may be set to zero instead of their default value. We'll see a real demonstration of this technique shortly when we look at the *Explosion* example.

Graphical customization

To allow easy modification of the particle and particle emitter, the component assets have been divided up into two sets of elements, those for the *designer* and those for the *developer*. Certainly no one is excluded from either set of elements, but some may feel more comfortable with one set or the other:

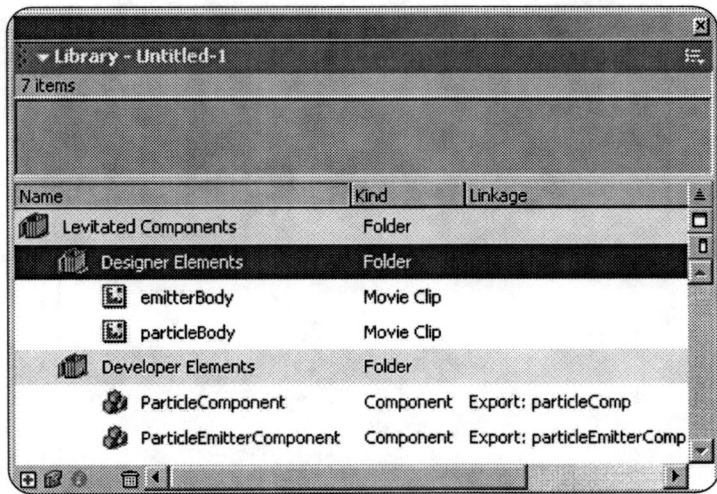

It is likely that you will have something special in mind for the graphical appearance of the particle. One of the elements in the designer set is called `particleBody`. The `particleBody` is a simple one-frame movie clip that contains a graphic shape. This is what one sees by default as the emitted particle. To change the graphic, just edit the `particleBody` movie clip. This might be something simple like replacing the graphic shape, or something more elaborate, where multiple frames or ActionScript is involved.

Changing the color of the particles is another simple modification. Since all particles are attached to the emitter, we need only apply a color transform to the emitter to affect all the particles that emerge from it. To apply a color transform to an object on the stage, select it and choose Tint from the Color attribute in the Property inspector. Transformations of opacity, scale, and rotation can also be applied this way. If you need a particle emitter that emanates particles of two different colors, just use two self-similar emitters, placed on top of each other, each with a different color transform applied.

Great rewards also await those who modify or extend the behavior of the particle through its prototype component definition.

Particle emitters in action

All of the following examples use the ParticleEmitterComponent in its unmodified form. The final two examples, *Poetry* and *Pens*, have been extended with additional movie clips embedded as part of the ParticleComponent.

Explosion

The explosion example, `explosion.fla`, uses a single emitter with a low number of maximum particles and an extremely high rate of emission:

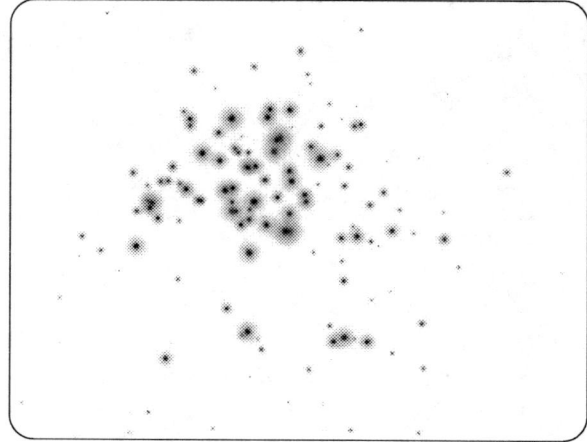

To allow the user some kind of control over the explosions, the emitters are dynamically instantiated with each click of the mouse. To facilitate this behavior, the following code exists on the main timeline of `explosion.fla`:

```
// Momentary, rapid creation particle emitter
// to simulate an explosion
_root.onMouseDown = function() {
        // dynamically attach particle emitter component
        var neo = "myExplosion"+String(this.depth++);
        // define the component parameters
        var initialization = {dustType:"Spray",
                              dustStrength:5,
                              dustSpread:360,
                              dustRate:5,
                              maxDust:30,
                              dustLife:30,
                              dustLifeVar:100,
                              dustSize:10,
                              dustSizeVar:100,
                              dustGrowFor:0,
```

```
                                    dustShrinkFor:80,
                                    dustFadeFor:50,
                                    dustSpin:random(11)-5,
                                    showEmitter:false,
                                    dustWanders:"Wander",
                                    gravity:5,
                                    wind:0};
        // Attach the movie and assign the parameters
        neoengine = this.attachMovie("particleEmitterComp", neo,
        ➥this.depth, initialization);
        // Position it over the mouse pointer
        neoengine._x=_root._xmouse;
        neoengine._y=_root._ymouse;
    };
```

Notice that the emit rate (dustRate) is a very fast 5 milliseconds. This means that approximately 200 particles will be created every second. Obviously, this is too much for most processors, so a limit (maxDust) of 30 particles is set to keep things reasonable.

The result is a momentary, explosive creation of high velocity particles in a fraction of a second. Everything happening at once – kind of like an explosion!

Falling snow

It's easy to waste time staring up into falling snow with your mouth open and your tongue out. Having recently moved to Austin, Texas, I have wasted very little time with this happy diversion – and I miss it!

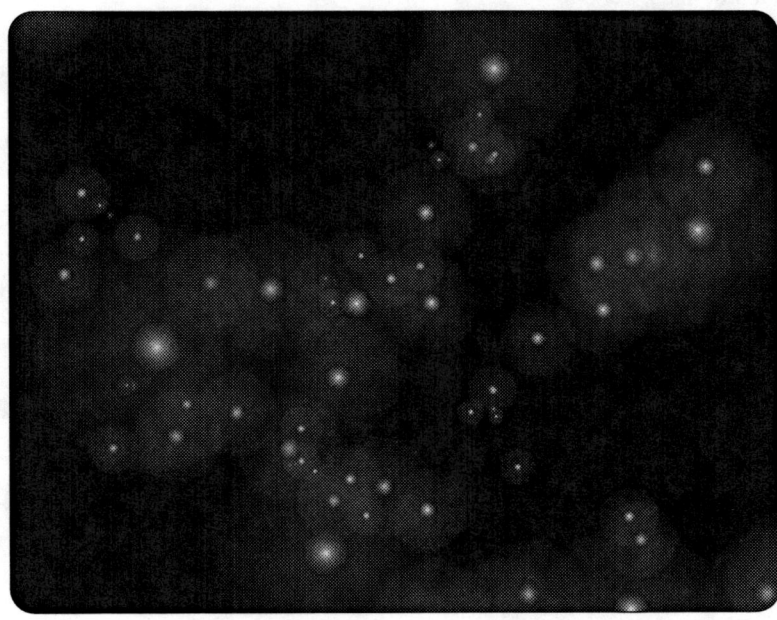

With the particle emitter, it's pretty straightforward to simulate snow using a few emitters with wandering particles that increase in size. To create the falling snow example, `snow.fla`, I used five emitters placed somewhat randomly on the stage, each with parameters set as follows:

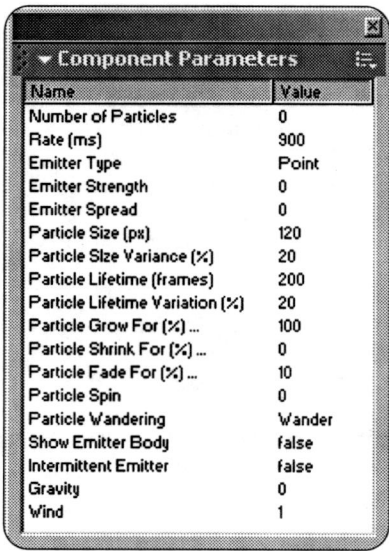

Name	Value
Number of Particles	0
Rate (ms)	900
Emitter Type	Point
Emitter Strength	0
Emitter Spread	0
Particle Size (px)	120
Particle Size Variance (%)	20
Particle Lifetime (frames)	200
Particle Lifetime Variation (%)	20
Particle Grow For (%) ...	100
Particle Shrink For (%) ...	0
Particle Fade For (%) ...	10
Particle Spin	0
Particle Wandering	Wander
Show Emitter Body	false
Intermittent Emitter	false
Gravity	0
Wind	1

Notice that the rate actually varies with each emitter by about 200 milliseconds to give a more chaotic effect. We've also got a slight wind – giving all the emitters this value for wind makes the particle field as a whole seem a little more coherent.

Disordered jet

In this example, `inkjet.fla`, a streaming jet of increasing disorder is created using a collection of four overlapping emitter components with various settings. In the FLA, you can select the emitters (hide the pipe graphic first) to take a look at their settings in Property inspector.

All four emitters are positioned very close to each other. Slight offsets in position produce a thicker stream. To demonstrate the ease in which particle emitters can be layered with other movie elements, the pipe graphic was split into two pieces (the front of the pipe and the inside of the pipe) and placed on layers just above and below the emitters, giving the appearance that the particles are being shot from inside the tube:

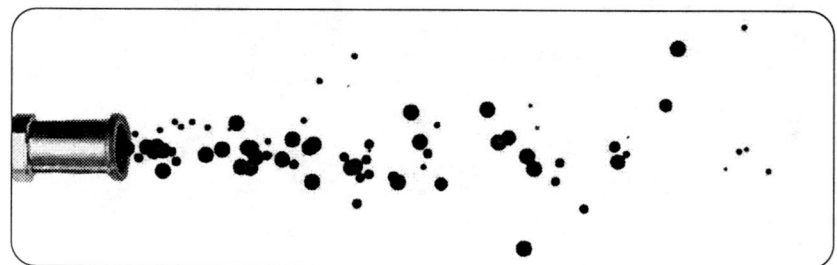

The disorder in the system is introduced by the Particle Wandering setting. Wandering particles randomly modify their own velocities, allowing them to deviate from their initial trajectories. As described earlier in the *Component parameters* section, particles can be set to not wander, wander, wander far, and wander further.

Bacteria

The bacteria.fla example is a demonstration of how a simple design-time transformation applied to the emitter can be used to modify the properties of all its particles:

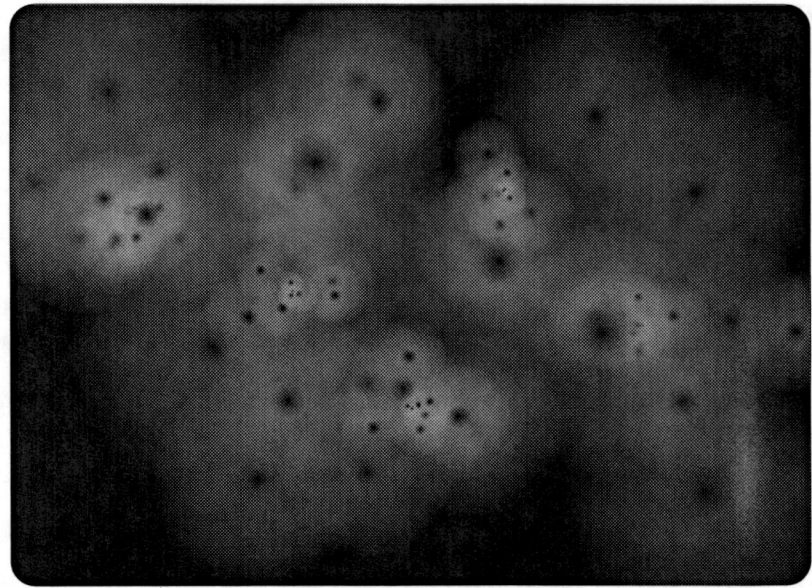

In this case, five distinct particle emitters have been placed onto the stage in random locations. Each instance was hand selected, and an Advanced color transform was applied. With the particle emitter instance selected, the color transformation can be applied via the Property inspector:

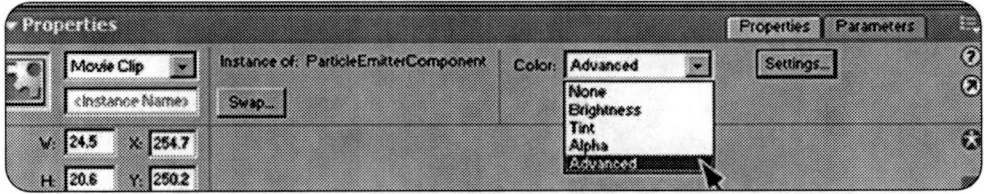

Random palettes

This is one of my favorite implementations of the particle emitter component – in `palettes.fla`, a gently rolling particle field of colored shapes drifts slowly across the screen:

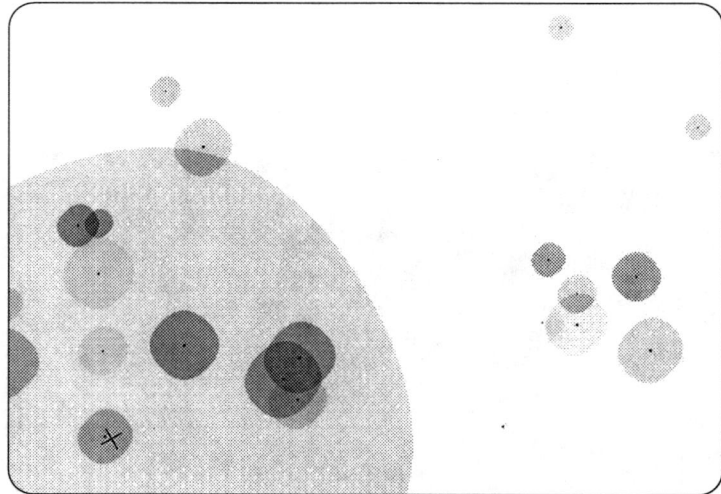

The `particleBody` movie clip in this example actually consists of many frames. Each frame contains a shape of a different color:

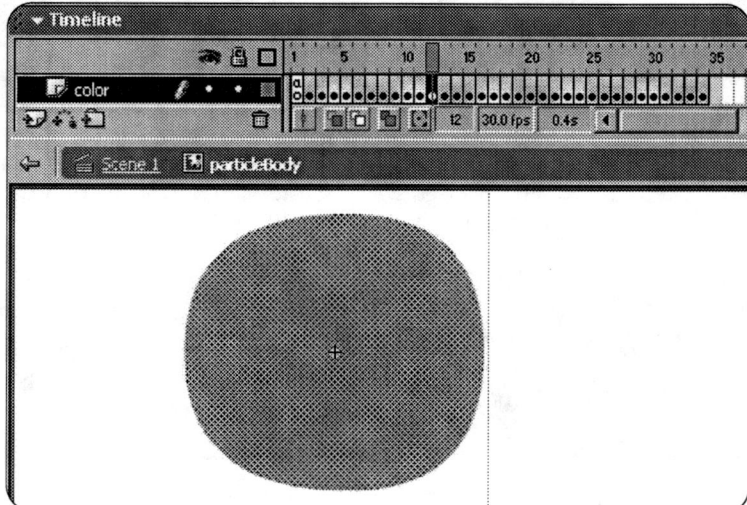

Code on the first frame of `particleBody` tells the movie clip to randomly `gotoAndStop` on one of its frames. There is also an instruction to decrease the opacity of the particle by somewhere within the range of 15 to 25 percent:

```
// Choose a color and shape at random
this.gotoAndStop(random(this._totalframes-1)+2);
this._alpha=15+random(10);
```

This is a common practice when many objects of different graphical appearances but similar behavior are required for a movie.

You may not immediately notice where the particle emitters have been placed within `palettes.fla`. This is because I have arranged all six particle emitters off to the bottom left of the stage:

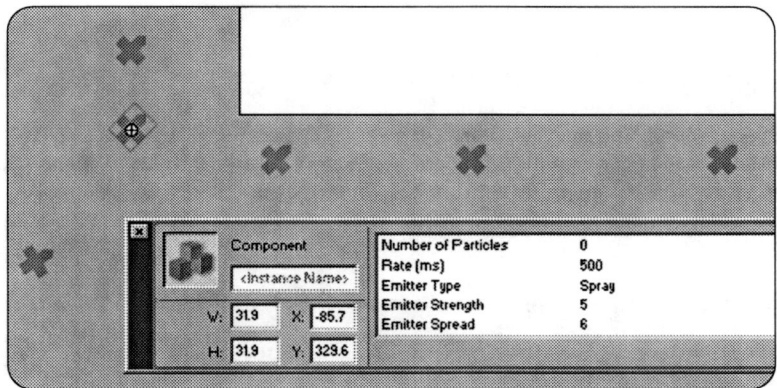

Why did I do this? I wanted to show particles coming onto the stage after they had had some time to wander. Also, since there is no 'fade in' property, I wanted to ensure that no particles suddenly popped onto the stage, as they do when they are created. Moving the emitters offstage allows the particle to come into existence fully before entering the viewing area.

There is a special feature with this example that you may notice only after some time of observation. The earlier illustration of the example in action provides a clue as to what exactly is special about. I won't give it away here, but finding this bonus effect may enlighten you to the possibilities of particle fields where multiple self-similar (or not so similar, for that matter!) emitters are present.

Poetry

In this example, `poetry.fla`, the simple particle graphic has again been replaced with something slightly more complex. Instead of a graphic shape, I have used a dynamic text box. The text box is assigned a word at random upon its creation:

The following code exists on the first frame of the `particleBody` movie clip:

```
textwords = "love, computation, peace,..."; // and so on...
var words = new Array();
words = textwords.split(",");
myword = words[random(words.length)];
stop();
```

Where `myword` is the variable used for the dynamic text box.

About once every second, the emitter creates a new word particle. The particle starts small and slowly expands to full size over the course of its lifetime. Just before it self-destructs, it spends the last 5 percent of its life fading into transparency. The result is the somewhat poetic display of a relaxed particle field.

Pens

This effect gives each particle a pen, so that it draws its path as it moves – the effect is unusual and striking:

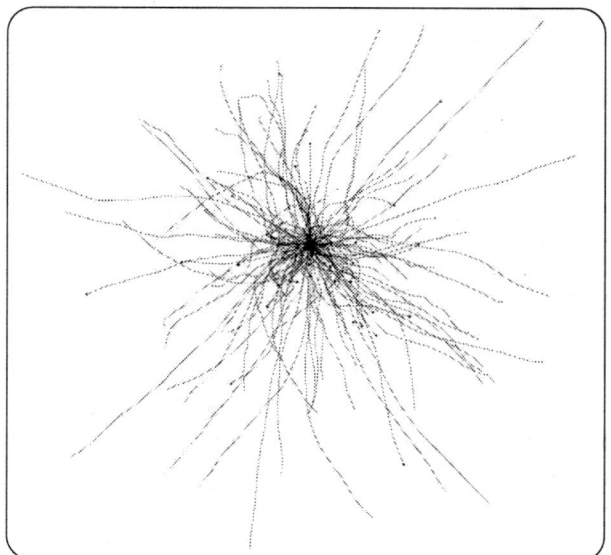

For this final example, `pens.fla`, a bit of additional programming was required. On the `particleBody` movie clip, the following code was added to the first frame:

```
// Make an empty clip at the root level
myLine=this._name+"line";
myLineObject = _root.createEmptyMovieClip(myLine,_root.depth++);
myLineObject._x = this._parent._parent._x;
myLineObject._y = this._parent._parent._y;
myLineObject.lineStyle(0,0x000000,20);
myLineObject.moveTo(this._parent._x,this._parent._y);
// Draw to it every frame until death
this.onEnterFrame = function () {
    myLineObject.lineTo(this._parent._x,this._parent._y);
};
stop();
```

Essentially, the first thing each particle does is create an empty movie clip positioned over the emitter. Then, for every frame, it uses the drawing API to trace a line following its path. When the particle self-destructs, the path it traced is left behind, and the result is a highly organic looking structure. The emitter in this example is using all the default parameter values – some pretty strange things can be drawn by playing with the parameters (especially the wind, gravity, and wandering behaviors).

There are many interesting applications of the particle emitter component, although, admittedly, not all are entirely productive! The component is a useful addition to an otherwise stagnant project where visual treats are desirable. They can be a highly effective complement when used well. Conversely, they can also be a massive drain on CPU resources if used without caution. Whether or not it fits in with your designs, people will always enjoy watching things that move, so this component should be a useful addition to your computational library and design toolbox.

Michael Montagna

Michael Montagna is an architect at Wagerworks Inc in San Francisco where he specializes in component architectures, enterprise UI and agile development processes. He discovered Flash several years ago while developing educational kiosk software for the Flandrau Science Center in Tucson, Arizona.

Michael considers Flash MX to be the reigning champion for web UI and sees an unbeatable match when Flash is teamed with Enterprise Java. He dreams of a command line Flash compiler and if you are reading this you should go make one right now!

For more information about Michael, please visit his website at www.haknam.com.

"Many thanks to Aaron Piland at apakstudio.com for the illustration and David Tudury for help with the geometry."

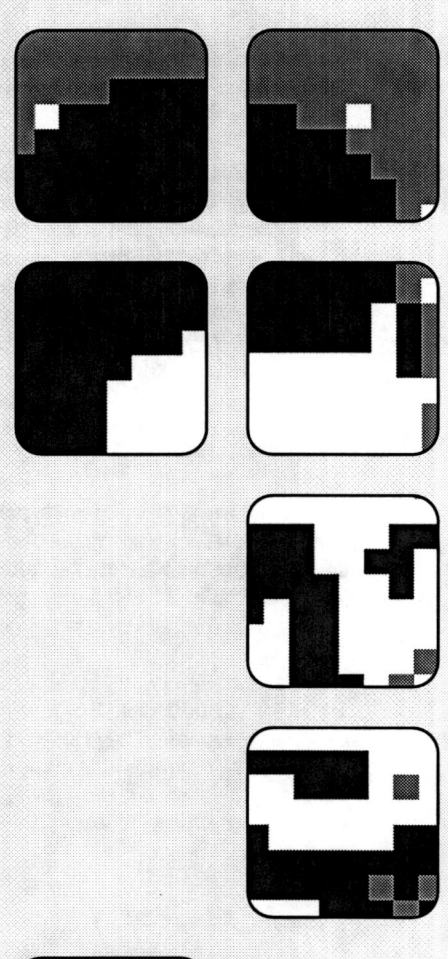

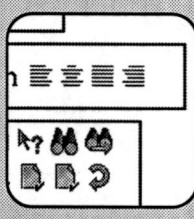

Component 14

Layout Manager

With the Layout Manager component, you can automatically layout components, place, arrange, and dynamically manage any number of components in your designs.

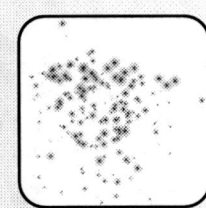

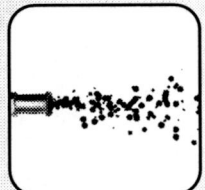
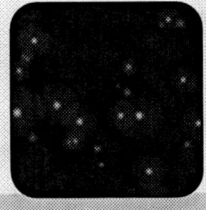
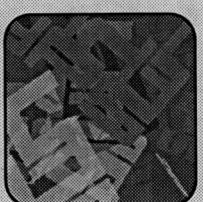
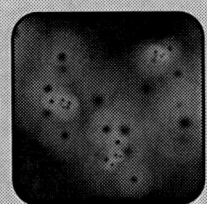

The Layout Manager component automates the placement of Flash MX components onto the stage. Essentially, you specify which components you would like to use and the Layout Manager automatically places and arranges the components within your project. This is a little different from typical Flash components because it is not a standalone component; in fact, it's a tool that helps you dynamically manage a complex group of other components through some simple but powerful ActionScript. This should make it easier to quickly construct a complex and dynamic user interface (UI) integrating a large number of components.

Because this component operates in rather different manner than you may be used to, it's worth looking at an example of its use early on – I recommend that you open the `InteractiveDemo.swf` file included in the examples folder in the download to get a feel for what the Layout Manager does. This sample file demonstrates the automated placement of over 40 components and UI elements through the use of two Layout Managers (denoted by the black bounding boxes):

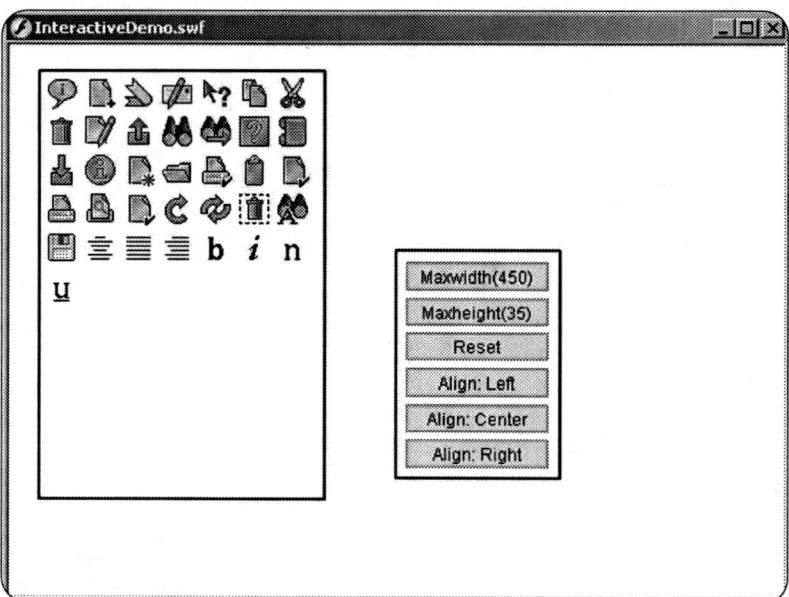

If you're already feeling confident, you could even open up `InteractiveDemo.fla` and experiment with the options (remember – this movie is generated entirely at runtime via ActionScript).

Components are extremely useful tools for speeding up development, reducing the chances of bugs in your projects, and for quickly expanding the range of functionality available in your Flash designs. The purpose of this book is to provide you with a host of new features for use in your next application, and in this chapter in particular we'll assume that you have some familiarity with the use of default Flash MX components (Flash UI Components Set 1), and that you're fairly confident with ActionScript. This includes the placing of components onto the stage via the `_x` and `_y` properties:

```
myComponent._x = 100;
myComponent._y = 53;
```

While this technique is straightforward for simple designs, placing and arranging lots of components onto the stage can be a tedious and time-consuming process. A sophisticated layout of components, all set 'by hand' via _x and _y properties, or arranged with the Align panel (CTRL/COMMAND+K) is neither easy to develop nor resilient to change. Change can occur internally across different states of the application, or externally after showing a UI design to a client, manager, or end-user. Constantly reworking a large set of dependent x and y coordinates is far from an efficient process! Likewise, relying solely on the Align panel in the Flash authoring environment is not always compatible with a dynamically changing UI.

What would be handy is a development tool that can address these issues by automatically instantiating and placing components onto the stage relative to each other. This would give developers the ability to quickly place a large number of components via ActionScript, and then focus on making fine-grained adjustments to those components in a straightforward and painless way.

This is what the Layout Manager component does by automatically arranging components according to the style parameters that you specify. This is analogous to how the words are placed on this page. Word processing software places the words on each line according to a set style. If a word does not fit on the current line, it is placed on the next line down. To see the utility of a word processor, imagine for a moment that each word on this page was a component. Consider how long it would take to position each word according to its x and y position! And what if you needed to edit the page? How long would it take to change the x and y positions to accommodate changing text? Obviously, word processors automate the placement of words on the page.

Likewise, the Layout Manager performs a task similar to that of the word processing software – it automates the placement of components on the stage. In doing so, it makes the x and y placement of Flash components transparent to the developer. This is done through a specific layout algorithm called the `FlowLayout` that works just like the Left, Center, and Right alignment of a word processor. This workflow allows a developer or designer to control the arrangement style of their design without having to wrestle with the details.

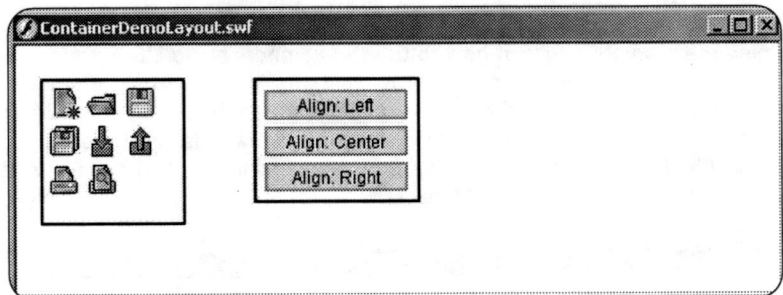

Above we see another example of the `Container` layout. The Layout Manager places each icon component within the height and width of the `Container`, which is illustrated by the black bounding box. Starting from the upper left corner and moving horizontally to the right, each component is instantiated and placed. When a row is filled with icons the Layout Manager moves down to the next row. This process continues until each component specified is placed within the `Container`. Try out the different alignment buttons in `ContainerDemoLayout.swf` and see how the `Container` will automatically shift the components. If you're eager to get into the technical details, open up `ContainerDemoLayout.fla` and look through the code on each layer.

How it works

The Layout Manager component is a pure ActionScript component that does not contain any graphics, and indeed is not visible when placed on the stage. Instead, it provides additional ActionScript functionality while leveraging the advantages of a Flash component so that you can use it and share it easily. Earlier, we touched upon the fact that the Layout Manager is made up of a couple of important ActionScript classes:

- The `Container` class is the core class in this object structure and contains the critical developer-accessible properties and methods such as `setLayout()`, `addComponent()`, and `doLayout()`. It should be noted that the `Container` does not actually hold the components added to it. Rather, attached components are 'contained' within its two-dimensional properties: `width` and `height`.

- `FlowLayout` is a subclass of `Container`. `FlowLayout` is the layout style class that actually does the specific layout. `FlowLayout` contains two important methods: `layoutContainer()` and `moveComponents()`. These methods contain the logic by which the attached components are placed into your movie.

To use the Layout Manager component in your next application, drag it from the Library of `LayoutManager.fla` (found in the download) to the Library of the intended Flash movie, then initialize and attach the component via ActionScript just like any other component. This component is primarily a scripting tool and it is not recommended that it be added to the stage by simply dragging it onto the stage.

Basic use

Let's now examine the absolute basics of how to use this component. To illustrate the use of the Layout Manager, I've created a demo component called Icon that simply displays one of many different toolbar icons – you'll notice this component in the Library of all the sample files associated with this chapter. This component is only for demonstration purposes and will not work outside of the included project files. Open up and test `BasicUse.fla` – you'll see a nice collection of icons appear in the output SWF representing the basic usage of the Layout Manager:

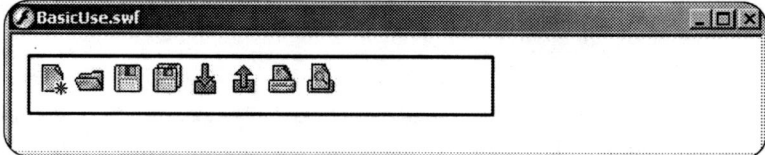

Now, returning to the authoring environment, note that the stage is completely empty – if you look on frame 1 of the root level of this FLA, you'll find the following code snippet:

```
// Init Layout Manager Component
var containerInit0 = {maxwidth:325, maxheight:40, debug:true};
//Add Container to the Stage
_root.attachMovie("MXContainer", "myContainer0", ++depth,
ÂcontainerInit0);
//Set Layout
myContainer0.setLayout(new FlowLayout("LEFT", 3, 3, myContainer0));
// Offset Container (ignore this for now)
myContainer0._x = 25;
myContainer0._y = 25;
// Init example component
var icon1 = {id:"New"};
var icon2 = {id:"Open"};
// and so on...
//
// Add Components
var i = 0;
myContainer0.addComponent("DemoIcon", "example" + ++i, ++depth, icon1);
myContainer0.addComponent("DemoIcon", "example" + ++i, ++depth, icon2);
// and so on...
//
//Execute Layout
myContainer0.doLayout();
```

The first thing to do is create an initialization object for the Layout Manager component. This object contains the width and height of the component. It also includes an optional debug parameter that draws a bounding box showing the dimensions of the Container:

```
var containerInit0 = {maxwidth:325, maxheight:40, debug:true};
```

Note that if the container is too small to fit the number of components specified, the Layout Manager will only place the components that fit. The additional components will not be made visible. A Container Exception is thrown and you will see a warning in the Output window.

Next, we add the Layout Manager component (with linkage name MXContainer) to a movie clip using the standard attachMovie() method. In the sample below, we add the component to the main stage by specifying _root:

```
_root.attachMovie("MXContainer", "myContainer", ++depth, containerInit);
```

You can double-check the component's linkage name by looking in the Library (F11):(See Over)

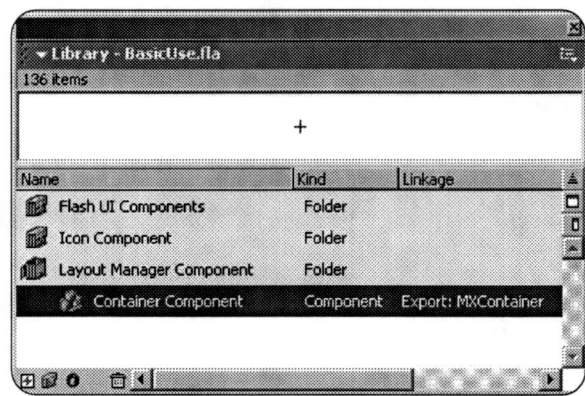

Now we get into the particulars of the Layout Manager. The `Container` uses a specific layout style to determine the actual placement of components. This style is set with the `setLayout()` method of the `Container`, and the component includes the layout style called `FlowLayout`. Later on we will see how to make a custom layout.

Returning to our original analogy, the `FlowLayout` style places components on the stage much like text is placed in a word processor, where letters and words can be aligned to the left, center, or right. Text is placed in lines left to right until it is filled, at which point it 'flows' down to the next line. The alignment adjusts the flow of the words. Similarly, the `FlowLayout` style allows you to select the type of alignment to be used for your component set. By using the LEFT alignment that is specified in `BasicUse.fla`, components are first placed in the upper left corner and then they're placed horizontally until each row is filled:

```
myContainer0.setLayout(new FlowLayout("LEFT", 3, 3, myContainer0));
```

The Layout Manager then begins a new row below the previous one, and so on until all components are placed or the `maxheight` of the container is reached. In this manner, components are placed left to right and top to bottom until the 'page', or stage in our case, is filled. Try out the CENTER and RIGHT options in the above line in `BasicUse.fla` line and re-test it to see the effect:

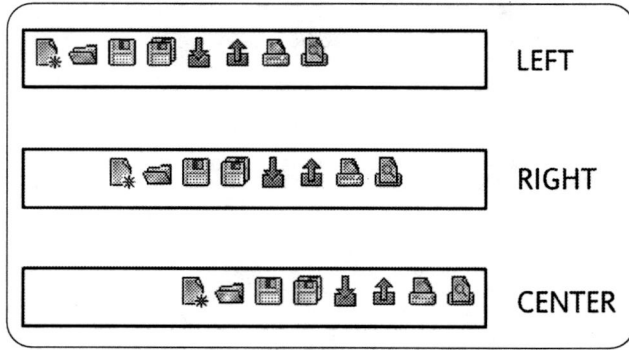

Note that if the alignment is invalid, a Container Exception is thrown and no components are placed on the stage. A warning will be displayed in the output window when you are testing in the Flash MX authoring environment.

`FlowLayout` also allows a developer to specify the spacing between components horizontally, and between rows of components vertically. These pixel spacings are called the `hgap` and `vgap` respectively – these parameters are specified after the alignment in the `FlowLayout` constructor (in `BasicUse.fla` I've set them both to 3):

You may want to adjust the distance between components horizontally, and between components vertically. These two parameters enable you to do just that:

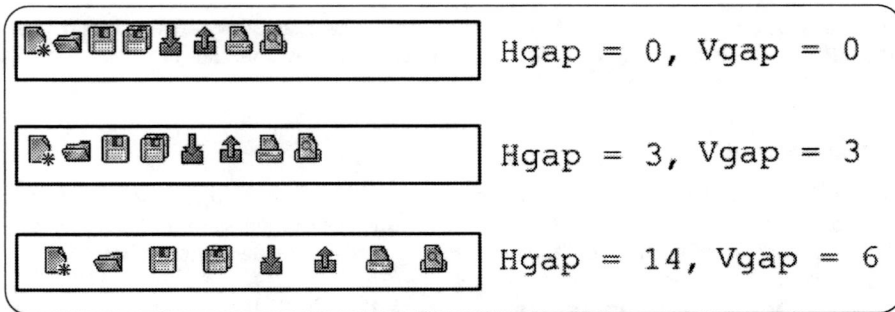

If the `FlowLayout` constructor is empty, a default alignment of `CENTER` and an `hgap` and `vgap` of 5 pixels is used.

Returning our attention to the code in `BasicUse.fla`, which was shown earlier, next step in the process, after specifying the position of `myContainer0` (discussed shortly in the *Container offset* section), is the initializing of the UI components that you wish to use. In the various examples discussed in this chapter we'll see the Layout Manger used in conjunction with some of the default components that are included with Flash MX, as well as a demonstration component called Icon. In the example project files in the download, all components have already been added to the Library. For your own projects, double-check that the components you wish to use are indeed added to your Library. Create initialization objects for each component, as instructed for that component. Typically, it will be something like this:

```
var icon1 = {id:"New"};
```

The `Container`'s `addComponent()` method is then used to add a component to be placed by the Layout Manager. You may notice in the line below that the parameters passed through this method are the same type as those required by the `attachMovie()` method of the `MovieClip` object. This is no coincidence; these parameters are in fact used by the container to execute an `attachMovie()` method for each added component. This happens under the covers, but here you are still given the opportunity to set the same parameters that you would normally do without the Layout Manager component:

```
myContainer0.addComponent("DemoIcon", "example" + ++i, ++depth, icon1);
```

179

The final step is to simply execute the Layout Manager. This is done with the `doLayout()` method of the `Container`, which doesn't take any parameters:

```
myContainer0.doLayout();
```

It's important to note that the Layout Manager cannot place components that are 'empty', that is, components that have no artwork placed within them. This should not be a major disadvantage in most cases. This is also the reason why you cannot place a container component within another container – nested containers are not supported.

Advanced use

There are many additional features to the Layout Manager that allow an advanced user to make sophisticated use of this component through multiple instances, manual and dynamic adjustments, and use of the `Insets` object.

Manual adjustment

In some cases, the uniform placement of a diverse collection of components will not be perfect usually due to the differing heights and widths of various components. To address this issue, we can manually adjust individual components after the Layout Manager has placed them.

Open up `ManualAdjustmentExample.fla` and notice that I've added the following lines of code that will shift the `example1` component slightly down and to the left:

```
// Manually adjust first component
example1._y += 12;
example1._x += -7;
```

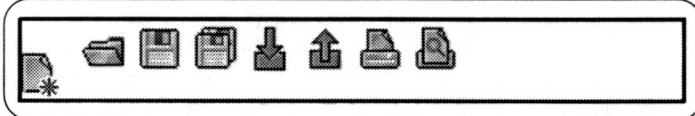

Container offset

The advanced user may also wish to offset the `Container` component from the origin of the stage. By default, the upper left corner of the stage is the origin for the Layout Manager. The `maxwidth` and the `maxheight` of the component are then determined from this starting point. This may be sufficient for most cases, but it's straightforward to add an x and y axis offset.

The examples that we've looked at so far have utilized a container offset; by default containers are placed at (0,0). This is generally sufficient when a container is placed within a non-root movie clip. However, there may be contexts where it is convenient or necessary to shift the container.

The first step consists of sending a reference of the `Container` component to the `FlowLayout` object through the `FlowLayout` constructor. This gives the `FlowLayout` object access to the properties of the `Container` component itself:

```
myContainer0.setLayout(new FlowLayout("LEFT", 3, 3, myContainer0));
```

The second step is the standard access to the `_x` and `_y` properties of the `Container` movie clip. The code below offsets the Layout Manager component down and to the right by 25 pixels in each direction:

```
myContainer0._x = 25;
myContainer0._y = 25;
```

Try experimenting with some different offset values to suit your requirements.

Multiple containers

Components are aligned relative to each other within a container. In most designs, this should prove adequate. More complicated UI, however, may require that components be arranged within several unique contexts. To this end, a developer can use multiple instances of the `Container` object and attach components to each container respectively. These containers then act independently of one another. The project file `MultipleContainers.fla` demonstrates the use of five separate containers, each with different layout parameters and dimensions:

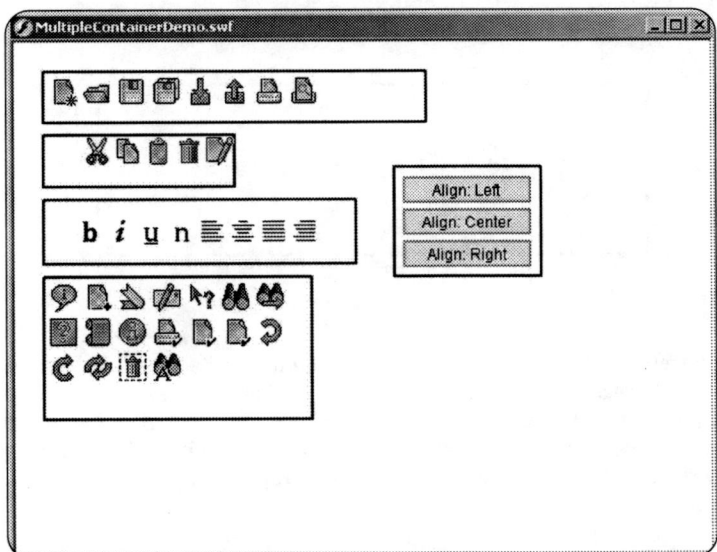

Remember, when using multiple containers the instance names of all components must be unique. Adding multiple containers will typically involve setting the offset of one or more of the discrete containers. This requires that a reference to each container be passed to the Layout Manager for that container. See the previous section for details on how to offset a container from the default origin (the upper left corner) of the stage.

Insets

The hgap and vgap settings that we examined in the *Basic use* section provide a convenient way of spacing components out. Similarly, offsetting the container also provides a useful means of adjusting the set of components relative to the stage. The Insets object provides yet another way of customizing the layout of components while still automating a large bulk of the work involved.

The Insets object provides discrete and adjustable 'padding' along the inside borders of the container component. It has four pixel dimension parameters: top, left, bottom, right. There is no default Insets object.

Refer to the project file InsetsExample.fla to experiment with the various parameters of the Insets object. Insets are constructed using in the following convention:

new Insets(top, left, bottom, right)

To add an Insets object to a Container use the getInsets() method passing a new Insets object (also see reference table at the end of this chapter). Note that in the Insets constructor, you must make any zero values explicit due to the way that Flash handles method signatures:

```
// Add insets (top, left, bottom, right)
myContainer0.getInsets(new Insets(30,30,20,10));
```

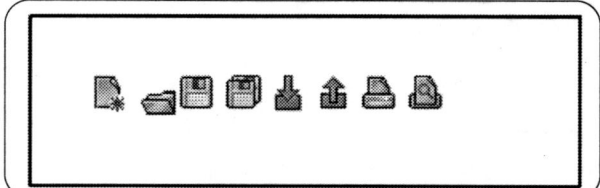

Dynamic update

Typical user interfaces change state often during the lifetime of a user's session. For this reason, it is sometimes necessary to rearrange components on the fly. You probably noticed that some of the example projects discussed earlier have included a container of gray PushButtons that adjust the alignment or width/height of a container. InteractiveDemo.fla is such an example. These buttons demonstrate one of the most important features and advantages of the Layout Manager component – it can dynamically update UI at runtime.

The Layout Manager component facilitates this with several methods. The update() method will rearrange the Container. This assumes that some property of the Container or the attached components has changed. For example, changing the _x or _y position of the Container would require a call to update() to make the change visible:

```
myContainer._x = 25;
myContainer._y = 25;
myContainer.update();
```

Resizing the `Container` is a common function and two methods are provided to facilitate this functionality: `setMaxheight(int)` and `setMaxwidth(int)` will resize the `Container` and automatically relayout the attached components. For example, the following code resizes the `Container` to match the current size of the stage:

```
myContainer.setMaxheight(Stage.height);
myContainer.setMaxwidth(Stage.width);
```

For some simple examples of how to script dynamic changes, refer to the code in the Dynamic Update Functions layer of the `InteractiveDemo.fla` project file. This contains several functions that update the root `Container`.

Custom layouts

The default layout manager included in this component, `FlowLayout`, is only one of many different algorithms that can be used to arrange components on the stage. Indeed, it is possible to implement your own custom layout by implementing the `Layout` interface. The interface defines several private methods that must be implemented and the `Container` object has been designed such that it will work with many different `Layout` implementations. An example implementation of the `Layout` interface is, of course, `FlowLayout` itself. To examine this class, add the Layout Manager component to your Library, open the Container Component to edit and view the ActionScript on the `FlowLayout` layer:

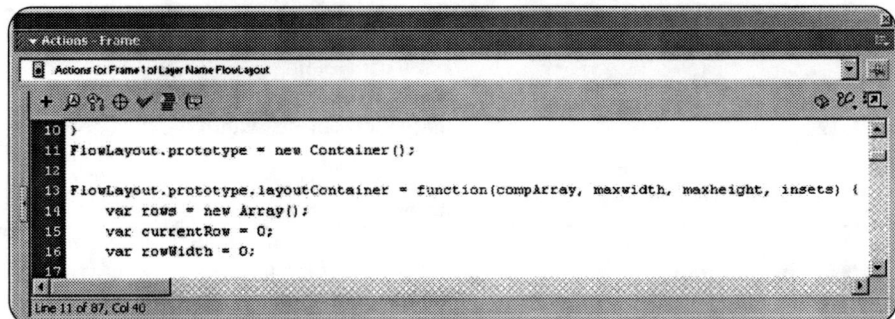

Here we see that `FlowLayout` inherits directly from `Container`. Note also the use of the `layoutContainer` function, which takes the following parameters:

- `compArray` – An array of component objects
- `maxwidth` – Maximum width of the container
- `maxheight` – Maximum height of the container
- `insets` – Support for the `Insets` object

Component methods

The component has several methods and constructors available to the developer – for reference, these are detailed in the following table. Methods are used in the format `ComponentInstanceName.MethodName(parameters)`.

Command	Description
setLayout(layout)	**Method**; attaches a layout object to the container for the purpose of laying out the components with a specific style. **Parameters**: Layout Object **Returns**: Nothing
getInsets(insets)	**Method**; attaches an `Insets` object for the purpose of defining the top, left, bottom, and right padding dimensions in pixels. **Parameters**: Insets Object **Returns**: Nothing
addComponent(idName, instanceName, depth [,initObject])	**Method**; adds a component to the `Container` for the purpose of adding that component to the stage. **Parameters**: `idName`: The linkage name of the component to be added. `instanceName` – The name of the component once instantiated. `depth` – An integer specifying the level of the component. `initObj` – An object containing the properties of the component. **Returns**: Nothing
doLayout()	**Method**; executes the current Layout. This method places the objects within the container onto the stage. **Parameters**: None **Returns**: Nothing
getMaxwidth()	**Method**; returns the value in pixels of the x dimension of the `Container`. **Parameters**: None **Returns**: Integer of the width of the `Container` in pixels
getMaxheight()	**Method**; returns the value in pixels of the y dimension of the `Container`. **Parameters**: None **Returns**: Integer of the width of the `Container` in pixels `setMaxwidth(width)`
setMaxWidth(int)	**Method**; takes the new integer and resizes the width of the `Container`. Components arranged within the `Container` are realigned in accordance with this new size.

Command	Description
	Parameters: Integer **Returns**: Nothing
setMaxheight(height)	**Method**; takes the new integer and resizes the height of the Container. Components arranged within the Container are realigned in accordance with this new size. **Parameters**: Integer **Returns**: Nothing
FlowLayout(alignment, hgap, vgap [,container reference])	**Constructor Method**; Instantiates a new FlowLayout object. This object is the mechanism by which components are placed on the stage according to a specific style. **Parameters**: alignment – string specifying the justification for use by the layout object. Valid parameters are: LEFT, CENTER, and RIGHT. hgap – integer that specifies the horizontal spacing in pixels between components and the container border. vgap – integer that specifies the vertical spacing in pixels between components and the container border. obj: a reference to the container object itself. Used if offsetting the Container from the stage origin. **Returns**: Nothing
Insets(top, left, bottom, top)	**Constructor Method**; instantiates a new Insets object. The insets object contains the dimensions of the top, left, bottom, and right borders within the Container. **Parameters**top – the margin between the top edge of the Container and the first row of components. left – the margin between the left edge of the Container and the first column of components. right – the margin between the right edge of the Container and the last column of components. bottom – the margin between the bottom edge of the Container and the last row of components. **Returns**: Nothing

Daryn Nakhuda

Daryn has spent the last six years living in Seattle and writing copious amounts of code. His first memorable project was building the entire web engine for a professional sports league in a proprietary scripting language that had more bugs than his own code. Since then, he's created award-winning Flash pieces and e-commerce systems at Altrec.com, developed domain registries for eNIC/VeriSign, and worked on various secret projects for eccentric local billionaires. Currently, Daryn is developing an anti-spam product called Spam Arrest.

When he's not working, Daryn likes experimenting with food and drink, snowboarding, playing with technology, and enjoying life... and thinking about what he's going to work on next.

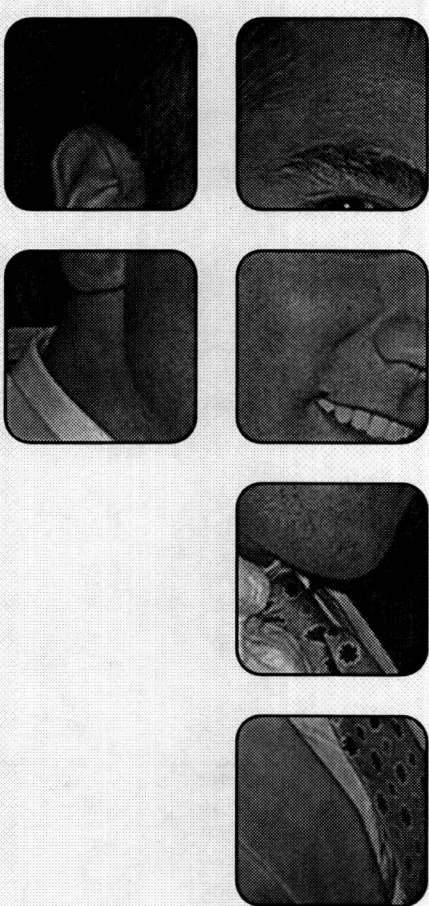

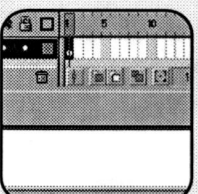

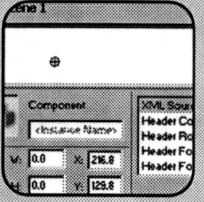

Component 15

Data Grid

You can use this Data Grid component to organize and present information in a clean, easy-to-use, and quick-to-understand manner. You'll wow your audience with features like sorting and scrolling, all tightly integrated into your user interface.

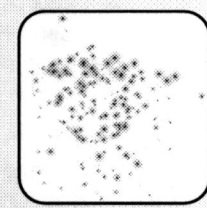

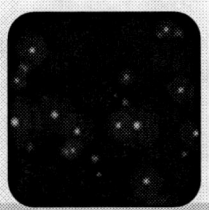

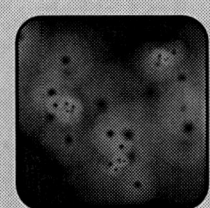

Although the name may not sound familiar to everyone, anyone who has used a computer in the past twenty years has probably seen and used a data grid in one form or another. A data grid is simply a tabular representation of information, most commonly associated with spreadsheet programs like Microsoft Excel, but also seen in word processing documents and web pages. It's the most common way of displaying record sets from a database or any other two-dimensional data source.

If you have a set of items that each have values for various fields, and you want to display them in a way in which you can compare them to one another, a data grid is perfect for you! (If, however, you're trying to display hierarchal data, such as genealogical (family tree) data, a data grid is probably not what you want – in such a scenario, consider using a tree-view schematic instead).

Here's a simple example of the Data Grid component in action:

In HTML, a table is most commonly rendered using the `<table>` tag. The HTML code for the above example would look something like this:

```
<TABLE>
<TR>
  <TH ALIGN="LEFT">First Name</TH>
  <TH ALIGN="LEFT">Last Name</TH>
  <TH ALIGN="LEFT">Company</TH>
  <TH ALIGN="LEFT">Title</TH>
</TR>
<TR>
  <TD>John</TD>
  <TD>Doe</TD>
  <TD><A HREF="http://any.com">ANY.COM</A></TD>
  <TD>CEO</TD>
</TR>
<TR>
  <TD>Bob</TD>
  <TD>Smith</TD>
  <TD>Bob's Autos</TD>
  <TD>Mechanic</TD>
</TR>
<TR>
```

```
        <TD>Madonna</TD>
        <TD><A HREF="http://www.madonnamusic.com">Madonna XMusic</A></TD>
        <TD>Musician</TD>
    </TR>
    <TR>
        <TD>Jane</TD>
        <TD>Smith</TD>
        <TD><A HREF="http://www.another.com">ANOTHER.COM</A></TD>
        <TD>President</TD>
    </TR>
    </TABLE>
```

This HTML script results in a table very similar to our Flash example shown above – so why would we want to do this in Flash when HTML will suffice? Is this a case of using a sledgehammer to crack a nut? Well, there are actually a number of important advantages to using the Data Grid component instead of the more traditional methods – the biggest of which are the interactivity and flexibility that Flash gives us.

The Flash Data Grid allows you to sort and re-sort the data by each column without amending the code or reloading the page, as well as scroll through the rows and columns of the grid. When displaying a simple table, these features may seem fairly unimportant, but with larger sets of data they can make a huge difference in your design and usability. For example, if we had 100 rows of data in the example above, the rendered HTML could take up the entire browser window. With the Flash Data Grid, we can set it to only show a certain number of rows at a time, say five, and then just let the user scroll through them. Additionally, an HTML table with 100 rows of data might also take a while to load for some users, and if they have to reload the page every time they want to sort by a different column, it can really detract from the table's usability.

By the way, Macromedia also provide an excellent data grid component as part of their Developers Resource Kit Volume 1 (www.macromedia.com/software/drk/productinfo/product_overview/volume1/), but that's an additional $99, and probably overkill for many projects.

Before we can use our Data Grid component, we need to make sure that our data is in a format that is readable by Flash, and the most natural format for that is XML.

Preparing the XML data source

If you are unfamiliar with XML, there is no need to be intimidated; it's simply a structured way of formatting data, and looks very similar to HTML. You can create and edit XML in Notepad, or your favorite text editor. In addition, some applications will let you export your data directly out of the program into an XML file (however, if you do choose to go this route, be forewarned that XML is not *one-size-fits-all* – different programs will export the XML differently, and each application that loads the XML is going to expect the XML to be in a particular format, which is not likely to be the same as what was exported).

For those interested, the syntax of an XML document is called its **schema**, and can be defined in various ways, the most common of which is known as a DTD (Document Type Definition). DTDs are extremely useful in many ways, because they can define any XML document, no matter how complex, using a standard grammar. However, they can also be very difficult to read, especially for people unfamiliar with the language. The easiest way to learn the syntax for a simple XML document is by example.

For the Data Grid component, open up the sample XML file from the download, `data.xml`, in a text editor – this shows us the data structure required to use the Data Grid component:

```
EditPlus - [C:\Book_Code\Components Most Wanted\Component15\data.xml]
File  Edit  View  Search  Document  Project  Tools  Window  Help

1    <LIST>
2      <HEADER WIDTH="100" NAME="fname">First Name</HEADER>
3      <HEADER WIDTH="100" NAME="lname">Last Name</HEADER>
4      <HEADER WIDTH="160" NAME="comp">Company</HEADER>
5      <HEADER WIDTH="100" NAME="title">Title</HEADER>
6      <ITEM>
7        <COLUMN NAME="fname">Steve</COLUMN>
8        <COLUMN NAME="lname">Rycroft</COLUMN>
9        <COLUMN NAME="comp" URL="http://www.friendsofed.com">friendsofed.com</COLUMN>
10       <COLUMN NAME="title">TE</COLUMN>
11     </ITEM>
12     <ITEM>
13       <COLUMN NAME="fname">Andrew</COLUMN>
14       <COLUMN NAME="lname">Tracey</COLUMN>
15       <COLUMN NAME="comp" URL="http://www.friendsofed.com">friendsofed.com</COLUMN>
16       <COLUMN NAME="title">CE</COLUMN>
17     </ITEM>
18     <ITEM>
19       <COLUMN NAME="fname">Bob</COLUMN>
20       <COLUMN NAME="lname">Smith</COLUMN>
21       <COLUMN NAME="comp">Bob's Autos</COLUMN>
```

Now let's examine each of the elements that make up this XML:

LIST

The `LIST` element is simply a container for the `HEADER` and `ITEM` elements, and does not have any additional attributes.

HEADER

The `HEADER` element is where you define the names of the columns to be placed in the header row of the Data Grid. The value of the element is used as the display label in the Data Grid. Additionally, you must specify two attributes for the element, the `column width` and the `column id`. The width is used for rendering the table correctly, and the ID is used for associating the columns with the appropriate data for each item:

```
<HEADER WIDTH="column width" NAME="column id">Display Label</HEADER>
```

ITEM

The `ITEM` element is a container for `COLUMN` elements, and does not have any attributes. An item can have any number of `COLUMN` elements within it, but only the column IDs referenced by the `HEADER` elements will be displayed. If an item does not have a value for a particular column, the `COLUMN` element can either be omitted, or included with a blank value.

COLUMN

The COLUMN element is where you define the individual columns of data for an item. The value of the element is what is shown in the Data Grid. The NAME attribute is required, and should correspond to the NAME attribute of a HEADER element. There is also an optional attribute, URL, which can be used to turn the cell into a hyperlink:

```
<COLUMN NAME="column id" URL="link url">Display Label</COLUMN>
```

Using the Data Grid

Once you have your XML created, the next step is to add the Data Grid component to your movie. As with all components, this is as simple as dragging the component from the Components panel or Library and onto your stage. If you're using the Macromedia Extension Manager, just double-click on the dgrid.mxp file to install the component. Otherwise, open up dgrid.fla and the Data Grid component will be available for you in the Library.

Once the component is on the stage (note that it is effectively invisible, aside from its registration point), select it and take a look in the Property inspector panel – here we can modify its properties (colors, fonts, and various other settings) by setting the appropriate parameters:

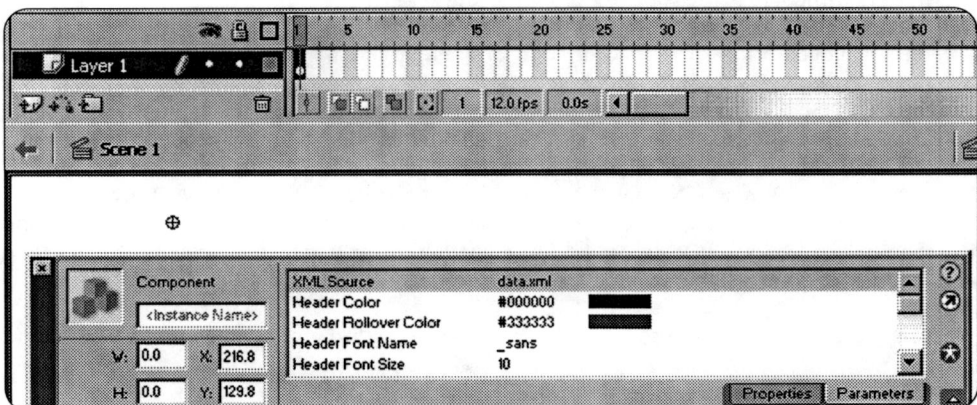

To test your component, just change the XML Source parameter to point to whatever XML file you want to load into the Data Grid – by default it points to a file called data.xml, located in the same directory as the FLA/SWF. Test your movie, and you should see your data presented in the grid.

Setting the component parameters

Let's now take a quick tour of all of these parameters – open up the Component Parameters panel (ALT/OPTION+F7) to see them all in full:

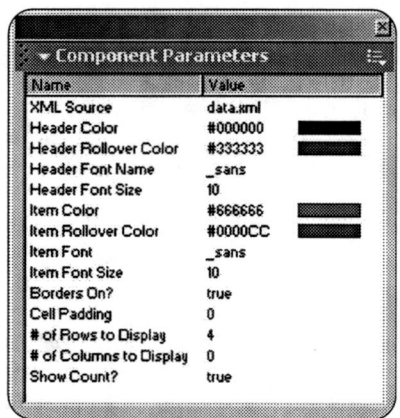

These parameters are defined as follows:

- XML Source – String describing the location of your XML data source, relative to the SWF.
- Header Color – The color of the header text.
- Header Rollover Color – The rollover color of the header text.
- Header Font Name – The font of the header text.
- Header Font Size – The font size of the header text.
- Item Color – The color of the item text.
- Item Rollover Color – The rollover color of the item text.
- Item Font Name – The font of the item text.
- Item Font Size – The font size of the item text.
- Borders On? – Boolean value determining whether to show a border around the item cells.
- Cell Padding – Amount of whitespace between cells.
- # of Rows to Display – Number of rows visible at once. Set to 0 to show all rows.
- # of Columns to Display – Number of columns visible at once. Set to 0 to show all columns.
- Show Count – Boolean value determining whether to show the line below the grid indicating the number of rows in the table and the current position.

The best way to understand these settings is to play around with them and see exactly what effect they have:

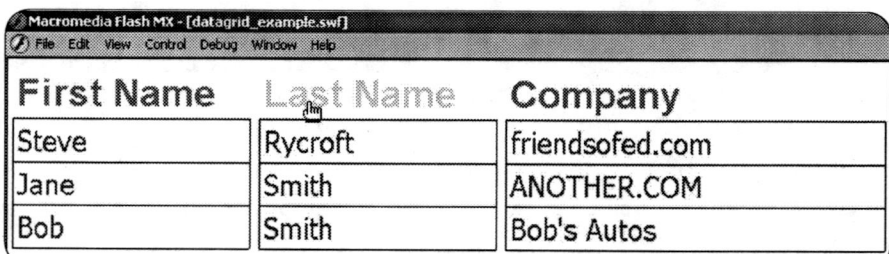

Now that you've got a grid of data, what else does this component do? As I've noted, this is a fairly simple data grid implementation, but there are a couple of additional features...

Sorting

Clicking on a column header will sort the Data Grid by that column. Click the header again, and the order will be reversed. Note that this is an alphabetical sort, so 'apples' comes before 'bananas', but 10 comes before 9.

Scrolling

Personally, I'm not a big fan of scrollbars on tables; they just seem like overdoing it for this type of data presentation. You have two choices with this Data Grid:

- Set # of Rows to Display and # of Columns to Display both to 0 and you will see all of your data at once – this works great if you have plenty of real estate available on your web page.

- Constrain # of Rows to Display and/or # of Columns to Display to reasonable numbers that let you fit your Data Grid into the rest of your interface.

If you choose the latter, you can move around between elements in the Data Grid using the following keyboard commands:

Key Press	Action
Up-Arrow	Move up one record
Down-Arrow	Move down one record
Left-Arrow	Move left one column
Right-Arrow	Move right one column
Page Up	Move up one page (NUMROWS records)
Page Down	Move down one page (NUMROWS records)
Home	Move to first page of records
End	Move to last page of records

Now that you're comfortable using the Data Grid, you may be wondering what other features might be useful to add to it. Here are some suggestions for functionality enhancements:

- **Numeric Sorting** – You'll probably have to set an attribute on the HEADER elements to tell your code when to use alphabetical order and when to use numeric order.

- **Navigation Buttons** – The keyboard is great for moving around, but if you are putting this grid onto a kiosk without a keyboard, you're going to need another way.

- **Scrollbars** – Personally, I don't like them on a Data Grid, but like navigation buttons, they can be really useful, especially in a keyboard-less environment.

- **Editable Fields** – Wouldn't it be cool if this thing worked like a simple spreadsheet?

- **Exportable Data** – If you make the fields editable, you'll probably want a way to get your changes to the data back out!

Aral Balkan

An interstellar marauder since age 12… oh, wait, I wasn't supposed to mention that! What I meant to say is: Born in Turkey a little over a quarter of a century ago, I spent most of my childhood and early teens in a tropical paradise called Malaysia and currently live in the murky wetlands of London (oh yes, the weather *is* that bad thank you very much!) Coding and design both grew out of hobbies that started at age seven, when my Dad brought home an IBM XT instead of a Commodore 64, leaving me to either write my own games or go without (thanks Dad!) My true passions in life are acting and singing, both of which I want to pursue professionally.

In between my globetrotting, I got the chance to produce a musical in North Cyprus (Jesus Christ Superstar) and grab a Master of Arts in Film & Video (emphasis Multimedia Design) from American University in Washington, DC. Nowadays, I run my own company in London called "Bits And Pixels", specializing in Flash for web and mobile applications.

Thanks to my amazing parents, Mehlika and Haluk, for making everything possible and for supporting me no matter what: I love and appreciate you more than you'll ever know. And of course, to the angel whom I am honored to be able to call my wife, Emilie, for sticking with me through late nights spent absorbing the glow of my monitors.

Aral's photo by Emilie Balkan.

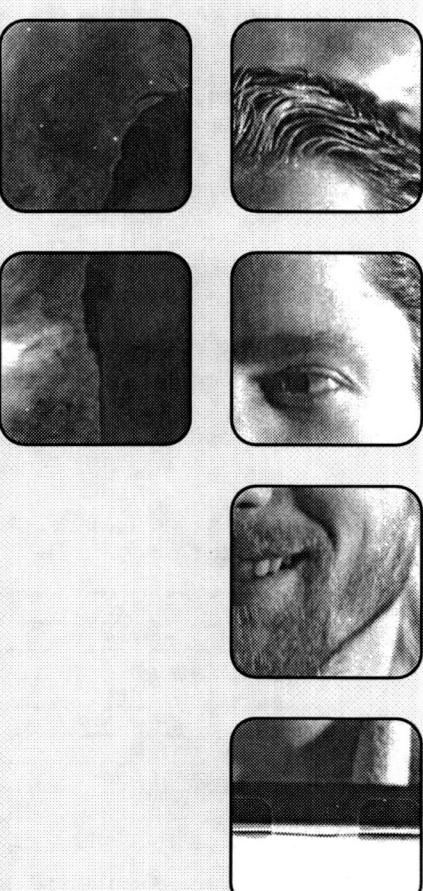

Component 16

Tornado: The Art of Movie Loading

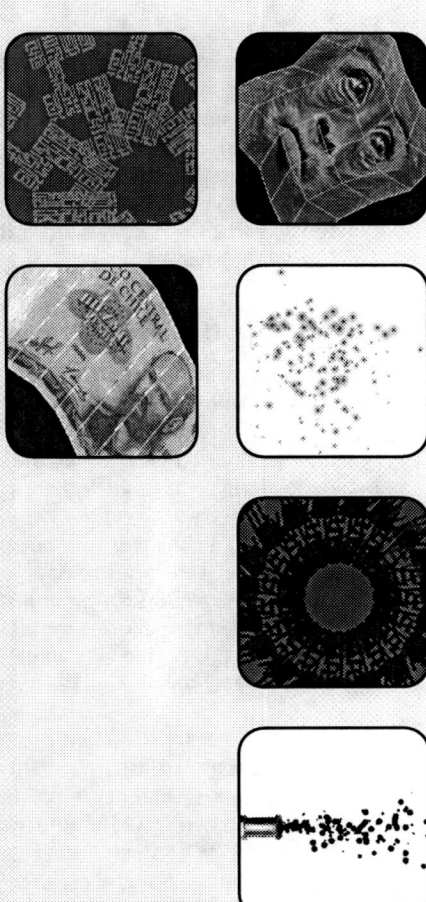

The Tornado Movie Loader component enables you to quckly and easily load in external movies and images into your Flash projects. It automatically queues multiple movies and loads them in order and can transparently handle the preloading of multiple movies, giving each its own preloader. With a little scripting, it allows for intelligent preloading based on user interaction by making it possible to influence the load order at runtime. To really separate it from the crowd, it is designed to handle the loading of multiple movies concurrently. All this, coupled with an easy to use Custom UI and Live Preview that let you visually layout external movies and images on the stage, and extensive Reference panel documentation make Tornado the most robust and user-friendly external movie loader currently available.

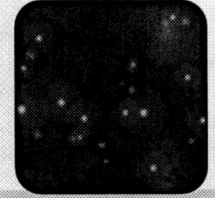

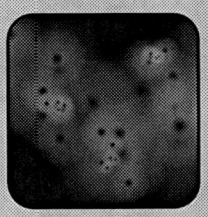

One of the great strengths of Flash is its ability to load in and run external movies dynamically at runtime. With Flash MX, this functionality has been extended to include the dynamic loading of JPEG images as well. Breaking up large Flash sites and applications into a series of smaller movies presents many advantages with regards to both the development process and the user experience itself. It allows team development and delegation, scalability and maintainability, as well as superior control over the streaming experience. Unfortunately, preloading is often incorrectly or inefficiently applied in Flash development today. Part of this comes from the complexity inherent in implementing systems that exhibit intelligent loading behavior. This is no longer the case, however, as you will soon see.

Once upon a project...

I first started thinking about abstracting out the movie loading process while working on a project late last year with Branden Hall and Charlie Cordova. The project was to create the Flash front-end for a virtual school and required us to load in and serve thousands of lessons, each of which were in separate Flash movies that had been generated offline (Charlie's since rewritten most of what Generator was doing using ActionScript alone... now there's a *scripthead*, if ever there was one!).

To get back to the story, Branden had created a wonderful movie-loading engine – in Flash 5 ActionScript, since these were pre-MX days – which we were using to queue up and load the SWFs. After getting a version upgrade on my brain just to understand his code, I started thinking about how the engine could be improved to make the movie loading process more intelligent (Branden actually released an improved version of this engine later under the guise of SWFQueue for his ACK! (ActionScript Component Kit) event engine – http://chattyfig.figleaf.com/ack/swfqueue.php).

After the project was over, I took some time off and devoted myself to creating a library of commonly used modules, or as I called them then, *components* – wrong choice of words, I was to find out later! Among others, there were components for simplifying data exchanges, for time-based animation and, of course, a movie loader component that I wrote from the ground up to allow more than one movie to load at the same time, and yet give me complete control over the loading process. This was all done in Flash 5 ActionScript and released as open-source (see FC-Lib at www.aralbalkan.com/index.php?article=7). If you take a look at it, you'll probably understand why I don't think anyone ever used it except for me: it's huge, with lots and lots of code and almost no documentation whatsoever.

With the introduction of components in Flash MX, I decided I'd be able to tackle the shortcomings of my Flash 5 movie loader by creating a component with an easy-to-use custom user interface (UI), Live Preview to enable visual configuration and layout of externally loaded movies, and extensive documentation (with Reference panel entries, code-hinting, and syntax highlighting). What resulted is the Tornado Movie Loader component and now it's yours to use, abuse, and enjoy!

My personal website, www.aralbalkan.com, is powered by a version of the Movie Loader component and exhibits intelligent streaming based on predicting the user browsing behavior:

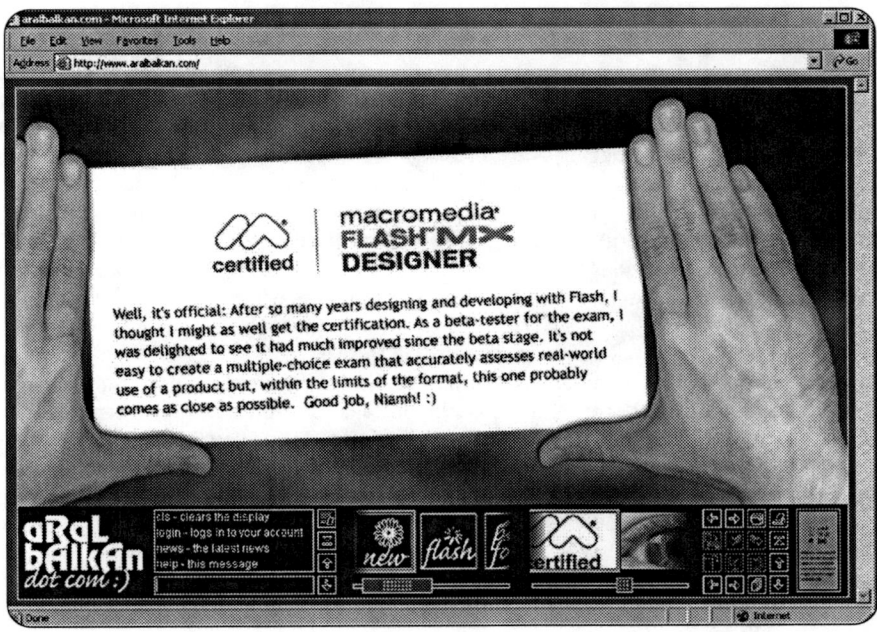

Another site built upon a previous version of Tornado is www.bitsandpixels.co.uk – play around with the interface and see how responsive it is to your browsing behavior:

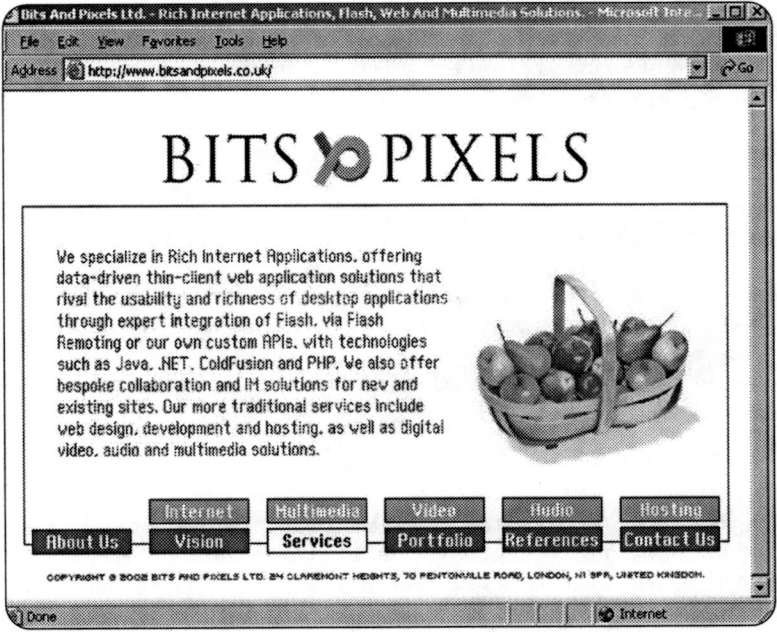

Tornado

Tornado allows you to quickly and easily manage the preloading and layout of external movies (SWFs) and external images (JPEGs) in your Flash movies – without even writing a single line of code (if that's the way you prefer it). By simply 'dragging and dropping' the component, you can visually layout external movies from within the authoring environment and see exactly how they will appear when loaded in at runtime. The layout engine is very flexible, giving you almost complete freedom in the arrangement of loaded movies and images. The preloading engine is similarly flexible: it can either use a custom preloader movie clip or call custom preloader functions that you specify. Creating your own preloader movie clip for use with the Movie Loader is very easy to do and this process will be explained in detail later.

If you haven't done so already, take a moment to install the component by double-clicking the setup file (`tornado.mxp`) in the book's companion download. The Macromedia Extension Manager will then automate the installation procedure, as usual. During installation, Tornado fully integrates into the Flash authoring environment with code hints and syntax highlighting (for all you ActionScripters out there) and a friendly custom UI and Live Preview (for everyone!). In addition, you'll find full documentation of all the component's methods and parameters in the Tornado Movie Loader entry of the Reference panel.

If you're anything like I am with a new toy, you're probably just itching to get your hands dirty... so enough waiting around, let's see what this baby can do!

Kicking up some dust

Using Tornado couldn't be simpler. In fact, you can use it without ever typing in a single line of ActionScript. Before starting the exercises, you'll probably want to copy over the contents of this chapter's examples directory from the download to your working directory. Here you'll find all the Flash movies for the exercises featured in this chapter, as well as some sample external movies and JPEGs that we'll be loading in using Tornado while we test it. Feel free to use your own external movies in place of the provided sample files while following along with the examples.

Let's get started:

1. Open a new movie in Flash (CTRL/COMMAND+N) and save it as `simple.fla` (or just refer to `simple.fla` from the download).

2. Drag an instance of the Tornado Movie Loader from the Components panel to your stage (or just double-click on it). The component should appear on the stage as a little icon:

3. Look in your Library (F11). You should see that a new folder has been added to it and inside you will find the Tornado Movie Loader component. From now on, whenever you want to another instance of the Movie Loader to your stage, you can just drag a copy from here instead of having to use the Components panel:

4. Click on the instance of the Movie Loader on the stage and look at the Property inspector (if you can't see it, select Window > Properties or just press CTRL/COMMAND+F3.) The Custom UI for Tornado is pretty huge and cannot fit in the Property inspector, so click the Launch Component Parameters Panel button here to make it appear in a pop-up panel:

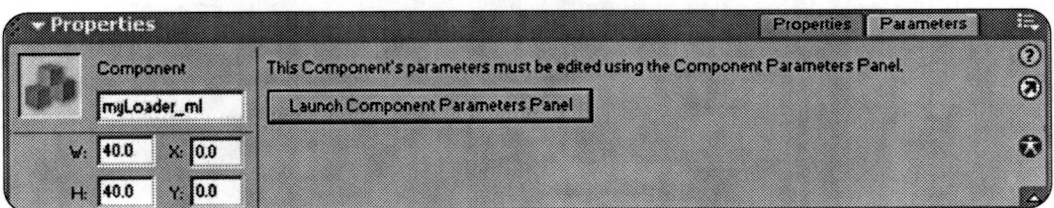

5. Look at your Component Parameters panel. If you see the Tornado icon telling you to expand the panel, make the panel larger until the UI appears. I told you it was huge!

6. OK, take a moment and catch your breath. The expanded Component Parameters panel showing the Tornado Movie Loader custom UI settings has quite a few options, but it should all make sense to you soon enough:

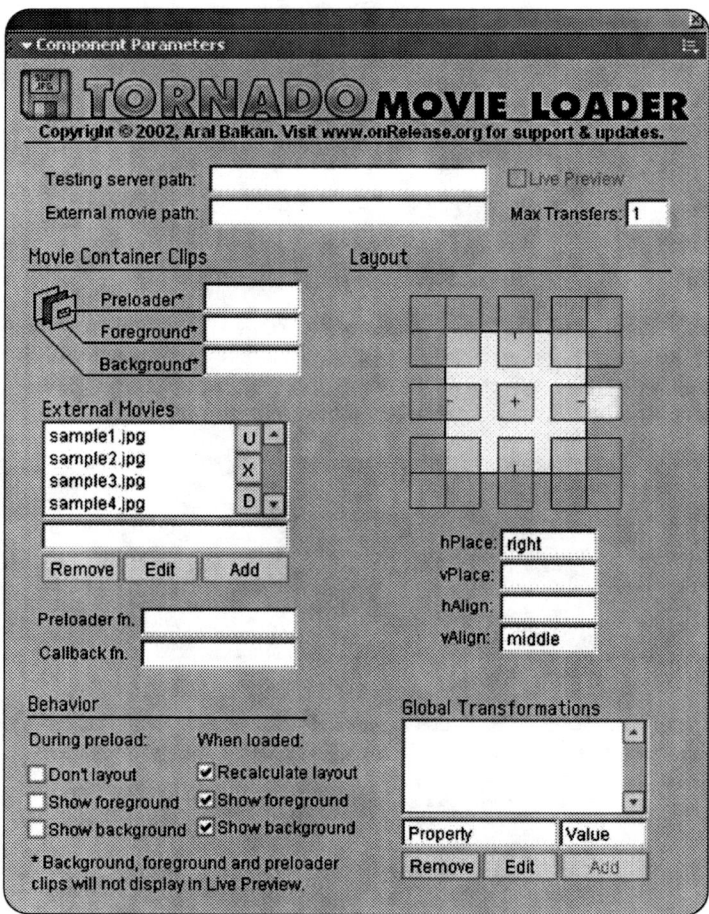

7. In the input box for the External Movies section, enter sample1.jpg and click the Add button. You should see the name appear in the External Movies ListBox, as shown above. Do the same for sample2.jpg, sample3.jpg, and sample4.jpg (you did copy them over from the download, didn't you?) If you need to change the position of a movie after you've added it, select it in the ListBox and use the U (up) and D (down) buttons to move it. Additionally, the X button is a shortcut for the Remove button.

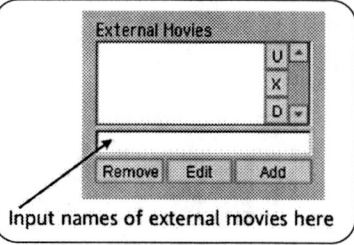

Input names of external movies here

8. Next, in the Layout section click the box that is farthest to the right and halfway down the side of the large white box, as shown in the previous screenshot. This tells Tornado to lay out the External Movies side-by-side, with each new movie appearing to the right of the previously loaded one. Notice that the entries for hPlace and vAlign have 'magically' received the values right and middle. These are the parameters you would have to pass to the component manually were you using ActionScript to attach it dynamically (we'll learn about that later).

9. Tornado's interface should now look exactly like the screenshot shown earlier. Making sure that the sample images are in the same directory as your main movie, test your movie (Control > Test Movie, or just press CTRL/COMMAND+ENTER). You should see the four images load in and get placed in a horizontal line, one after the other. Not bad for a few seconds work, eh? I have to tell you though, I think the baboon is up to something!

You have seen first hand how easy it is to load in and lay out external movies using Tornado, but what about the really exciting features? Where are the automatic preloaders we mentioned? And why couldn't we see a 'live preview' of the layout in the authoring environment? Not to mention all that talk about intelligent movie loading and stuff... Well, relax, we're going see all these and more, but to make use of these more advanced features you first need to have a deeper understanding of how Tornado works – this is exactly what we'll be discovering next.

The eye of the storm

Let's break down the Interface (no, no, drop the hammer, I meant it figuratively!), starting from the very top. Immediately, you should notice that the Live Preview checkbox is dimmed, signifying that it is disabled. So we have to do something before we are even allowed to turn Live Preview on and what we have to do is tied directly to the Testing server path input box:

The reason you can't have Live Preview until after you enter a testing server path is due to a peculiarity with Flash MX whereby the Live Preview movie doesn't know where the main movie is located and thus can't access any external movies that may be in the same directory. There is a workaround, however, that involves using a **testing server**. So what, pray tell, is a testing server?

A testing server, plain and simple, is a web server. In order to have live previews with Tornado, you either need to have a web server installed on your development machine or have a web hosting account that you can use. All you need to do is put any external movies you want to load in a directory that is within your web server's root.

There are many advantages to having a web server installed on your development machine, such as not having to upload the files to your hosting account every time you want to test something, and not paying for a hosting account just so you can develop. So, you may want to consider doing so even if you don't care too much for Live Preview. There are many web servers out there and one of the best ones, Apache, is free (http://httpd.apache.org/). If you're on Mac OS X then you already have it, and if you're on a PC you might want to download the FoxServ installer from www.foxserv.net , which is the easiest way I know of installing Apache (and it comes with lots of other goodies too, like PHP and MySQL!).

Once you've installed a web server (or have a hosting account somewhere that you can upload your external movies to), you are ready to use Live Preview. The best way to test this is to see if you can reach your external movies by entering their URLs in a standard browser (for example, `http://localhost/myExternalMovies/someMovie.swf`). If you don't have a web server that you can use, you can skip ahead to the *Containing the movies* section where we delve deeper into the inner workings of the Tornado Movie Loader. Everyone else, read on for some fun with Live Preview!

Show me the movies!

We're going to continue with the example above and enable Live Preview, so if you've closed that movie just open up `simple.fla` (from the download) in your working directory, ensuring that this is under the root directory of your web server. Then you'll be ready to follow along:

1. In the Testing server path input box, enter the absolute URL (starting with `http://`) to the directory that your movie is in. For example, if the root of your web server is on `C:\Foxserv\www\` and your movie is in `c:\Foxserv\www\my_movie\`, you should enter `http://localhost/my_movie/` in the box (you should be able to access your web server's root as localhost on your development machine). Don't forget the trailing slash or it won't work!

Testing server path:	http://localhost/dev/my_movie/	☐ Live Preview
External movie path:		Max Transfers: 1

2. You'll notice that as soon as you enter the protocol (the `http://` part of the address), the Live Preview checkbox will light up to signal that it is now enabled. Tornado just wants to make sure that we have entered something resembling a URL in the box. It doesn't (and cannot) check that the path we've entered is correct, or even whether or not we have a testing server (you'll soon notice though, because your movies won't show up!).

3. Don't enable Live Preview just yet – we still have a decision to make. We specified the URL to our main movie for the Testing server path but we can choose to house the external movies we want to load in a different directory, as long as it is located under the directory that our main movie is in. If you want to create a separate directory for your external movies, do it now. If your external movies are in the same directory as your main movie, you can skip the next step (but it's worth reading through anyway to find out what the External movie path box is for).

4. If your external movies are in a separate directory under the one that your main movie is in, you need a way to tell Tornado where they are. You do this by entering the relative path to the movies in the External movie path box. To continue our example from Step 1, above, if your external movies are housed in a directory called external_movies under the my_movie directory, you could enter external_movies/ in the External movie path box. Again, notice the trailing slash: it's very important that you don't forget this or Tornado won't work properly. The top of the Tornado interface should now look similar to the screenshot below (with your own directory-specific entries for the paths, of course):

| Testing server path: | http://localhost/dev/my_movie/ | ☐ Live Preview |
| External movie path: | external_movies/ | Max Transfers: 1 |

5. And now, the moment you've all been waiting for... make sure that you have an uninterrupted view of the stage and your instance of the Movie Loader and click on the Live Preview checkbox to turn on Live Preview:

| Testing server path: | http://localhost/dev/my_movie/ | ☑ Live Preview |
| External movie path: | external_movies/ | Max Transfers: 1 |

You should see the sample JPEGs load in and place themselves exactly as they had when you ran the movie earlier, but this time within the Flash authoring environment! Go ahead, play around with the settings and get a feel for how Live Preview works. Fun, isn't it?

203

Live preview

If you tried to move the component around after Live Preview had loaded some movies into it, you most probably came up against another of Flash MX's Live Preview hiccups. This one leads to all sorts of junk being left around the stage. Until Macromedia releases a fix for this, there are, thankfully, two workarounds:

- The first is to select the component (although it appears much larger after content has been loaded into it, you will still have to click within the small square area of the Tornado icon at the upper left of the Live Preview area to select it). Once selected, resize the component so that it covers all of the Live Preview area (so that it encompasses all of the loaded movies). Don't worry about making the component larger than its content area (it'll work, trust me!).

- The second workaround is to turn Live Preview off, move the component, and then turn Live Preview on again. You may also want to do this for those times when you're loading in a large number of movies, since resizing the component may not be practical in these cases. You may also want to keep Live Preview off while making a large number of changes to the component, since every change will cause an update and this can get distracting. It's better to enter all the changes you wish to make and then turn Live Preview on. Of course, in actuality you will probably use all these methods at different times, depending on your workflow.

Well, now that we've tackled the top of the interface and found out how to activate Live Preview, let's journey down a little further and examine the Movie Container Clips section and see if we can't unravel the mystery of the preloaders while we're at it.

Containing the movies

The way Tornado works is by creating container clips, called Movie Containers, to hold each external movie that is loaded.

Apart from the actual movie to be loaded, Movie Containers can also hold a preloader clip, background clip, and a foreground clip. The external movie is sandwiched between the background clip and the preloader and foreground clips – the structure of this movie container is shown in the figure below:

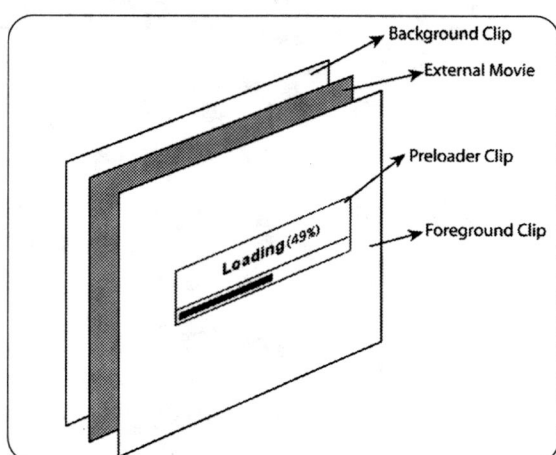

The background and foreground clips are just normal movie clips that Tornado takes from the Library and places behind and in front of the external movie. The background clip can contain a background graphic or animation that you want repeated behind every external movie, and the foreground clip is a good place to put a border around your external movie and perhaps also a button. These clips are there to allow you complete freedom in customizing the appearance and functionality of the Movie Containers – I'm sure you'll find uses for them that I haven't even thought of.

By default, your Movie Containers will only contain the external movie and you must specifically tell the Movie Loader if you want to use a preloader, background, and/or foreground clip by specifying their respective symbol identification (Linkage IDs) in the External Container Clips section of the interface:

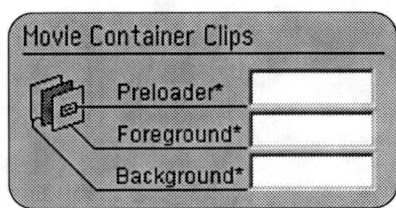

So, now we know that in order to add a preloader we must first create a preloader clip and specify its Linkage ID in the Preloader box. At this point, you might be wondering what sort of a creature a preloader clip really is. Well, as it turns out, it's quite a simple little critter that we'll soon have wagging its tail and fetching our movies for us.

Preloader clip workshop

As I mentioned previously, a preloader clip is just a plain old movie clip. What makes it special is that it needs to have a handler called `onPreload` defined in order to function correctly. To save you the tedious details of creating a simple preloader, I've included one such clip in the `preloader.fla` example, which you should open up in Flash to follow along with the exercise.

Keep in mind that you cannot test preloaders from within the authoring environment since there is no way to make external movies stream in, even when you use the Bandwidth Profiler. I have tried to inflate the size of the SWFs so that they should take some time to load when testing over a server. Also, remember to clear your cache after every test or else you won't see the loading process.

1. Double-click on the Sample Preloader movie clip in the Library to open it up for editing. Notice how the clip is laid out.

2. Click on frame one in the Actions layer and look in the Actions panel. You should see the `onPreload` handler:

```
onPreload = function(bytesLoaded, bytesTotal) {
        // constants
        WAITING_CODE = -1;
        PAUSED_CODE = -2;
        ORIGINAL_WIDTH_OF_BAR = 118;
```

```
            if (bytesTotal == WAITING_CODE) {
                    preloader_txt.text = "Waiting...";
                    bar_mc._width = 0;
            } else if (bytesTotal == PAUSED_CODE) {
                    preloader_txt.text = "Paused...";
                    bar_mc._width = 0;
            } else {
                    preloader_txt.text = "Loading...";
                    // set width of bar
                    bar_mc._width = ORIGINAL_WIDTH_OF_BAR *
                    ➥bytesLoaded/bytesTotal;
            }
    };
```

3. Test the movie over a web server to see the preloading process. It looks like some of our old friends are making an appearance:

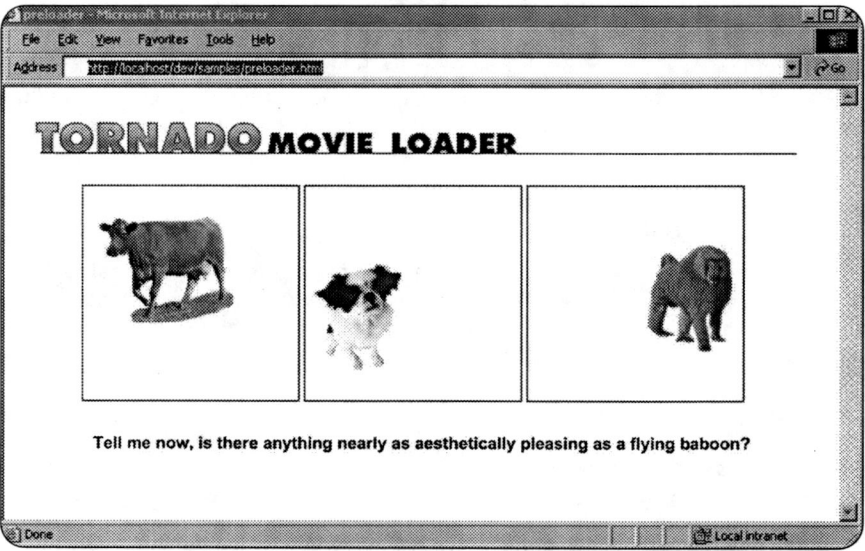

As you can see, the `onPreload` handler has two parameters: `bytesLoaded` and `bytesTotal`, these refer to the number of bytes loaded for the current movie and the total number of bytes in the current movie.

The code is pretty much self-explanatory: at any given time, the preloader can either be waiting for a download to start, be in a paused state, or loading – in which case, the width of our status bar is updated to reflect the amount loaded.

Once you specify a movie clip to be used as the preloader by entering its Linkage ID into the Preloader input box in the Movie Contrainer Clips section of the interface, Tornado will attach a copy of that movie clip to the Movie Container of each requested movie. While a movie is loading, the onPreload handler of its preloader will be called automatically with the current bytesLoaded and bytesTotal values.

There are two special codes that the Movie Loader can send back in place of the actual bytesLoaded and bytesTotal values, these are -1 to signal that the download has not started yet and -2 to signal that the movie has been paused (maybe some other movie has been forced). In these instances, you can either choose to make this information available to the user (as is the case in the example above), or simply not display the preloader during these times using something like this:

```
if (bytesTotal < 0) _visible = false;
```

We will cover movie forcing and intelligent loading in detail later on, when we tackle issues involving a little more ActionScript. For the moment though, let's skip the rest of the External Movies and Behavior sections for now and look a little deeper into how the Layout functions work.

Layout functionality

The Movie Loader component was designed to be as flexible as possible in what it can do with external movies, as far as layout is concerned. There are three separate, yet related, controls that determine the layout of loaded movies:

- Placement
- Alignment
- Transformations

Each of these affects the physical position of the loaded movies on the stage and in relation to each other, and do so in a predetermined and predictable manner.

Placement

Placement refers to the relative position of each loaded movie in relation to the movie prior to it. It affects layout in the horizontal and vertical axis, as reflected by the component parameters for hPlace and vPlace, respectively. Hori zontally, a movie can be placed on either the left or the right of another movie, and vertically, either on top or on the bottom of it.

Alignment

Movies can also be aligned to each other on the horizontal and vertical axis. Horizontally, you can align one movie to the left, middle, or right of another and vertically, you can align the tops, middles, and bottoms of two movies. To set horizontal and vertical alignment, set the hAlign and vAlign parameters of the component.

Tornado's custom UI visually represents the results of the various placement and alignment combinations that are available. Try loading in different sized images and playing with the layout control to see the different ways in which the alignment and placement settings work. The alignment controls can actually offer even more options through the use of ActionScript and numeric values for hAlign and vAlign. For more information on this, see their respective entries in the Tornado Movie Loader > Parameters > Layout section of the Reference panel.

By default, the placement and alignment rules are applied twice, once for the Movie Containers before any transformation rules have been applied at the very start of the preloading process, and again after the external movie has loaded.

When they are first applied, since the external movie has not even begun to load, the Movie Loader applies the placement and alignment rules using the dimensions of the Movie Container. The Movie Container at this point may contain any combination of a preloader, background, and/or foreground Clip. The combined dimensions of any content within the Movie Container will determine the visual result of the placement and alignment rules. You have the option of altering this default behavior, however, using two of the component parameters that we previously chose to ignore. These are the Don't layout (during preload) and Recalculate layout (when loaded) CheckBoxes listed under the Behavior section.

With the Recalculate layout box checked, the Movie Loader will reapply the placement and alignment rules after the external movie has completed loading. Instead of applying the rules to the Movie Containers, however, it will now apply them to the actual loaded movie itself. This way, for example, if you have irregularly sized movies that need to be placed one after the other in a horizontal line, you can set the hPlace parameter to right and have them perfectly placed once they have loaded.

If you do not wish to have your placement and alignment rules applied to the Movie Containers at the start of the preloading process, check the Don't Layout box. You may want to do this if you do not aim to display the loading process for individual clips. Turning on Don't Layout (during preload) while Recalculate layout (when loaded) is off will lead to any placement or alignment rules you have specified in the component parameters being ignored.

Transformations

In addition to the placement and layout controls, Tornado offers even more control over the layout of your movies with transformations. Using transformations, you can modify any valid movie clip property for your loaded movies (for example, the _x and _y properties). For instance, you can make each successive movie that loads 10% more transparent than the one before it by entering _alpha in the Property input box and 10 in the Value box under the Global Transformations section.

Transformations can be applied to every Movie Container in a Movie Loader by setting the Global Transformations parameter, and also to individual Movie Containers by passing a transform object as an argument when calling the addMovie() method through ActionScript (we'll look at this later). Both a global transformation and an individual transformation can affect the same clip. In these cases, the global transformation is applied first and any individual transformations for the Movie Container are applied afterwards.

As noted above, to add a global transformation, enter the Property to be transformed and the relative Value you want to offset the property by. You can specify absolute values for the properties by passing a string instead of a number for the value argument (for example, if you pass "100" instead of 100 for _x, then all of your external movies will load at x = 100, instead of each being offset to the right of the previous movie by 100 pixels). As stated earlier, you can choose to transform any valid movie clip property. The most common ones are _x and _y (which affect horizontal and vertical placement), _width and _height (which affect Movie Container dimensions), _alpha (transparency), and the movie clip's _rotation.

Transformations are either applied as *relative* or *absolute*. **Relative transformations** take the value of the property to be transformed from the previously loaded movie and calculate the value of the property for the new Movie Container as the offset. To specify a relative transformation, just pass the value you want to add (or subtract) from the property each time a movie is loaded. For example, to move each loaded movie 300 pixels to the right, enter a Value of 300 for the _x property in the Global Transformations box. Note that these values do not have to be positive – for example, if you instead wanted each new movie to appear 300 pixels to the left of the previous one, you would enter -300 for _x.

Global transformations are applied to every Movie Container and are only applied once, before loading of the actual movie has begun. Thus, they affect the Movie Containers that your movies will load into and not the movies themselves. The contents of the Movie Containers at this time may include a preloader clip, background clip, and/or a foreground clip.

Issues with alignment in Flash MX

Although these do not directly affect the functionality of the Movie Loader component, there are several issues that plague ActionScript-based alignment in Flash MX, all of which exist due to a couple of interrelated bugs in the Flash player. You should be aware that if your movies contain static text, the horizontal alignment may be slightly off. This is due to a bug in the player where movie clips with Static Text sometimes report their widths incorrectly. A way to circumvent this problem is to make the static text selectable. Although this will remedy the problem with horizontal alignment, vertical placement may still be slightly off (by about one pixel.) This is similarly due to a bug in the player where the _y coordinates of movie clips containing static text are sometimes reported incorrectly.

The only surefire way to avoid these potential problems is to use either device text or input text for your text fields. Depending on the typeface used and the font size, you may never experience these issues but it is documented here so that, in case you do, you don't end up pulling out your hair (believe me, it takes a really long time to grow back and your workmates start giving you weird looks! Don't ask me how I know...). Hopefully, these bugs will be fixed in the next version of the Flash Player.

It's taken a while, but we've made a lot of progress and covered all the interface elements save for Max Transfers at the very top, the Preloader fn. and Callback fn. input boxes under the External Movies ListBox, and four remaining CheckBoxes in the Behavior section.

First, let's get those CheckBoxes out of the way. The Show Background/Foreground (during preload/when loaded) CheckBoxes, quite simply, determine when to display the background and foreground clips. Of course, if you haven't specified either of these clips, they won't have any affect. The default behavior is to hide these clips during preload and make them visible automatically once the external movie has loaded.

A thousand ways to preload a movie

We created and used a custom preloader in the previous exercise and you saw how Tornado attaches a copy of the preloader clip from your Library and uses it each time a new movie is loading into it. But what if you wanted to have a single function somewhere that handled the preloading of all the movies in a Movie Loader? Perhaps you want to display a single preloader that shows the progress of all the movies within the loader? To do this, you would create a preloader function and enter its name in the Preloader fn. box. Here's a sample preloader function:

```
function myPreloader(theMovie, bytesLoaded, bytesTotal) {
    var percentLoaded = bytesLoaded * 100 / bytesTotal;
    trace ( theMovie + " is " + percentLoaded + " complete!" );
}
```

This doesn't do anything terribly exciting but does illustrate how the preloader function works. You'll notice that it has an additional first parameter that tells it which movie Tornado is sending it information about. If you wanted to, you could create an array for all the different movies and total their `bytesLoaded` and `bytesTotals` to give the current total for a specific Movie Loader instance.

Free callback

In addition to a global preloader function that gets called as each movie in the component is loading, you can specify a callback function that is called each time a movie completes loading. Here's an example of a callback function:

```
function myCallback(theMovie) {
    trace ( theMovie + " has completed loading!");
}
```

Of course, in real life you could do something exciting like ask the external movie to start playing from frame two. It's a good idea to leave frame 1 of your external movies empty with nothing but a single `stop()` – this will accomplish a couple of things:

1. Stop the movie from playing before it is fully loaded.

2. Circumvent an ugly one-frame glitch where the first frame of your movie will appear half-drawn between the time that the movie loads and the frame after when it initializes.

By the way, the `theMovie` reference returned is a reference to the Movie Container and not directly to the external movie itself. You will remember that Movie Containers may contain a preloader, background, and foreground clip in addition to the external movie. You can access all of these clips separately through ActionScript. Here's an example that shows you how to do just that:

```
function myCallback(theMovie) {
    // Set the visibility of the preloader to false manually
    // (by default, Tornado does this for us automatically)
    theMovie.mcPreloader._visible = false;

    // Set the transparency of the background and
    // foreground clips manually
    theMovie.background_mc._alpha = 75;
    theMovie.foreground_mc._alpha = 25;

    // Instruct the newly loaded movie to play from frame 2
```

```
            theMovie.mcMovieShell.gotoAndPlay(2);
    }
```

Thus you can see that `theMovie.mcPreloader` addresses the preloader clip, `theMovie.background_mc` and `theMovie.foreground_mc` address the background and foreground clips, respectively, and the external movie itself is referenced by `theMovie.mcMovieShell`.

In addition to specifying the preloader and callback functions using the custom UI in the Component Parameters panel, you can also call the `setPreloaderFunc()` and `setCallbackFunc()` methods of the component. For full details of this, refer to their respective listings in the Reference Panel.

Last, but definitely not least, we have Max Transfers...

Max transfers

The Max Transfers parameter determines the maximum number of movies that can load at the same time. By default, this is set to one so that only one external movie can be loading at any given point in time. This is the safest setting and will work across all platforms. You can set this higher to allow multiple movies to load at the same time, but be aware that there are certain limitations surrounding this feature on certain browsers and platforms (notably Microsoft Internet Explorer 5.1 on a Mac). For a full discussion of these issues, refer to the section below on *Features and limitations*.

Now that we've covered the user interface and used some of Tornado's basic and intermediate features, let's crank up the engine and see what it's really capable of. Of course, as for all things advanced, we will need to delve a little deeper into ActionScript from this point on. But don't worry, the ActionScript interface isn't too complicated to grasp and you should have a much easier time now that you have a conceptual idea of how the component works.

Tornado unleashed with ActionScript

To truly realize the potential of the Movie Loader component, we have to go beyond simple *drag and drop*, and use a little bit of ActionScript to dynamically add the component to the stage and add the movies to be loaded to the component.

ActionScript basics

The simplest way to add the component to the stage dynamically is to create an object to hold the component parameters that we were previously setting via the Component Parameters panel, and pass this to the Movie Loader using `attachMovie`. Open up `actionscript101.fla` – this example file already has the preloader clip from our previous example in the Library:

1. You should notice right away that the Tornado component is not on stage. This is no accident, since it will be added dynamically using ActionScript.

2. If you right-click (or CTRL-click on a Mac) on the Tornado component in your Library and select Linkage..., you will see its Linkage ID is `MovieLoader`. This is the name that we will use to tell Flash that we want to attach a copy of the component onto the stage. By the way, I gave it this

generic but descriptive ID, instead of calling it something like Tornado, to make it simpler to understand when reading the code (especially for someone who may not know what a 'Tornado' is supposed to do in Flash!).

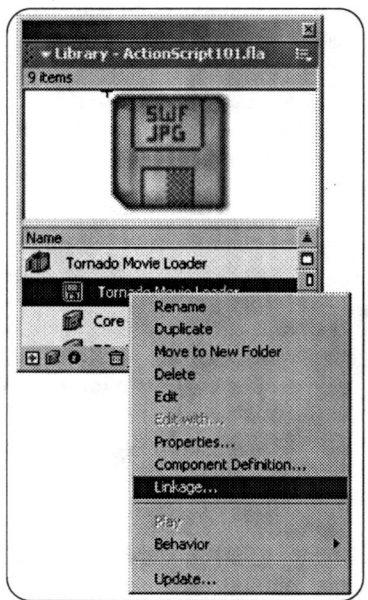
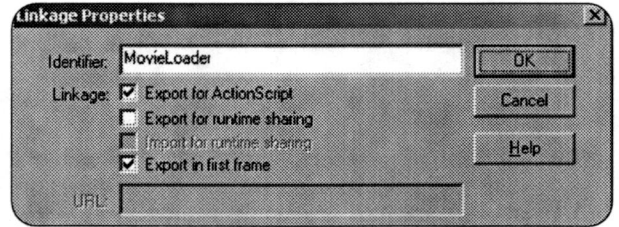

3. Next, let's take a look at frame 1 of the Actions layer, where you'll see the following code:

```
// Create an object to hold the settings
movieLoaderSettings = new Object();

// Add the movies to load
movieLoaderSettings.movieURLs = ["sample1.swf", "sample2.swf",
"sample3.swf"];

// Make each movie appear 210 pixels to the
// right of the previous one
movieLoaderSettings.globalTransforms = { _x : 210 };

// Specify the clip to use as the preloader
movieLoaderSettings.preloaderClip = "samplePreloader";

// This isn't necessary since maxTransfers defaults to one
movieLoaderSettings.maxTransfers = 1;

// Attach a copy of the Movie Loader component
_root.attachMovie("MovieLoader", "myLoader_ml", 1000,
➥movieLoaderSettings);
```

```
// Put the Movie Loader in a good spot
myLoader_ml._x = 60;
myLoader_ml._y = 73;
```

As you can see, with this code we're simply mirroring what we were doing using the custom UI. Namely, we're setting values for certain parameters and specifying the movies that we want loaded. In fact, this way of attaching the component through ActionScript doesn't actually allow us any advantages over using the custom interface. However, you'll see in the next section how a slight modification to this script will allow us control over every aspect of the loading process, so a little knowledge of how it works can't hurt. Let's start from the end of this code and work our way up.

The `attachMovie()` function tells Flash to attach an instance of the Tornado Movie Loader component (`MovieLoader`) to the `_root` timeline and give it an instance name of `myLoader_ml`. The `_ml` suffix tells Flash that this is a Tornado Movie Loader and Flash uses this information to help you out with code hints when you next refer to it. It also allows Flash to highlight your code's syntax. The third parameter here specifies the depth of this dynamically created component.

In the final argument of the `attachMovie()` method, we pass it an object containing the parameters that we wish to initialize. This object contains settings for parameters defined earlier in the code, such as the preloader clip (`preloaderClip`) and `maxTransfers`. It also contains the list of movies that we want to load (`movieURLs`). As I mentioned earlier, by passing the list of movies in an array as we have done here, we are merely mirroring the functionality of the custom UI. If we want to have control over the loading process, we need a way to refer to each of the movies we add to the component, so that we can intelligently ask it to stop loading one and start on another if and when the need arises to deviate from the initial loading queue.

To do this, we attach the component using the same code as above, but without passing the `movieURLs` parameter. Instead, we add the movies to be loaded individually and keep track of their movie IDs. Later, you'll see how this technique is used to create a simple interface to demonstrate intelligent loading techniques.

The Right Stuff: taking it further with scripting

Now we're prepared to take our ActionScript to the next level:

1. Open up `actionscript201.fla` and note how the script in the first frame of the Actions layer has been modified:

    ```
    // Create an object to hold the settings
    movieLoaderSettings = new Object();
    movieLoaderSettings.globalTransforms = { _x : 210 };
    movieLoaderSettings.preloaderClip = "samplePreloader";
    movieLoaderSettings.maxTransfers = 1;

    // Attach a copy of the Movie Loader component
    _root.attachMovie("MovieLoader", "myLoader_ml", 1000,
    movieLoaderSettings);
    ```

```
// Put the Movie Loader in a good spot
myLoader_ml._x = 60;
myLoader_ml._y = 73;

// Create an array to hold movie IDs
_global.movies = new Array();

// Add three movies to the loader
for (var i = 1; i <= 3; i++) {
    movieID = MyLoader_ml.addMovie("sample"+i+".swf");
    movies.push(movieID); // add the movie id to the array
}
```

So why go through all the trouble of creating an array to contain the details of our external movie clips? The reason is so that we can take advantage of one of the most powerful features of the Movie Loader: the ability to force particular movies to load.

Use the Force!

The Movie Loader can happily go through the movies you have specified, loading each one in turn, without any further action on your part. However, there are times when it is imperative that we interrupt the Movie Loader and tell it to load a movie that may be further along in the queue.

Imagine that you are loading the content for a Flash site and the user decides to click on a section that is at the end of the loading queue. You can either do nothing and make the user wait while the Movie Loader loads every other movie before the one the user is waiting for (and end up with a very agitated user on your hands!), or you can take action and make the Movie Loader stop what it is currently loading and jump ahead to load the movie that the user wants to see. This is called forcing a movie and there are four states in which a movie can be forced, influenced by two modes.

When a movie is forced **exclusively**, all other movies that were downloading are paused. It is usually a good idea to force a movie to load exclusively, unless you are certain that most users in your target audience are on high-bandwidth connections and/or you are developing an intranet application. In a **non-exclusive** force, the forced movie starts loading but other movies can still continue loading alongside it, up to the number of simultaneous movies allowed (as set by the maxTransfers parameter).

In a **returning** force, the Movie Loader continues loading from where it left off prior to loading the forced movie, whereas in a **non-returning** force, it continues with the next movie after the movie that was forced. If you have a site where the content is broken off into sections and the user clicks on the section opener, you could initiate a non-returning force that will load the section opener and then continue loading the movies in that section, making the assumption that the user's next step would be to look at the content within that section.

The following table describes these four different ways that we can force a movie:

	Exclusive	Non-Exclusive
Returning	The forced movie is exclusively loaded (all other downloading movies are paused) and the Movie Loader returns to loading the movie it was on prior to the force.	The forced movie is loaded along with any other movies that may be loading (limited by maxTransfers). The Movie Loader returns to loading the movie it was on prior to the force.
Non-returning	The forced movie is exclusively loaded (all other downloading movies are paused.) The movie loader continues loading with the movie after the forced movie and down the line until it reaches the end of the queue. It then returns to the start of the queue.	The forced movie is loaded along with any other movies that may be loading (limited by maxTransfers). The movie loader continues loading with the movie after the forced movie and down the line until it reaches the end of the queue. It then returns to the start of the queue.

So, let's put our newfound knowledge of movie forcing to use by refining the previous exercise even further.

Brute force

We're going to continue where we left off in our previous example (actionscript201.fla). Find and open brute_force.fla and follow along:

1. You'll notice that there's a green arcade button on the stage. If you click on it to select it you'll see that it has the instance name forceButton_mc.

2. The first frame of the Actions layer has the script that you should be familiar with from the previous exercise, but with the following code added at the end:

```
// Make the forceButton force the 2nd movie to start loading
forceButton_mc.onRelease = function() {
        // Note that array indices start at 0,
        // so 1 actually refers to the 2nd movie
        _root.myLoader_ml.forceMovie(movies[1]);
};
```

3. In order to see the preloading, you have to test the movie on a web server – remember, the Flash authoring environment cannot simulate a streaming connection for external movies. You should be fine if you have a hosting account somewhere, or if you have a local web server installed on your development machine. I've inflated the file size of the sample external movies so you should be able to see them preload even over a fast connection. Press the force button as soon as the movie appears. Pretty neat, huh?

215

Integration

Although the Movie Loader component is powerful in its own right, it truly shines when used in conjunction with other components in the creation of user interfaces. The first component that comes into mind is the ScrollPane component included with the Flash UI Components Sets 1 and 2 (which are available as free downloads from the Macromedia website.)

Why can't we all just get along?

In order to use the Movie Loader with other components, we need to again use ActionScript to attach it. We can't just drag an instance of it from the library and configure it using the custom interface since the other component would have no way of pulling the Tornado in after it has been placed on the Stage.

Here, then, is a simple example of using the Movie Loader component inside the ScrollPane component. Open up the `scroll_pane.fla` file and follow along!

1. On the stage, you'll find an instance of the ScrollPane component from the Flash UI Components Set 2, with the instance name of `myPane_sp`.

2. Look at the first frame of the Actions layer – you should see the following script (with additional commenting showing you how to include a ScrollPane with Tornado):

    ```
    /*
    ```

```
        Remove the border of the ScrollPane (Note: requires the modified
version of the scrollpane included here)
*/
// Create a new style format
myPaneStyle = new FStyleFormat();
// Change the face (bounding box border) to white
myPaneStyle.face = 0xFFFFFF;
// Make scroll pane component listen to style changes
myPaneStyle.addListener(myPane_sp);
// Tell subscribed components that the style has changed
myPaneStyle.applyChanges();
// Add the movie loader component as the
// content clip for the ScrollPane
myPane_sp.setScrollContent("MovieLoader");
// Get a reference to the movie loader component
scrollContent = myPane_sp.getScrollContent();

/*
        Set up the initial parameters of the movie loader component
*/
// Set number of simultaneous transfers to one
scrollContent.setMaxTransfers(1);
// Move each loaded picture 300 pixels to the right
scrollContent.globalTransforms = { _x : 300 };
// Set the clip to be used as the preloader
scrollContent.preloaderClip = "samplePreloader";
// Add the movies to be loaded
scrollContent.addMovie("sample1.jpg", null, null, null, this,
➥"onMovieLoad");
scrollContent.addMovie("sample2.jpg", null, null, null, this,
➥"onMovieLoad");

/*
        NB. The last two parameters define the callback function - the
function that is called after the movie has loaded. In this case, we use
it to call the refreshPane() method of the ScrollPane component to make
it resize the component and the ScrollBars each time a new movie is
loaded.
*/
// Create the callback function
onMovieLoad = function() {
    // Movie has loaded, recalculate size of the ScrollPane
    myPane_sp.refreshPane();
};
```

Note that for this example, I had to modify the original ScrollPane component to make it possible to change the color of the border (in this case, to hide it by changing it to white). You'll find this version of the ScrollPane in the movie and you can use it for your other projects, if you like.

Instead of the ScrollPane component, you can also use the Movie Loader inside the DraggablePane component. In fact, the code for doing this is almost identical to the code above. The only things you have to change are the suffix of the instance name (from _sp for ScrollPane to _dp for DraggablePane) and the method that is called from the callback function (the DraggablePane has a `refreshScrollContent()` method that should be called in place of the ScrollPane's `refreshPane()` method).

The more the merrier

In case you were wondering, you can use as many Movie Loader components as you like in your movies. There are, however, certain issues you should be aware of when doing so. Most importantly, no matter how many Movie Loaders you have on stage (or add via ActionScript), there can only ever be one global movie queue. In other words, all of the movies you add to each separate Tornado get put into a single queue, starting with the first movie added. Thus, it is important that you add your movies to your Movie Loaders in the order that you want them to load. When adding multiple Tornados via drag and drop, you don't have any control over the order in which they get initiated, so if load order with multiple Tornados is important for your application, you should use ActionScript to attach them.

You should also keep this point mind while using the `forceMovie()` method, especially in the *non-returning* and *non-exclusive* modes (refer to the table in the earlier section on forcing movie loading) ,since it can easily lead to undesired behavior.

There's an example movie called `multiple_loaders.fla` in the companion download to this book that showcases the behavior of multiple Movie Loaders.

Features and limitations

In any development process, it is imperative that you know both the features and limitations of the various components you are using, since these will ultimately determine the ultimate quality of the product itself, and usage restrictions. As far as the Movie Loader component is concerned, here is what it can do and what its limits are:

Features

- Queues multiple movies and loads them in order.

- Automatically handles the preloading of multiple movies.

- Allows for the visual layout of loaded movies and includes robust controls for placement, alignment, and both relative and absolute transformations.

- Implements a single, global loading queue and allows multiple Movie Loader components to be used within a movie without conflicts.

- Lets the movie load order be influenced dynamically at runtime, allowing complete control over the streaming experience.

- Can load multiple movies concurrently (but refer to the *Limitations* section, below, for important notes on this feature).

- Displays a live preview of exactly how movies will look when loaded and laid out (requires a testing server and has some limitations, covered below).

Limitations

- The HTTP 1.1 specification limits the number of consequent HTTP requests to two and on some browser and platform combinations, this limit is enforced on the client side. This limit doesn't make much sense today and will make even less sense as broadband uptake increases, so hopefully it will be raised to some higher number in a future revision of the specification. What it means for us is that you should assume that no more than two movies are being loaded simultaneously by the Movie Loader component. You can set the maxTransfers property to any number you like, but it may be limited to two on platforms that comply with the HTTP 1.1 specification. Be warned though, that setting the number too high can cause the performance of your movie to drop.

- Microsoft Internet Explorer 5.1 on the Mac platform can be somewhat unpredictable (note the subtle euphemism for 'buggy') in its handling of simultaneous HTTP connections and you will find that certain load requests get dropped randomly. The only workaround is to limit maxTransfers to 1 on this platform, effectively imposing a serial loading queue. If you want to get really crafty, you can detect the platform by exploiting another bug that is particular to it: IE 5.1 on the Mac cannot pass query string arguments to Flash through the Object and Embed tags. You can thus easily test for the platform by passing a query string argument to your SWF in the Object and Embed tags of the page (for example, my.swf?notMacIE = true) and checking in your movie to see if the value is received:

```
if (notMacIE == "true") {
        // this platform is not Mac IE, so set as
        // many simultaneous transfers as you like
        myMovieLoader_mc.setMaxTransfers(4);
} else {
        // It's Mac IE, so make sure that movies load serially
        myMovieLoader_mc.setMaxTransfers(1);
}
```

- The Live Preview function in Flash MX allows you to see exactly how your movies will look once loaded and laid out. Unfortunately, due to a bug with embedded live preview SWFs in Flash MX, the live preview does not know where the external movies you want to load are located. The workaround to this is to have a web server installed on your development machine and to provide the URL to the directory where your external movies are housed in the Testing server path box. This is only necessary if you want to use Live Preview, not for the component to function at runtime.

- There is yet another bug with Live Preview corrupting the screen if you try to move the component around after the Live Preview has loaded the movies. There are two workarounds that you can implement to solve this problem:

1. You can turn Live Preview for the Movie Loader off, move the component and then turn Live Preview back on again (I'd also recommend turning off Live Preview for the component before deleting an instance of the component from the stage, since the same bug causes parts of the loaded movies to remain on the stage). If you do experience screen corruption, a quick double-click on the magnifying glass icon in the toolbox will clear it up.

2. Thanks to Paul Spitzer from the *Flashcoders* list for this one: resize the component instance on the stage to fit the loaded content shown by the Live Preview. You can now move the component without Flash corrupting the screen.

- You cannot have different `maxTransfers` settings for different instances of the Movie Loader component – only the latest setting will be used. This is because the `maxTransfers` setting is global to the movie itself.

- There is currently no way to stop downloads on a single instance of the Movie Loader component. You can halt and resume movie downloads across all instances by calling the `stopLoader()` and `startLoader()` methods of any one of the instances (note that currently these are private methods).

- You cannot preview the background and foreground clips in the authoring environment since they are dynamically added from your movie's library at runtime, and currently there is no way to display a clip from your movie's Library in the Live Preview.

- The Live Preview may take quite a while to load in all external movies, especially if you have many of them. Each time you make a change using the Component Parameters panel, Live Preview has to recalculate how the movies will look once loaded. Accordingly, you may want to turn Live Preview off when making lots of changes and then back on again to see how your changes look.

Tips and tricks

Here are some handy tips to make the most out of the Movie Loader component. If you discover any of your own, let me know and I'll put them up on my blog at www.onRelease.org for all to share.

The perils of the _root

When creating Flash movies to be included in other movies, don't refer to _root in your ActionScript statements. Although the movies will work by themselves, they won't work once loaded into another movie since all references to _root will now point to the root timeline of the parent movie. One easy way to work around this problem is to save an explicit reference to the timeline of your movies and use this in place of _root. So, instead of referring to root directly in your movies, like this:

```
_root.myMovieClip_mc._visible = false;
```

Do this:

```
// On frame 1 of the root timeline,
// save a reference to the local _root timeline:
_global.myRoot = this._root;
```

And use that reference in your movie in place of _root:

```
myRoot.myMovieClip._mc._visible = false;
```

Note that by placing your reference in the _global namespace, you make it available from any timeline, but there is also a 'gotcha' that you have to be aware of – if you have multiple movies and use the same variable name for the reference, they will overwrite each other since they share the same namespace. The best thing to do in these cases is either to use relative addressing throughout (that is, use _parent a lot), or make sure that your variable names are unique.

Runaway SWFs

Don't be surprised if the movies you're loading start playing before they're completely loaded. It just means that you forgot to put a good old stop() action on the first frame!

Don't go changing!

Although the movie loader will wait until a movie has completely loaded before making it visible, it will take another frame (yes, one whole frame!) for the loaded movie to initialize itself. During this time, you can have a single unsightly frame appear with all the junk that's on the stage during the first frame of your loaded movie, before your ActionScript code has had a chance to execute and hide the behind-the-scenes details. The best thing to do to make sure this never happens is to leave the first frame of your movies completely empty, except for the life-saving stop() action mentioned above.

But the client wants Flash 5...

What, they still want Flash 5? Are you kidding? Seriously though, if you have to develop for Flash 5, all is not lost. The Movie Loader component is based on a Movie Loader class that I originally wrote for Flash 5 and which is available as open source as part of the FC-Lib library from www.aralbalkan.com/index.php?article=7. It's not as robust as the Movie Loader component, and doesn't have its fancy placement and alignment functions (and of course, no Live Preview), but the core functionality is pretty much the same and since the code is open, you can adapt it as you like.

I've tried to make the Tornado Movie Loader component as flexible as possible so that it can be completely customized for different applications. I've also tried to make it easy to use with an intuitive yet powerful custom user interface and Live Preview. If, however, you have a feature request or wish it would do something differently, you can email me at aral@BitsAndPixels.co.uk with your comments and suggestions. Of course, you can also always right-click on the component, choose Edit..., and have a go yourself!

Lifaros

Lifaros is an experimental Flash developer who enjoys combining code, design, math, and art to create fun visual effects and interactive Flash/ActionScript-based multimedia presentations. His most recent projects have involved utilizing Bezier splines, modulation dynamics, physics effects, and image manipulation. At the moment Lifaros is developing complex interactive Flash applications for the United Nations, and teaching ActioScript for advanced users.

"There are a lot of different ways to build an interactive design or application, no rigid rules or frontiers to the creative process. Personally, my inspirational input comes from nature, books, TV, the Internet, the city, and from my relationship with other people. I think it's important to recognize that there is also an internal inpirational source: the voice of our heart and in our dreams."

Lifaros has been reviewing and writing advanced ActionScript books and articles with friends of ED for some time now. Most recently, he has collaborated as a co-author on Flash Math Creativity and Fresh Flash. Right now, Lifaros is working on another exciting new project – Flash Video Creativity.

"I'd like to thank Chris Matterface, Steve Rycroft, and the foED technical review team for their determined efforts in trying to understand my horrible English!"

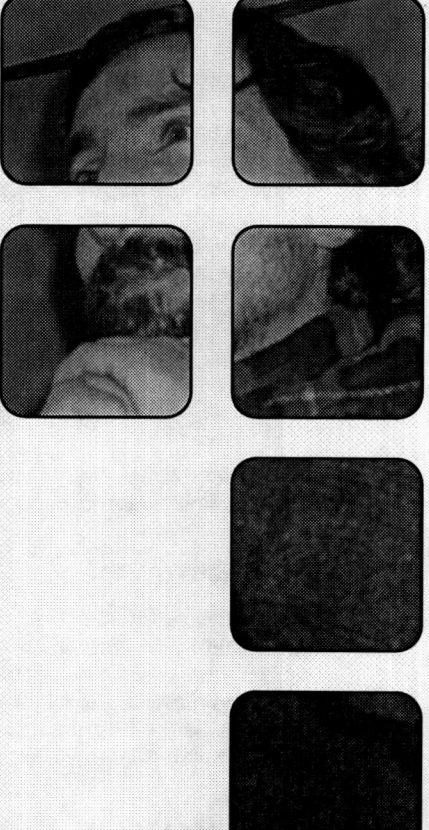

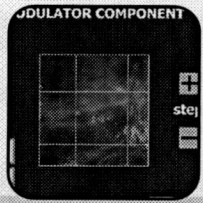

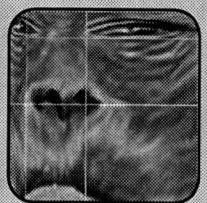

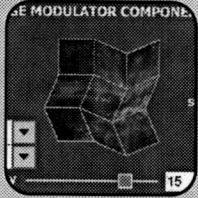

Component 17

Image
Modulation

These cool components can be used to modify the shape of an image, preserving its integrity, producing a static or dynamic effect. Best of all, there are hundreds of variations that can be configured through a very friendly user interface".

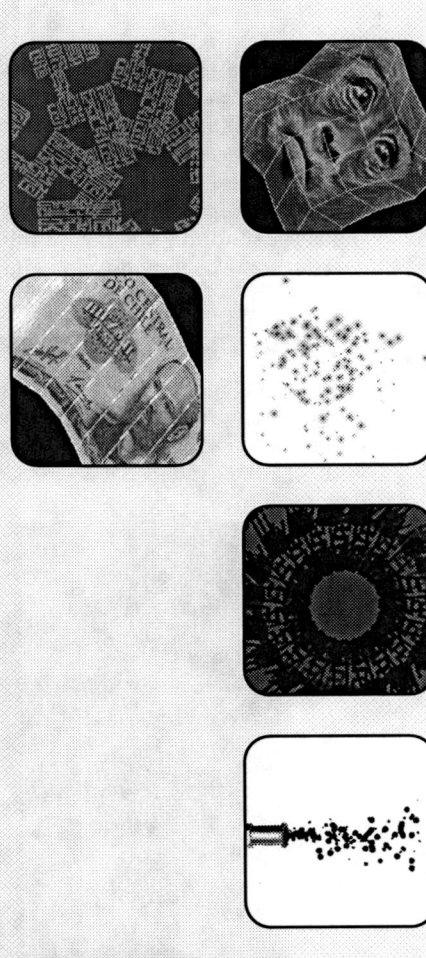

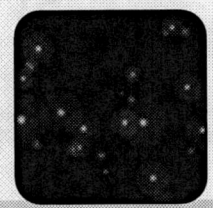

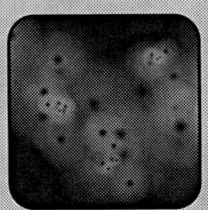

One of the great benefits of using components is that they can dramatically speed up the development process. It's incredibly easy to use the ScrollBar, the ComboBox, and all the other components included in Flash MX and incorporate them within our projects. But better still, we can also develop other kinds of components using some fairly simple math concepts.

I'm always playing with raster or bitmap images. I really enjoy applying distortion and discovering new shapes, so for my addition to this book my goal was to develop a couple of components that allow us to apply some cool modulation effects to any image in our movie.

Liquid image modulator component

This component can be installed using `FLiquidMatrixComp.mxp` and will modify the vertical and horizontal proportion of the image without losing its integrity, similar to the effect of playing with a convex or concave mirror. By modulating certain parameters, using sinusoidal waves essentially to gently change their values, we can expand and shrink an image without 'breaking' it:

This component works by dividing the whole image into a number of small pieces, generating a matrix with horizontal and vertical slices. Each cell is modulated independently, so as to gently modify the overall size.

First of all the application generates the matrix, calculating the vertical and horizontal size of each cell according to the size of the source image and a specified number of columns and rows. Then all the nested movie clips and masks are moved and scaled properly, so the cells are perfectly joined side by side. Finally the modulation parameters such as the frequency, amplitude, and phase are applied (these terms will be defined shortly).

Component parameters

We can obtain a huge number of effects and variations by setting up the appropriate parameters. Accordingly, I've developed a custom user interface in order to make things easier. Before looking at some specific examples of this component in action, we'll take a moment to highlight what each parameter in the Component Parameters panel can do.

Assuming that you've already installed this component from the `FLiquidMatrixComp.mxp` file in the download, drop an instance of it on the stage and then open the Component Parameters panel to launch the custom user interface:

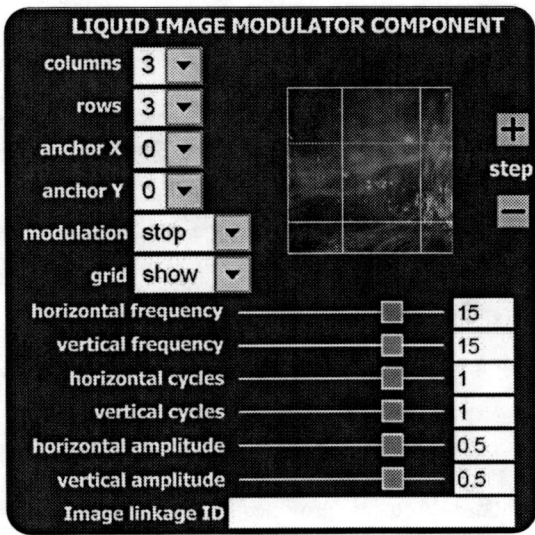

The UI has the following ComboBoxes, sliders, and buttons with which we can modify every parameter of the liquid image modulator component:

- Columns ComboBox – You can modify the number of vertical slices or columns (up to 1 0). The more columns and rows (next parameter) the better the effect, but notice that the modulation is a very intensive on the CPU (there are a lot of sine and cosine math calculations involved), so try using a small number of columns and rows in order to speed up the animation. As ever, it's a compromise between smooth animation and a cool effect!

- Rows ComboBox – You can modify the number of horizontal slices or rows (up to 1 0).

- Horizontal anchor X ComboBox – You can select the column of the cell that will be fixed during the modulation process.

- Vertical anchor Y ComboBox – You can also select the row of the cell that will be fixed during modulation. If you want a fixed upper left corner, both anchor values must equals to 0.

- Modulation Combo Box – You can turn on/off the modulation, so the component can be used as a static or dynamic effect.

- Show grid ComboBox – The white grid shows the bounds of each cell. You can turn on/off the grid visibility. You might turn off the grid in order to speed up the modulation, but in the examples in this chapter we'll keep the grid on to demonstrate how the cells are manipulated by this component.

- Step buttons – If you want to modify the look of a static image just modify the minus and plus step buttons.

- Horizontal frequency slider – The width (`_xscale`) of each cell will be expanded and shrunk at the same given frequency but a different phase in order to accomplish the effect. If you want a 'soft' animation use a value of 10-15 degrees.

- Vertical frequency slider – You can also modify the modulation frequency of the height (`_yscale`) of the cells.

- Horizontal cycles slider – When we modify the modulation phase of the cells we are also modifying the number of horizontal modulation cycles or waves. A value of `0.5` means 180 degrees, `1` refers to 360 degrees, and so on. It's worth experimenting with the slider to understand this parameter thoroughly (and the next one).

- Vertical cycles slider – You can also modify the number of vertical modulation cycles.

- Horizontal amplitude slider – The modulation amplitude (expansion and contraction) of each cell can be modified using this slider. You must enter a number somewhere between `-1` and `1`.

- Vertical amplitude slider – You can also select the amplitude of the vertical modulation of each cell.

- Image linkage ID input text field – You need to enter the linkage ID of the movie clip you want to use in the input text field at the bottom of the custom UI. This is the ActionScript reference name of the Library object you wish to manipulate, defined by right-clicking on the movie clip in the Library (or Ctrl-clicking on a Mac) and selecting Linkage.... Note that you can't apply the effect directly to a movie clip (with a nested image) present on the stage because you couldn't give it a linkage ID. Once it's given a linkage ID in the Library, you can use any movie clip or graphic symbol as the source image, for instance you can even use a text field.

Liquid image samples

Now that we're ready to play with our image modulator, let's take a look at some of the possibilities.

Liquid monkey: horizontal cell modulation

First of all, I want to show you how to configure a simple modulation effect. Take a look at the Component Parameters panel in `liquid_monkey_01.fla` – here we have 10 columns and just 1 row, so the result when we link to the movie clip in the Library with the specified linkage ID (`monkey`) is a fun horizontally modulated mutated monkey face. You can appreciate that the position and size of the image does not change because we are using the first cell (0,0) as the anchor point and just one horizontal cycle (360 degrees). We've also turned on the grid option so we should be able to see the white lines bounding the cells:

Test the movie to see what we end up with using these parameters:

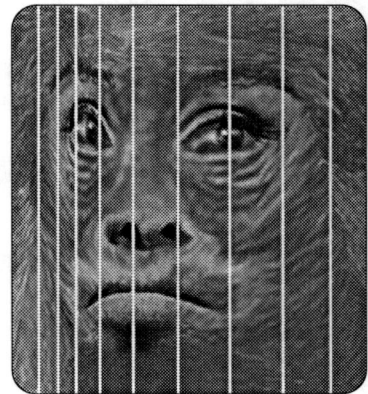 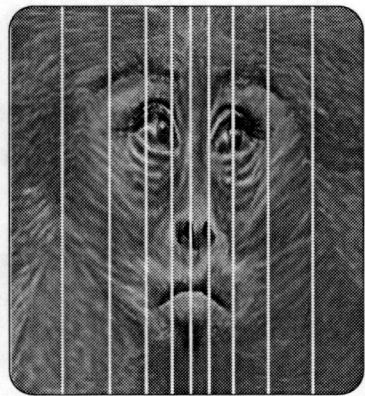 

Liquid monkey: vertical cell modulation

In `liquid_monkey_02.fla` we have 1 column and 5 rows this time – the result is a nice vertical modulation. We have incremented the modulation amplitude value so the distortion is more evident. Here's what the resultant effect looks like now:

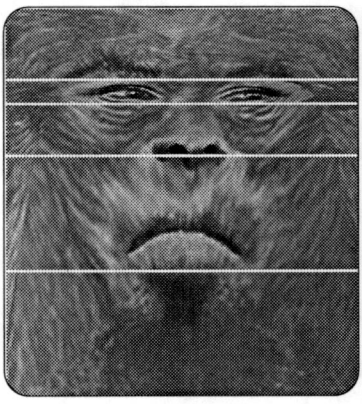 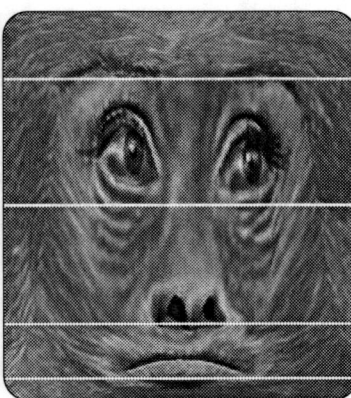 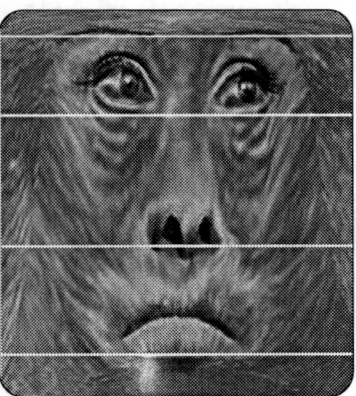

Liquid monkey: both horizontal and vertical cell modulation

With the example file `liquid_monkey_03.fla` we've set both vertical and horizontal modulation, each one with its own amplitude and frequency values. There are 5 columns and 5 rows so we have 25 image cells growing and shrinking harmoniously. This is what the result looks like:

  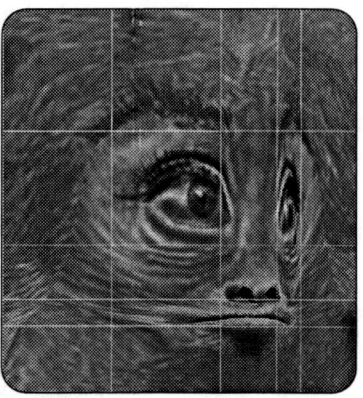

Liquid monkey: attaching the component dynamically

Finally, in `liquid_monkey_04.fla`, we dynamically create the component at runtime with the `attachMovie()` method. We use the optional fourth `attachMovie` parameter to send an object with all the properties values of the `FLiquidMatrixClass`. The code is attached to frame 1 of the single layer in `liquid_monkey_04.fla`:

```
properties = {};
properties.linkid = "monkey";
properties.columns = 3;
properties.rows = 3;
properties.anchorx = 1;
properties.anchory = 1;
properties.ampx = .7;
properties.ampy = .7;
properties.nx = 1.3; // horizontal cycles
properties.ny = 0.8; // vertical cycles
properties.wx = 20; //horizontal frequency
properties.wy = 15; // vertical frequency
properties.showgrid = true;
properties.modula = true;
properties.step = 0;
this.attachMovie("FLiquidMatrixSymbol", "img", 327, properties);
img._x = 100;
img._y = 125;
img._xscale = 50;
img._yscale = 50;
```

With the `properties` object we modify the anchor cell such that the image will appear to dance, moving in all directions. The size of the image is growing and shrinking because we modified the number of vertical and horizontal cycles. Note that `FliquidMatrixSymbol` is the linkage ID of the liquid image modulator component.

For reference, you can also set and retrieve the following properties at runtime:

Property	Description
_linkid	Image linkage ID
_columns	Columns
_rows	Rows
_anchorx	Horizontal anchor
_anchory	Vertical anchor
_wx	Horizontal frequency
_wy	Vertical frequency
_nx	Horizontal cycles
_ny	Vertical cycles
_ampx	Horizontal amplitude
_ampy	Vertical amplitude
_showgrid	Grid
_modula	Play/Stop modulation
_step	Step

Finally, I added two buttons that trigger a different configuration (a normal and a 'crazy' state) at runtime using the properties shown above:

```
normalButton.onPress = function() {
    img._columns = 7;
    img._rows = 7;
    img._nx = 1;
    img._ny = 1;
    img._anchorX = 0;
    img._anchorY = 0;
    img._wx = 10;
    img._wy = 10;
    img._ampx = 0.5;
    img._ampy = 0.5;
    img._showgrid = true;
};
crazyButton.onPress = function() {
    img._columns = 3;
    img._rows = 3;
    img._nx = 1.3;
    img._ny = 0.8;
    img._anchorX = 1;
    img._anchorY = 1;
    img._wx = 20;
    img._wy = 15;
```

```
            img._ampx = 0.7;
            img._ampy = 0.7;
            img._showgrid = true;
        };
```

Note that the buttons have been given instance names of normalButton and crazyButton:

In this way you are ready to start creating your own interfaces (featuring buttons, sliders, ComboBoxes, and so on) so that users can interact with your designs and modify the parameters whenever they want. Test the movie to see the difference between the normal and crazy states:

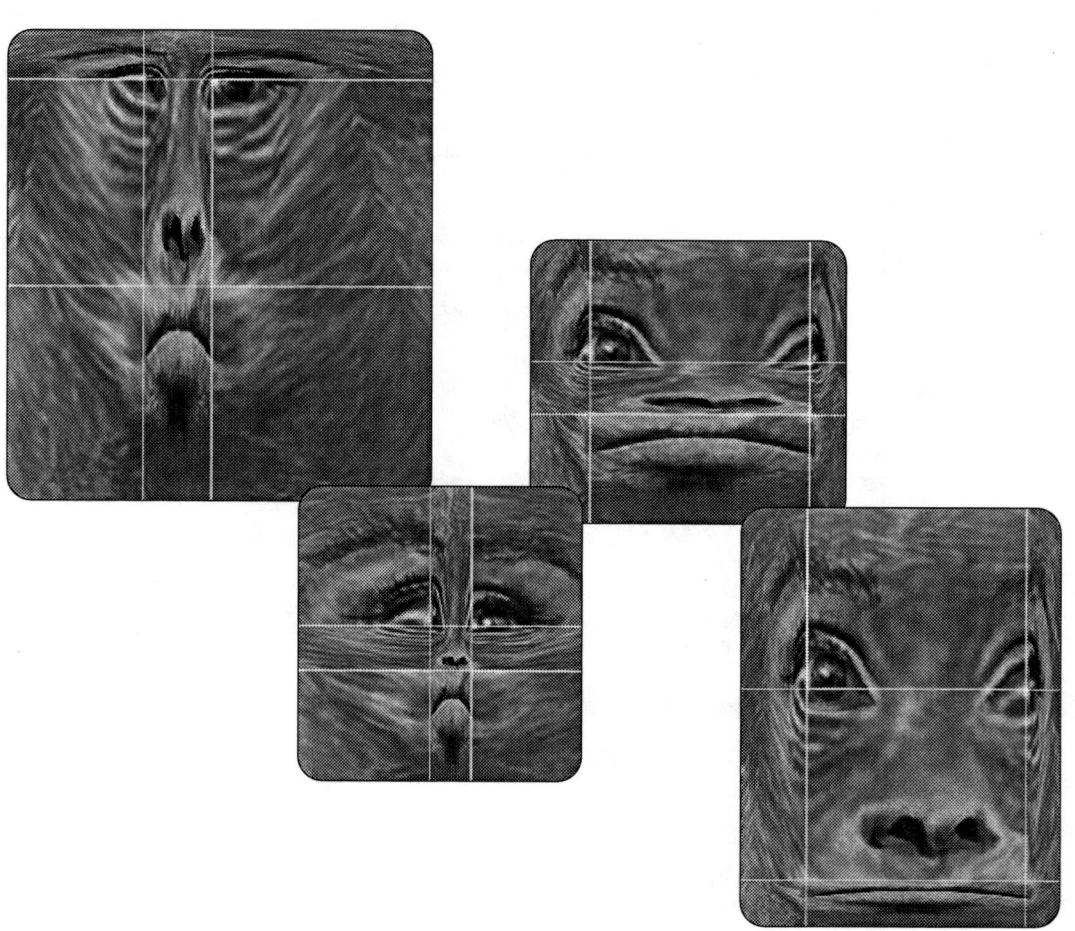

Skewed image modulator component

We can create another family of image modulation effects by utilizing the skew feature as the modulated parameter – that's exactly what we've done with the skewed image modulator component, which can be installed using `FSkewedMatrixComp.mxp`. In both of the image modulation components discussed in this chapter the class structure (the methods and properties that make up the component) are very similar, but this time we are modulating the vertical and horizontal *skew* of each cell instead of simply its width and height.

When we skew an image, we can modify its inclination angles, but we must not change the length of its sides. ActionScript does not actually have a skew property so I have developed my own skew function – feel free to use this skew method in your projects. The component class in this case is called `FSkewedMatrixClass`. As in the liquid modulator we need a matrix because the image will be divided into horizontal and vertical slices.

Once generated, every cell of the matrix needs another nested movie clip named `holder`, in order to perform the skew. Then we scale and move every cell – each cell will be modulated independently, gently modifying both the vertical and horizontal skew angles. Then all the cells are joined side by side. Again, this effect is extremely intensive on the processor and taxes Flash to the max, so it's optimized using a small number of cells (as a precaution, it's even worth saving any unsaved data before playing with this component).

Component parameters

The UI is very similar because we have the same ComboBoxes, sliders, and buttons, although we have included a couple of new sliders:

- Horizontal offset: – Adds a horizontal skew angle. The image appears to rotate around the vertical axis producing a neat 3D effect.

- Vertical offset – Adds a vertical skew angle.

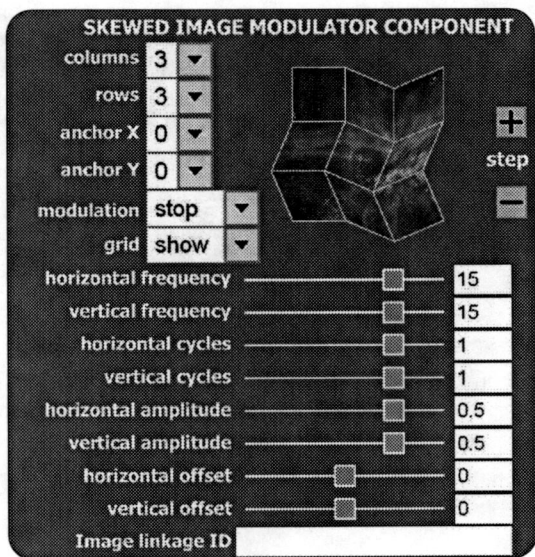

231

Skewed image samples

Once we have all of the necessary parameters set up, we are ready to discover new effects. As with the liquid image modulator component, we'll discuss some variations of this component in the sections that follow – open up each example file, and examine the parameter settings that produce each effect.

Skewed galaxy: skew modulation

Let's start with `skewed_redgalaxy.fla` in which, when tested, the image appears to be swimming across the sky because it has both vertical and horizontal skew modulation, each one with the same frequency and number of cycles, although it has opposite values for vertical and horizontal amplitude. These settings give us the following movie:

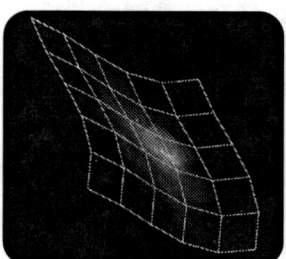 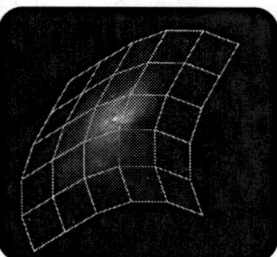 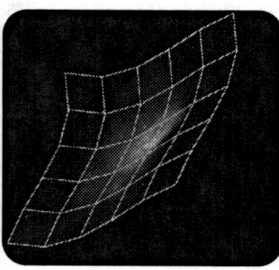 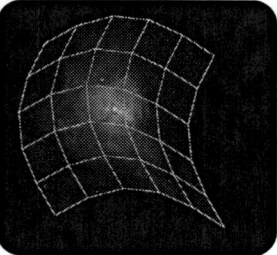

Skewed monkey: skew modulation and offset

With `skewed_monkey.fla` we have both vertical and horizontal skew modulation, each one with its own amplitude and frequency value. We have also added an offset of about 45 degrees to both axes. The image looks like a piece of paper moved by the wind because 25 image cells are skewing harmoniously. Here's the result using a 10x10 grid (running on a Pentium 4 processor):

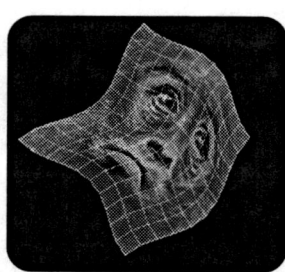 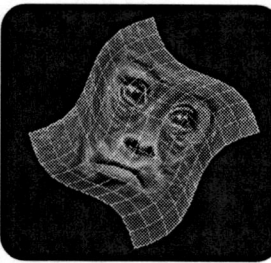 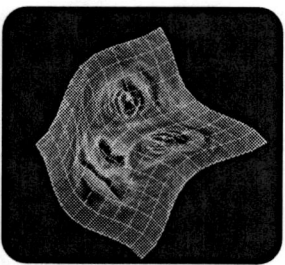

Skewed money: horizontal skew modulation and offset

In this final example, `skewed_money.fla`, I'm modulating a Chilean 10000 Pesos note. We have 10 vertical slices skewing side by side, and their vertical and horizontal offset values are equal to around 40 degrees. Here's the finished design:

Notice that I've set a maximum number of 10 columns here. However, if necessary, you can modify the component code to allow more slices to produce more realistic effects – although be careful that your CPU doesn't explode!

Now that we've finished our quick tour of these two tools, I'm sure you will find interesting applications for them. If you are an ActionScript addict, you can try to code other similar effects yourself using the power of OOP, masking, the drawing API, and all the other cool features of Flash MX. The task is not exactly easy, but the results will always be impressive!

Mike Pearce

Mike followed the usual path to a career in Flash: training for 12 years as a classical ballet dancer before deciding that sitting in front of a computer was much better for his posture. Mike now works for Nectarine, a multimedia company based in Melbourne, Australia, as a developer and designer. When not punching keys, Mike's love of breakbeat and Kung Fu take over – though not usually simultaneously...

"Big thanks to Minty and Bek."

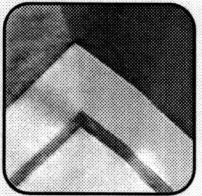

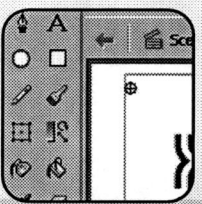

Component 18

XML-to-ActionScript Parser

Streamline the process of using XML with this powerful conversion utility. Take the headache out of XML and put your time back into the fun stuff! Easy enough for the XML novice to use, powerful enough for production projects, the XMLto ActionScript parser component will have you developing dynamic, content driven sites and applications in no time.

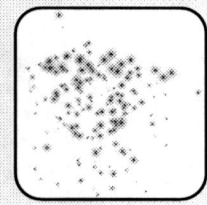
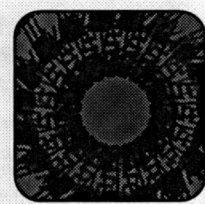

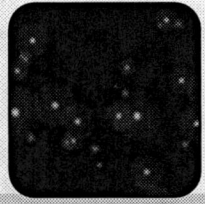

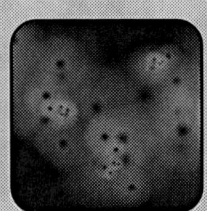

When XML first started to make its mark on Macromedia Flash, just the thought of using it seemed quite daunting to some. In fact, coming more from a design background, I held off from using XML for as long as I possibly could! I was quite intrigued by it all, but no matter how many times I was told what an easy concept it is to grasp, I still had trouble getting over my psychological block that working with XML must be *really hardcore programming*! Of course, I was entirely wrong – after much procrastination, I finally sat down and got to grips with XML, and soon realized that there are numerous advantages to using XML with my data. I still don't know why I had such trepidation in those early days, so if you're in those boots... read on!

As simple as the concept of XML is, I still find it quite tedious to use in Flash. Each new project I create, I end up writing yet another XML parser to grab my data and turn it into something I can use easily in Flash. Well, that sounds like the perfect criteria for a component! Let's quickly run through the basics of my XML to ActionScript parser component, and then take a brief look at what exactly XML is and why on earth we'd want to use it.

The XML to ActionScript parser (XMLtoASparser) is a little utility that, in its simplest form, will take your XML document and turn it into a native Flash object, retaining the hierarchy of the XML document. Your data will then be accessible using dot syntax, so all you need is a basic understanding of ActionScript objects and dot notation to use it.

Of course, the XMLtoASparser component is not necessarily just for beginners. The more advanced features will enable you to explore your XML document, restructure the converted ActionScript object, and preview your changes, all at authoring time – without having to run your movie. The XMLtoASparser component is extremely user - friendly, but it does assume that the user should put a little thought and care into using some of the more advanced features. Automatically checking for and correcting user input errors would increase parsing time considerably, so this component relies, to some extent, on receiving correct information. Accordingly, it's useful to arm ourselves with the basics of XML and a little background knowledge of how the component works.

The mechanics behind the component are fairly straightforward – an XML document is loaded and runs through a recursive parse function, which identifies the nodes and attributes contained within the file. That is, each node is explored and dealt with, and if another node is nested within that node, the function is executed again, this time exploring the nested node. This process creates a type of 'self-sufficient' routine in which the entire document can be processed with a relatively small amount of code.

If some of these terms have you looking towards the exit already, it's probably worth reading the next section to familiarize yourself with XML. After a solid grounding in XML concepts, we'll be ready to make use of XMLtoASparser.

XML basics

XML, or e**X**tensible **M**arkup **L**anguage, is just a standardized way of *describing* data. You see, it really doesn't matter where the XML ends up; the point is that the same XML file could be used by countless different applications on many different platforms. Wait a minute, so why such a complicated sounding name for such a supposedly simple concept? It's what's known as a tag-based markup language. All that means is that each bit of data is contained within a tag – just think of tags as you would headings in a simple document; all the information for a particular section is contained under the appropriate heading. Additionally, XML is extensible in the sense that it allows users to define their own tags and data structure.

Take a look at the following XML:

```
<chapter18>XML to ActionScript Parser</chapter18>
```

The tags are easily identified because they are contained by angled brackets (< and >); between these brackets you'll find the tag name. In the above example we have one tag named chapter18. At the end of the line we see a closing tag, which has a forward slash (/) in front of the tag name. Every tag in XML must have a corresponding closing tag to let the parser know it's come to the end of that bit of data.

Now, let's try using some of the 'technical' terminology. Once a piece of data or text is turned into usable XML, we refer to these sections (the tags and the data they contain) as **nodes**. We could say that the example above consists of one node named chapter18 and contains the text XML to ActionScript Parser. Not surprisingly, if there's text within a node like the one above, that section of text is referred to as a **text node**.

Nodes may be *nested* inside one another. Nesting simply means that they reside inside another node. By nesting nodes in this fashion, we can build up quite complex data structures, while maintaining a lot of flexibility over the type and content of data. For instance, our earlier example might be part of a larger XML document looking something like this:

```
<Components_MW>
  <chapter16>Tornado Movie Loader</chapter16>
  <chapter17>Image Modulation</chapter17>
  <chapter18>XML to ActionScript Parser</chapter18>
</Components_MW >
```

Another thing we need to discuss before we move on are **attributes** – these are just little snippets of information relating to a particular node, which we can include in the opening tag. For example:

```
<Components_MW publisher="Friends Of ED">
  <chapter16 author="Aral Balkan">Tornado Movie Loader</chapter16>
  <chapter17 author="Lifaros">Image Modulation</chapter17>
  <chapter18 author="Mike Pearce">XML to ActionScript Parser</chapter18>
</Components_MW >
```

Notice that inside the opening tags in the sample above there is a bit more information – these are the attributes. Attributes are added in the form: attributeName="attributeValue", and you may have as many attributes as you like. Just make sure each one is separated by a space and the value is enclosed with inverted commas.

One final thing to note is that every XML file must have *all* its data contained within one node. This is known as the **root node** and sits at the very top of the document's hierarchy.

OK, so this introduction is far from a complete guide to XML, but hopefully now we're all up to speed so we can get the most out of this component – for more details about XML, see www.xml.org and www.xml.com.

One of the major advantages of using XML with Flash is that you can keep all your data outside of your Flash file, after adding some well-thought-out ActionScript. This means that every time your client picks up a spelling mistake they missed, or wants to update the weekly special on their restaurant's website, all you'll be doing is opening up a simple text editor. The process of updating becomes so easy that you can even show your clients how to update their content themselves!

Another plus for XML is file size – if you've got a fair bit of text in your Flash file, that's going to start to push up the size a bit. It's easy to forget that text can actually take up a large amount of memory, so why not just use XML to dynamically load the text into your graphical interface as and when you need it? Sounds like a good plan? OK, let's get down to the fun stuff...

Using the component with the custom UI

Open up `XMLparse.fla` from the download, and select the instance of the XML to ActionScript parser component that has already been dragged from the Library to the stage:

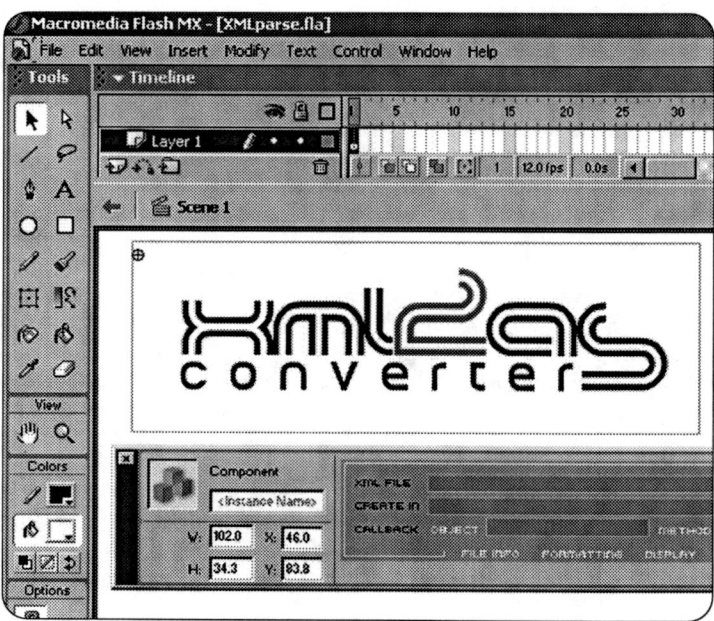

The first thing we should emphasize at this point is that this component really only needs to be as complex as you require – don't assume that every parameter in the custom user interface needs to be filled-in. For simple applications, only one parameter is required – the file name! Nonetheless, there are quite a few features available, so let's check them all out.

File Info

Focusing our attention on the custom UI in the Parameters tab of the Property inspector (Window > Properties), the File Info button is the first on the left. This is where the basic parameters are set regarding the location of your XML document and the soon-to-be-created ActionScript object:

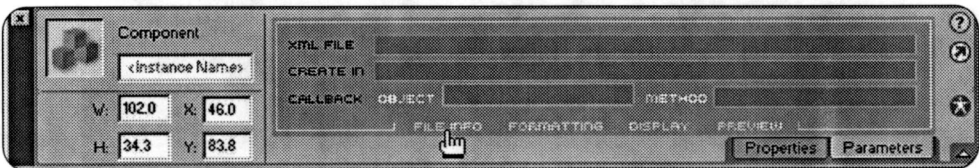

You can also set a callback function here – this is simply a function you can specify to execute when the conversion process is complete. Say, for example, I was using the component to bring in some XML data with which I was going to use to construct a menu. When the XML file had been loaded and the conversion process was complete, I might want to immediately set about building the menu from the data provided. If I had written a function to handle that process called buildMenu and it was located on the main timeline, I would specify _root as the callback object and buildMenu as the method. So, as soon as all my data was ready, the component would automatically call the buildMenu function, and the construction of my menu would be well under way!

On the other hand, I might just want to play a simple animation to let the user know the menu data has loaded OK. Accordingly, if I had made a movie clip named menuLoadedAnim_mc on the main timeline, I could enter _root.menuLoadedAnim_mc as the callback object and play as the method.

Note that the term *method* used here is just another name for *function*. It is usually used when a function belongs to an object. In the example above, play is referred to as a method of the movie clip in question.

For reference, the parameters on this screen are as follows:

- XML file – The name and path (if required) of your XML document. A useful tip here is to use your mouse to paste text into one of these text fields (right-click or CTRL-click and select Paste from the menu); using the shortcut keys (CTRL/COMMAND+V) won't work here. For example, on a PC you can just copy and paste the full path from your Windows Explorer window.

- Create in – The location in which the converted ActionScript object is to reside. By default, the object will reside inside the component instance, so this parameter is optional.

- Callback – This line has two parameters: object and method, the method referring to a function belonging to the object. When the callback is executed it will be passed one parameter – a reference to the component instance.

239

Formatting

The next button along is Formatting. In this screen you will be able to modify the structure of the converted ActionScript object:

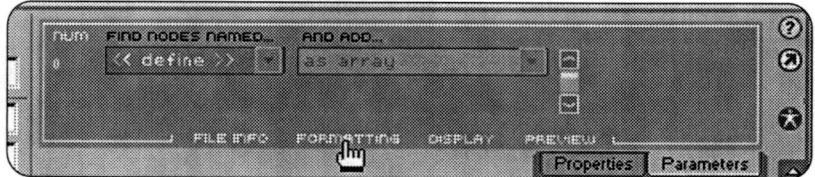

You may remember back at the start of the chapter we learned that the beauty of this component is that it will take your XML files and turn them into ActionScript objects, while retaining the original documents' hierarchy. Now, that's all well and good for some situations, but take a look at the following XML snippet, which presents the same data but involves a subtle restructuring from the previous sample:

```
<Components_MW publisher="Friends Of ED">
  <chapter number="16" author="Aral Balkan">Tornado Movie
➥Loader</chapter>
  <chapter number="17" author="Lifaros">Image Modulation</chapter>
  <chapter number="18" author="Mike Pearce">XML to ActionScript
➥Parser</chapter>
</Components_MW >
```

OK, so the neat thing about our component is that we can use dot syntax to access this data once the conversion is complete. But what would happen if I tried to access Components_MW.chapter? You can see that we're going to run into some problems as there are three nodes named chapter in this case, and in Flash you can't have multiple properties of an object with the same name.

This is where the Formatting options come in handy. With these parameters we can give the component some rules to follow so the data you end up with in Flash best suits your needs and gets past the problem that we've just encountered. One thing to note here is that for many of your projects you won't even need to visit this screen. By default, if more than one node in a given level of your XML file shares the same node name, the parser will put them into an array for you so you won't have to worry!

Just to demonstrate, if you were working with the above XML and didn't set any parameters in the formatting screen, the component would realize our little naming problem and package the information from each chapter node into an *array* called chapter. If we needed to grab the author data from the chapter number 16, we could access it like this:

```
myXMLtoASparser.Components_MW.chapter[0].author
```

where myXMLtoASparser is the instance name that you give to your component. Remember, all the XML data is converted to an ActionScript object *within* the component, unless you've specified otherwise in the Create in parameter of the File Info screen.

More generally speaking, we can look in the Output window after the above XML has been loaded and begin to picture how the XML data and structure is converted over to ActionScript objects:

```
Output                                                    ×
                                              Options
:: XMLtoASobj: loading XML document: C:\Documents
:: XMLtoASobj: loading 0%
:: XMLtoASobj: loading 0%
:: XMLtoASobj: loading 100%
:: XMLtoASobj: XML conversion in: 74ms


CONVERTED OBJECT "Components_MW"
chapter: [Array]
    2: {Object}
        text:XML to ActionScript Parser
        author:Mike Pearce
        number:18
    1: {Object}
        text:Image Modulation
        author:Lifaros
        number:17
    0: {Object}
        text:Tornado Movie Loader
        author:Aral Balkan
        number:16
publisher:Friends Of ED
```

You can also see this data in the Preview screen of the custom UI, but we'll look at this in more detail later.

If you're unsure about what an array is or how to access the elements in an array, make sure you read the appropriate Flash documentation. For instance, the *Flash MX Designer's ActionScript Reference*, from friends of ED (ISBN: 1-903450-58-6) provides a wealth of information, tutorials, and examples for everyday scripting in Flash, including detailed reference sections on using arrays.

Returning to our current example, now that we know what will happen if we *don't* specify any special formatting options, let's take a look at some of the options we *do* have available. With our book data XML, we already know that all the data inside pertains to specific chapters of the book, so the most important thing to know to classify each item is the actual chapter number. Wouldn't it be great if we could alter the formatting of the object so that instead of having all the items in an array, we could simply add the data based on its most important attribute? Of course it would! So let's look at how we'd go about it.

If you take a look at the formatting screen, you'll notice two drop-down menus. Above the first one we see Find nodes named…, and above the second one we have And add…. Hopefully you'll catch on to what's going on here, it's fairly intuitive, but we'll run through it anyway, again using the book data example.

We know that the node which we want to add a rule for is chapter, so select <<define>> from the first drop-down menu and type in chapter. We've just specified that we want the component to 'find nodes named' chapter, and now we need to tell it what to do when it finds one. Click on the second drop-down menu and have a look at the options. If this is the first time you've been to this screen, you'll see two options, as array and by attribute. The first option is essentially what we went through earlier – choosing this option is the same as not specifying any special instructions for that node, as it is the default option. So in this case it's the second option we're after. Adding the data *by attribute* will let us specify which attribute we would like to use as the property name. In this case we want to add by the number attribute, so select by attribute and type in number.

If all goes according to plan, you'll now be able to access data like this:

```
myXMLtoASparser.Components_MW.chapter[16].author;
myXMLtoASparser.Components_MW.chapter[17].text;
myXMLtoASparser.Components_MW.[18].author;
```

Note that we use the array access operators as in this example to address the properties that are made up of numbers. In ActionScript, you cannot use a number or a string with spaces as the name of a property (that is, in a variable, object, or array) to address it. So, for example, if we were to format our array with the values chapter and author as the Find nodes named... and the And add parameters, the data would be structured like this:

```
Output                                                                [X]
                                                              Options
CONVERTED OBJECT "Components_MW"
chapter: {Object}
        Mike Pearce: {Object}
                text:XML to ActionScript Parser
                author:Mike Pearce
                number:18
        Lifaros: {Object}
                text:Image Modulation
                author:Lifaros
                number:17
        Aral Balkan: {Object}
                text:Tornado Movie Loader
                author:Aral Balkan
                number:16
publisher:Friends Of ED
```

Accordingly, we might access data as follows:

```
myXMLtoASparser.Components_MW.chapter["Aral Balkan"].text;
```

This would produce the result: Tornado Movie Loader (refer to original XML data, above).

However, we could also quite happily load data directly if it has a single reference name:

```
myXMLtoASparser.Components_MW.chapter.Lifaros.text;
```

You might recall we also touched on text nodes in our *XML basics* section. Whenever this component comes across a text node, it will simply add that text to its object as a property called `text`.

If at any stage you would like to remove a formatting rule, just select <<none>> from the Find nodes named... menu.

Here are a few useful hints and tips to keep in mind when using the formatting options:

● If you have already previewed your XML in the Preview screen, the drop-downs will be populated with a list of the attributes and nodes contained in your document!

● Selecting as array from the formatting options will only create an array if there is more than one node in that level with the same name. Otherwise, it will simply add that node by its name.

● Be careful when entering an attribute to add by in the formatting options. If the component can't find the attribute it is looking for, it will ignore that node.

● When adding by an attribute in the formatting options, make sure the attribute you are adding by is unique, otherwise subsequent nodes will not be added. That is, if you choose to add by an attribute called `name` and two of the nodes have the same value for their `name` attribute, you're going to run into problems.

Display

Here you'll find the display options for the component:

The visual part of this component is quite minimal. Most of the time all you'll really want to do is have this component do all the hard work behind the scenes and then gracefully disappear. However, if you'd like to let the component display some feedback to your users, there are a few options available – but you should keep in mind that when you are running the component locally, the loading of the XML will happen so fast that you will most likely only see a full loading bar and the text message "done" (if you choose to make the component visible). The logo you see during authoring is only there to give you an indication of where your components are on the stage of the authoring environment. Your users will not see the component's logo.

Most of the options shown above are pretty straightforward, but let's take a look anyway:

● Show component – Specifies whether or not the component is visible.

● Show load progress – Specifies whether loading progress text appears.

- Show load bar – Shows/hides load progress bar.

- Hide component when complete – Makes the component invisible when processing is complete.

- Remove component when complete – Removes the component when processing is complete. Remember, by default the converted ActionScript object is created inside the component instance, so make sure you don't check this option unless you have specified a different location for the object to reside. Doing so will remove all the data we just created! You can specify a different location for the converted object in the Create in parameter of the File Info screen.

- Swap to depth – Movie clips that are added to the stage during authoring time cannot be removed. To get around this, you must first swap the clip onto another depth using this input box to specify a free depth (alternatively, you can dynamically load the component – refer to the section on using the component with ActionScript below).

Outputting data to the display screen is a fairly CPU-intensive process. If your converted object is extremely large and complex and all that data is contained in very few properties, it may cause Flash to get bogged down. If you are working with huge objects like this, it is recommended you don't visit the display screen. Instead, just test your movie and watch the trace output in the Output window. It will give you the same output as the display screen but the process is much quicker. If you would like to turn off *all* object tracing to the Output window, just go into the code inside the component and follow the commented instructions.

Preview

The last of the option screens is Preview – here you can load in and explore the XML document and see how the changes you've made affect the structure of the ActionScript object:

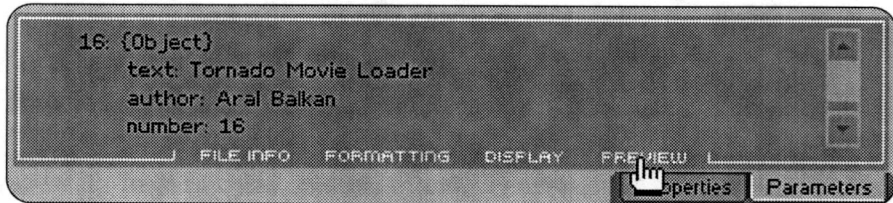

Remember, each time you visit the Preview screen the component will compile a list of nodes and attributes to make life easier in the Formatting screen.

Using the component with ActionScript

You can also create instances of the component entirely through code – you just need to ensure that the component is in your Library. The format for dynamically using the XMLtoASparser component is as follows:

The create() method will return a reference to the converted object, so you can assign it to a variable to make life easier, like this:

```
myNewObj = XMLtoASobj.create(parentObject, name, depth, url, call-
back, createIn, formatOptions, displayOptions);
```

These `create()` method parameters are described in the following table:

Parameter	Description
`parentObject`	Specifies the timeline in which the component will be created.
`name`	Specifies the name of the new component instance.
`url`	The file name (and path) of your XML file.
`callback`	The function to call when complete. This parameter is an array with the elements: `[callObject, "method"]`.
`createIn`	An optional parameter specifying where the converted object is to be created. By default the object is created *inside* the instance.
`formatOptions`	A two-dimensional array. Each element in the array is an array itself containing `["nodeName", "addBy"]`. To add by array, set the `addBy` value to `null`.
`displayOptions`	An object containing any of the following properties: `showComponent`, `showLoadingText`, `showLoadingBar`, `hideWhenDone`, and `removeWhenDone`. Each of these properties will have a Boolean (`true` or `false`) value.

If you do not wish to set any of these parameters, simply pass `null` in place of the parameter.

In the download you'll find a fully commented example of how we might dynamically create an instance of the `XMLtoASparser` component (dynamicXMLtoAS.fla).

This example takes advantage of the `createIn` parameter. Although the instance is created inside `_root.holder_mc`, you'll notice that the actual converted object is created in the `_root` timeline. Use this feature when you would like to convert your data to a specific location then get rid of the component.

245

James Palmer

James graduated in 1998 from the Texas A&M Computer Engineering program. In 2000 he completed his M.S. degree in Computer Visualization. Deeply technical and profoundly visual, James has been working professionally both in print and on the web since 1994. James founded Caramba Designs in 2001 to develop web-based applications and end-to-end solutions for unique problems.

James would like to extend his thanks to his beautiful wife, Yaya, who he is madly in love with, his free-thinking parents, his little sister and her husband, and the entire Tiger Marmalade clan for being the great friends that they are.

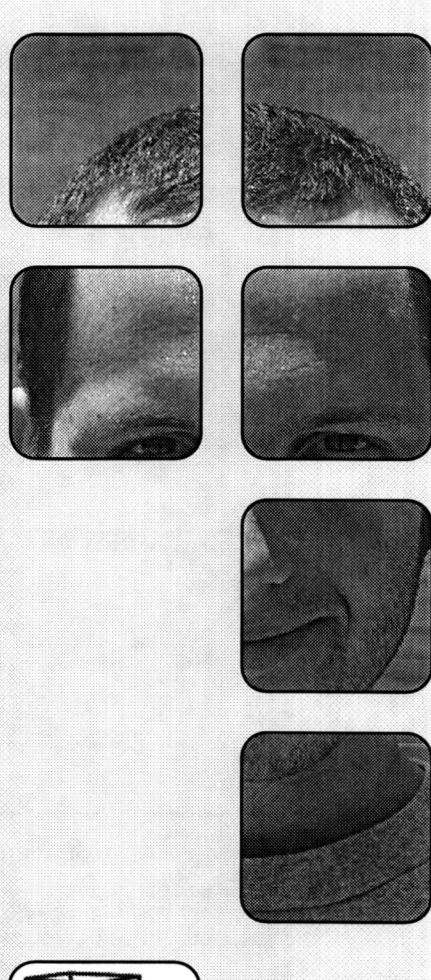

Component 19

Virtual Trackball

This component offers an elegant ActionScript-based interface for providing three dimensional rotation information, which can then be applied to interactive 3D graphics. Its smooth intuitive feel and extreme flexibility makes complex 3D transformations easy for any Flash application.

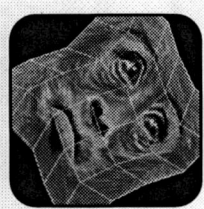

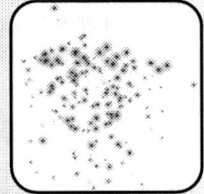

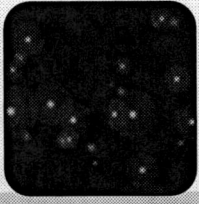

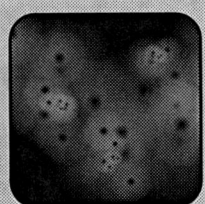

One of the most powerful features of Flash MX is the drawing API. These drawing methods allow developers to create dynamic content using lines, curves, fills, and gradients. At first glance, the movie clip drawing methods may seem fairly basic, but they are actually the fundamental elements that make up many more advanced applications. One of the most impressive applications is being able to dynamically draw virtual 3D geometry.

That said, 3D content in Flash MX certainly won't compete with solutions based on specific 3D packages, like OpenGL or DirectX, in terms of speed. Currently Flash doesn't take advantage of 3D rendering hardware that make games like Doom and Quake possible. Nevertheless, while the next big first-person shooter from ID (www.idsoftware.com) probably won't be written in ActionScript, we can still do some very interesting and useful work with the tools available.

There are many interesting and often difficult challenges associated with 3D content. Indeed, manipulating 3D geometry in an intuitive way can be the first stumbling block. In two dimensions, it's relatively simple to translate and rotate an object with the mouse. Most input devices are two-dimensional in nature, so there is a very intuitive and obvious mapping between the motion of something like a mouse and operations on 2D geometry. In three dimensions, it's not completely obvious what the most instinctive way to manipulate geometry is, especially when you only have 2D input devices to work with.

Consider the rotation operation in three dimensions. One approach would be to create three sliders for the x, y, and z axes. Each slider would represent the rotation about the associated axis. While the code for this is relatively trivial to write, there are few people who can effortlessly decompose an orientation into separate rotational axes.

In the 80s, pioneers in the field of computer graphics began to look at more complex user interface mappings for this problem. In 1988, Chen, Mountford, and Sellen suggested enclosing the 3D object to be transformed in a virtual sphere. The path between two points on the virtual sphere is then used to define the rotation applied to the object. The resulting interface has a very intuitive feel and has since gained a wide acceptance. This interface is usually referred to as a **virtual trackball**. The component that I am introducing in this chapter is based on Gavin Bell's implementation of the virtual trackball, which was originally written for Silicon Graphics, Inc.

The Trackball component differs from many of the components described in this book in that we are going to have to get our hands dirty with some ActionScript programming. In this respect, the component is geared more to those renaissance designer-programmer types who are comfortable doing a little programming in order to create really stunning visual effects.

In this chapter we'll touch on some of the fundamental concepts of 3D rendering, covering the core Trackball methods, and we'll show how to use the component to create a very intuitive user interface for manipulating 3D geometry.

Using the Trackball component

After installing the component via its MXP file in the usual manner, you'll find the Virtual Trackball Component within the Caramba Components group in the Components panel. Before we get into demonstrating the component in action, let's get familiar with its main elements. Drag an instance of the Trackball onto the stage of a new Flash movie:

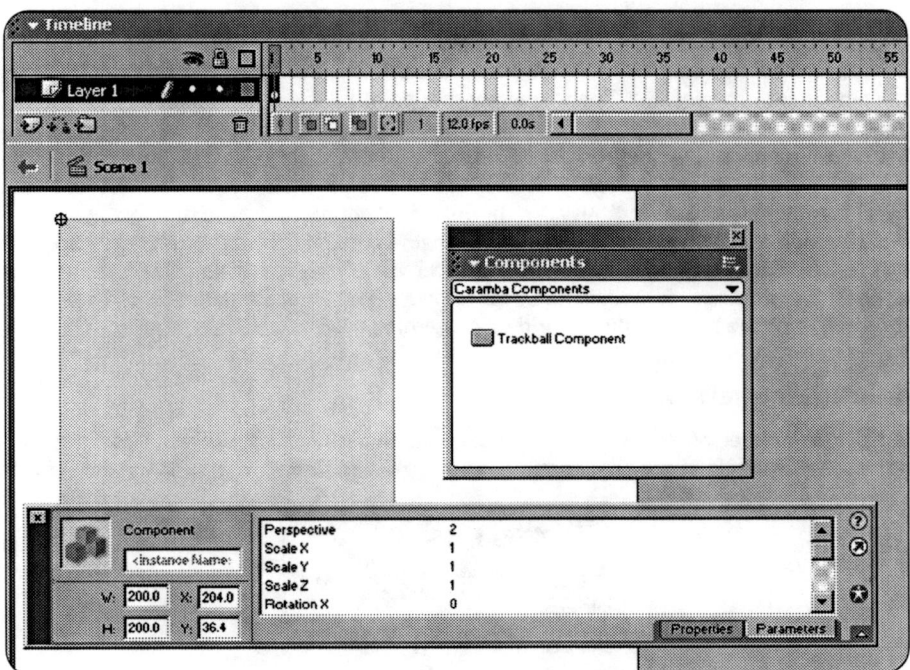

The Trackball component implements a virtual trackball interface and is represented in the authoring environment by a large blue square. At runtime, the component does not have a visible interface, but instead it acts like a giant *hot spot* in your movies. When you click and drag the mouse on the component it modifies an internal rotation matrix.

Component methods

There are four important methods that the Trackball component provides to access this rotational information:

- `transformVertex(x, y, z)` – This method is a convenience function that multiplies a point (`x, y, z`) by the rotation matrix created by the Trackball component. The result is a transformed or rotated point.

- `increment()` – This method causes the Virtual Trackball component to update its internal rotation matrix based on the position and state of the mouse.

- `getQuaternionRotation()` – This method returns the rotational value of the virtual trackball as a quaternion (that is, a four-dimensional description of the rotation). While we won't discuss quaternions here, this method is useful for advanced ActionScript programmers who might use this component with their own 3D geometry engine.

- **`getRotationMatrix()`** – This method returns the rotational value of the virtual trackball as a transformation matrix. In order to rotate or transform a point by the rotation that the Trackball component provides, we simply multiply that point by the rotation matrix.

We won't be using the last two methods in the examples in this chapter. In fact, the `transformVertex()` method uses these functions internally so we don't have to do so much serious coding. They are mentioned for completeness and may be useful for ActionScript programmers working on more advanced 3D graphical displays. For instance, a 3D engine designer could use `getRotationMatrix()` to extract a rotation matrix for multiplication with another transformation matrix. The `transformVertex()` method does this work for us behind the scenes and makes it possible to do some simple 3D work without delving into the mathematical world of quaternions and matrices.

Component parameters

There are also a number of useful parameters that can be set, in the Property inspector or Component Parameters panel, that effect the transformation performed by the `transformVertex()` function:

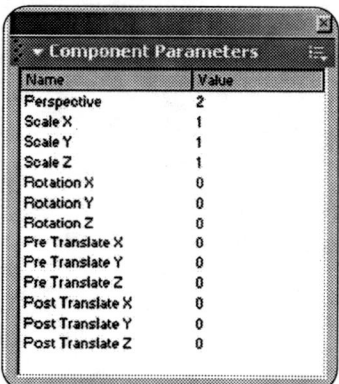

Name	Value
Perspective	2
Scale X	1
Scale Y	1
Scale Z	1
Rotation X	0
Rotation Y	0
Rotation Z	0
Pre Translate X	0
Pre Translate Y	0
Pre Translate Z	0
Post Translate X	0
Post Translate Y	0
Post Translate Z	0

- Perspective – This parameter determines how much perspective is used in the transformation. Low values (above zero) result in a large amount of perspective, whereas using a higher value will decrease the amount of perspective. A value of 0 indicates no perspective.

- ScaleX, ScaleY, ScaleZ – These parameters apply a scale operation on the transformation that occurs after rotation (see next parameter).

- RotationX, RotationY, RotationZ – These parameters indicate the initial rotation that will be used by the Trackball component. The rotation is performed in X-Y-Z order.

- PreTranslateX, PreTranslateY, PreTranslateZ – These parameters translate the input coordinates *before* any other transformations are applied. These are useful for moving the center of rotation.

- PostTranslateX, PostTranslateY, PostTranslateZ – These parameters translate the output coordinate *after* all other transformations are applied. These are useful for moving the transformed coordinates to a new final position. While the PreTranslate parameters effect the rotation and perspective of the transformation that is performed, the PostTranslate parameters do not.

Now that we have a comfortable background knowledge of the Trackball component, let's look at some examples of its use.

Example 1: Manipulating points in 3D space

A very straightforward technique for rendering 3D scenes on a two-dimensional plane (the computer screen) is to let the x and y axes of the screen correspond to the x and y axes of the scene. The imaginary lines, or rays, that we use to project points in 3D space onto the 2D projection plane will be parallel. Thus, we are creating a parallel projection:

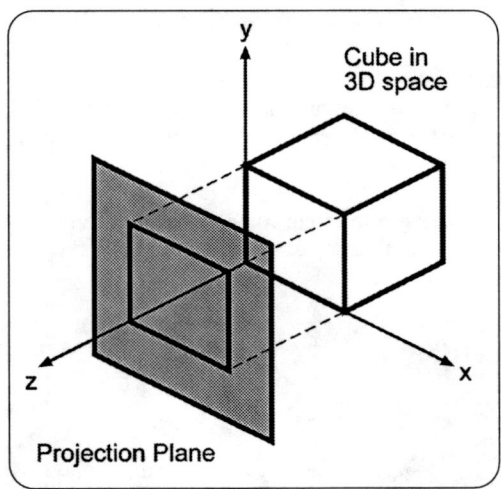

In this scenario, the z-axis represents depth in the scene. However, because our projection is strictly parallel it has no effect on the x and y coordinates and does not create perspective. Instead, in this example we will scale the points at the vertices of the cube based on each point's z value. It's amazing how changing the size of the point helps create the illusion of three dimensionality!

Open up `3D_example1.fla` from this chapter's source files in the download, and take a look on the stage. For this sample file, I've dragged the Trackball component onto the center of the stage and given it an instance name of `trackball`. Also note that I've strategically set the document window size to 200x200 pixels because this is the default size of the Trackball component (but we could easily scale the component to any size).

Now, with the component selected, check in the Component Parameters panel to see what parameters I've set here (see over):

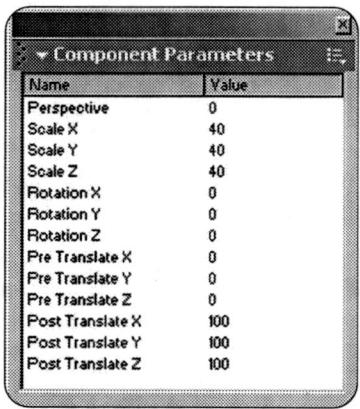

This creates a parallel transformation (that is, one with no perspective). It will scale the result of the rotation by 40 on each axis and then translate each axis by 100 units. This final translation of 100 units per axis is used to make the center of the rendered object correspond with the center of the movie at coordinates (100, 100).

Next, focus your attention to the group circle movie clips that I've positioned just off the lower left perimeter of the stage. These are eight instances of the same movie clip, myPoint, that I've given instance names b0, b1, b2, and so on, up to b7:

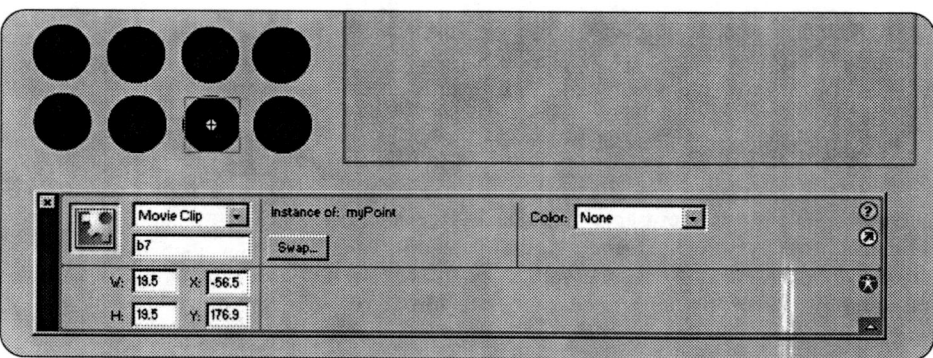

OK, now that we're aware of the parameters and movie clips, we're ready to examine the all-important ActionScript – first, notice how I've structured the timeline of this movie:

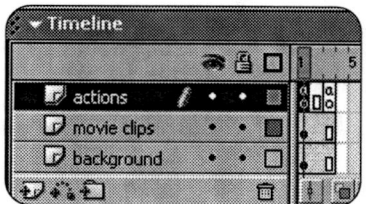

On frame 1 you'll find the following code:

```
// Create the vertices of the cube,
v = new Array(3);
v[0] = new Array(8);
v[1] = new Array(8);
v[2] = new Array(8);
v[0][0] = -1; v[1][0] = -1; v[2][0] =  1;
v[0][1] = -1; v[1][1] =  1; v[2][1] = -1;
v[0][2] =  1; v[1][2] = -1; v[2][2] = -1;
v[0][3] =  1; v[1][3] =  1; v[2][3] = -1;
v[0][4] =  1; v[1][4] = -1; v[2][4] =  1;
v[0][5] = -1; v[1][5] =  1; v[2][5] =  1;
v[0][6] = -1; v[1][6] = -1; v[2][6] = -1;
v[0][7] =  1; v[1][7] =  1; v[2][7] =  1;
```

And frame 3 contains this script:

```
// Transform each vertex that makes up the cube,
for (i=0; i<8; i++) {
    trackball.increment();
    var w = trackball.transformVertex(v[0][i], v[1][i], v[2][i]);
    setProperty("b" +  i, _x, w[0]);
    setProperty("b" +  i, _y, w[1]);
    setProperty("b" +  i, _xscale, 200-w[2]);
    setProperty("b" +  i, _yscale, 200-w[2]);
}
gotoAndPlay(2);
```

So, each time we loop over frame 3 we recalculate the position of the cube's corner points. We update the points b0 through b7 in the scene with these new coordinates using the setProperty() method. We also use setProperty() to set the scale factors on b0 through b7 to correspond with their respective z-axis positions.

When you test your movie (CTRL/COMMAND+ENTER), you should be able to rotate the cube by clicking on the invisible Trackball component and dragging the mouse around. The points on the cube will move in the x-y plane and their size will change as their z values change:

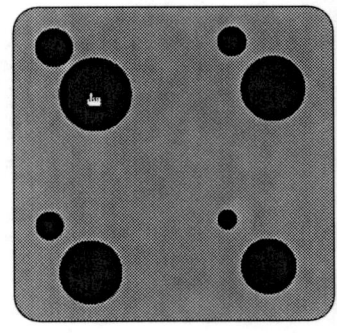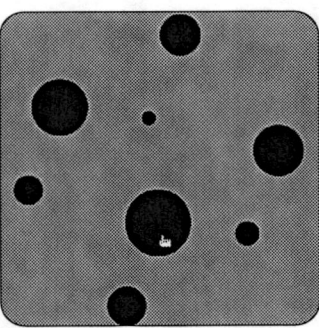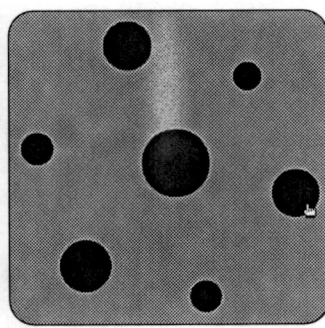

Example 2: Drawing a dynamic 3D polygon

The previous example illustrates how easily the Trackball component can be incorporated into a movie. We kept things relatively simple to show how transforming points with the `transformVertex()` method works. We can use the same technique in combination with the drawing methods in Flash MX to draw and rotate polygonal objects.

We'll also add perspective to this example. I won't go into a deep derivation of how or why it works, but when the Perspective parameter is set to a non-zero value, `transformVertex()` multiplies the x and y axes by `perspectiveValue/(perspectiveValue+z)` to create a fairly convincing perspective effect. In a nutshell, the imaginary projection lines we have been using to transform 2D coordinates to 3D coordinates will no longer be parallel – instead, they'll converge at a point called the center of projection:

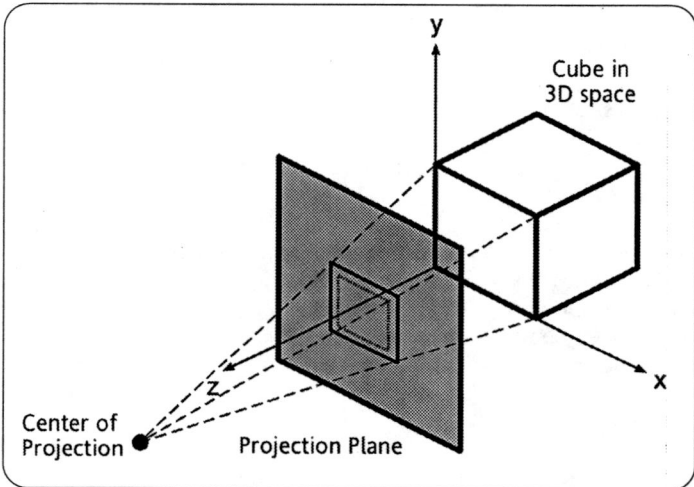

Before we jump into the implementation, we need to decide how we are going to draw our polygonal model. We can do a little sketch on graph paper or even in Flash to plot out what the vertex coordinates should be. For more complicated scenes, you could use a 3D modeling package to generate the raw data. Here's what I came up with for a simple L shape:

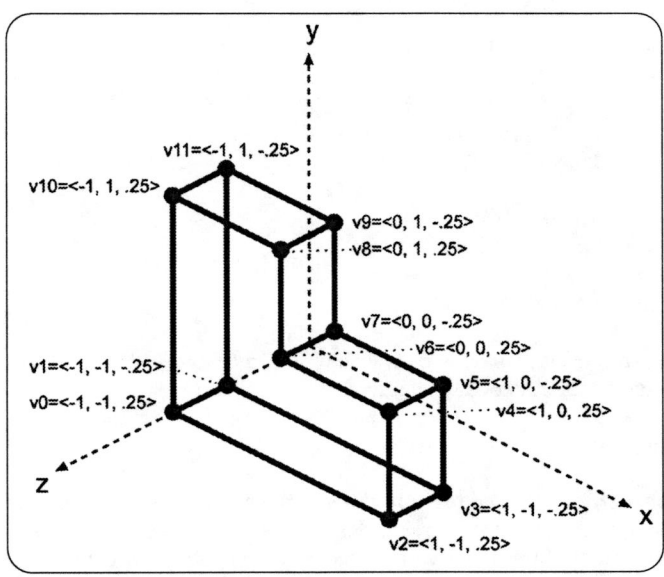

So, if we wanted to draw the very front face, we would draw a polygon with the vertices v0, v2, v4, v6, v8, and v10. The left face is made up of vertices v0, v1, v11, and v10, and so on for each other face. Obviously, the order in which we draw the faces is also important – if we drew the top face in the order: v10, v9, v8, v11, we'd be drawing a bowtie instead of a rectangle. You may want to refer back to this drawing as you read the ActionScript code of this next example in order to keep everything straight in your mind.

Open up 3D_example2.fla, where you'll find a very similar setup to the previous example. You'll see the first obvious difference when you examine the Component Parameters panel:

This time, I've set the Perspective to 3, which will introduce a moderate amount of perspective, and the Scale values to 40 each.

On frame 1 of the actions layer you'll see the following ActionScript to set up the vertices of our 3D polygon:

Name	Value
Perspective	3
Scale X	60
Scale Y	60
Scale Z	60
Rotation X	0
Rotation Y	0
Rotation Z	0
Pre Translate X	0
Pre Translate Y	0
Pre Translate Z	0
Post Translate X	100
Post Translate Y	100
Post Translate Z	100

```
// Create the vertices of the cube
v = new Array(3);
v[0] = new Array(12);
v[1] = new Array(12);
v[2] = new Array(12);
v[0][0] = -1; v[1][0] = -1; v[2][0] =  .25; // v0
v[0][1] = -1; v[1][1] = -1; v[2][1] = -.25; // v1
v[0][2] =  1; v[1][2] = -1; v[2][2] =  .25; // v2
v[0][3] =  1; v[1][3] = -1; v[2][3] = -.25; // v3
v[0][4] =  1; v[1][4] =  0; v[2][4] =  .25; // v4
v[0][5] =  1; v[1][5] =  0; v[2][5] = -.25; // v5
```

```
v[0][6]  =   0; v[1][6]  =   0; v[2][6]  =   .25; // v6
v[0][7]  =   0; v[1][7]  =   0; v[2][7]  =  -.25; // v7
v[0][8]  =   0; v[1][8]  =   1; v[2][8]  =   .25; // v8
v[0][9]  =   0; v[1][9]  =   1; v[2][9]  =  -.25; // v9
v[0][10] =  -1; v[1][10] =   1; v[2][10] =   .25; // v10
v[0][11] =  -1; v[1][11] =   1; v[2][11] =  -.25; // v11
tv = new Array(3);
tv[0] = new Array(12);
tv[1] = new Array(12);
tv[2] = new Array(12);

// Create an empty movie clip that we can draw in
this.CreateEmptyMovieClip("canvas", 4);
canvas._x = 0;
canvas._y = 0;
```

The multi-dimensional array v is used to store the vertex coordinates of our object. The first subscript is used to access the x, y, and z values of a point, denoted by 0, 1, and 2 respectively. The second subscript is used to specify the index of the point whose values will be retrieved. Using arrays will make it easy to iterate through all the points using a for loop (described shortly). The multi-dimensional array tv is identical in structure to the array v, this is used to store the *transformed* vertex coordinates.

The last three lines in the code snippet above initialize a new movie clip named canvas that will be used to draw our 3D polygon. We set the center of the canvas movie clip to coincide with the center of the stage.

Now, turn your attention to the code on frame 3 of the actions layer in 3D_example2.fla:

```
trackball.increment();

for (i=0; i<12; i++) {
    // Get the transformed vertex
    w = trackball.transformVertex(v[0][i], v[1][i], v[2][i]);
    tv[0][i] = w[0];
    tv[1][i] = w[1];
    tv[2][i] = w[2];
}

// Clear any previously drawn lines from this movie
canvas.clear();

// The lines will be 2 pixels wide and blue
canvas.lineStyle (2.0, 0x0000FF);

// Draw front face
canvas.moveTo(tv[0][0], tv[1][0]);
canvas.lineTo(tv[0][2], tv[1][2]); // p0 to p2
canvas.lineTo(tv[0][4], tv[1][4]); // p2 to p4
```

```
canvas.lineTo(tv[0][6], tv[1][6]); // p4 to p6
canvas.lineTo(tv[0][8], tv[1][8]); // p6 to p8
canvas.lineTo(tv[0][10], tv[1][10]); // p8 to p10
canvas.lineTo(tv[0][0], tv[1][0]); // p10 to p0

// Draw back face
canvas.moveTo(tv[0][1], tv[1][1]);
canvas.lineTo(tv[0][3], tv[1][3]); // p1 to p3
canvas.lineTo(tv[0][5], tv[1][5]); // p3 to p5
canvas.lineTo(tv[0][7], tv[1][7]); // p5 to p7
canvas.lineTo(tv[0][9], tv[1][9]); // p7 to p9
canvas.lineTo(tv[0][11], tv[1][11]); // p9 to p11
canvas.lineTo(tv[0][1], tv[1][1]); // p11 to p1

// Draw lower right side face
canvas.moveTo(tv[0][2], tv[1][2]);
canvas.lineTo(tv[0][4], tv[1][4]); // p2 to p4
canvas.lineTo(tv[0][5], tv[1][5]); // p4 to p5
canvas.lineTo(tv[0][3], tv[1][3]); // p5 to p3
canvas.lineTo(tv[0][2], tv[1][2]); // p3 to p2

// Draw upper right side face
canvas.moveTo(tv[0][6], tv[1][6]);
canvas.lineTo(tv[0][8], tv[1][8]); // p6 to p8
canvas.lineTo(tv[0][9], tv[1][9]); // p8 to p9
canvas.lineTo(tv[0][7], tv[1][7]); // p9 to p7
canvas.lineTo(tv[0][6], tv[1][6]); // p7 to p6

// Draw left side face
canvas.moveTo(tv[0][0], tv[1][0]);
canvas.lineTo(tv[0][10], tv[1][10]); // p0 to p10
canvas.lineTo(tv[0][11], tv[1][11]); // p10 to p11
canvas.lineTo(tv[0][1], tv[1][1]); // p11 to p1
canvas.lineTo(tv[0][0], tv[1][0]); // p2 to p4

gotoAndPlay(2);
```

This script begins by incrementing the Virtual Trackball component's internal values using its `increment()` method. We then use a `for` loop to transform each vertex in the array `v` and store the transformed vertex coordinates in `tv`. Next, we clear the `canvas` movie clip and draw the faces of our 3D object using these transformed values. This process is repeated every time Flash executes the script for this frame.

After a close reading of this code, you may notice that we haven't drawn all the faces in our model! Since this is a simple wire-frame model, not every face needs to be drawn in order to draw every edge. In fact, we could have developed a slightly better representation of our model and drawn *only* the edges.

257

Test the movie to see the results – this example really shows the potential of Flash MX as a tool for delivering interactive three dimensional content:

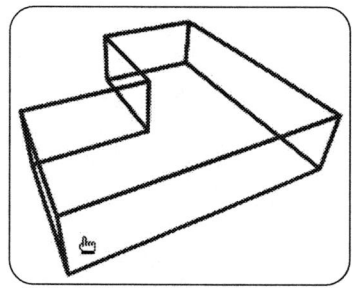 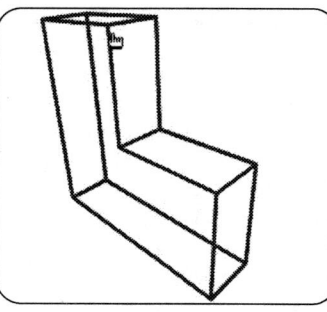 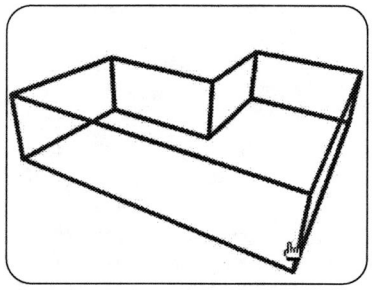

Remember, the parameters set in the Component Parameters panel effect the transformation that takes place. Play around with different values to get a feel for how changing the perspective, scale, rotation, and translation effects the scene:

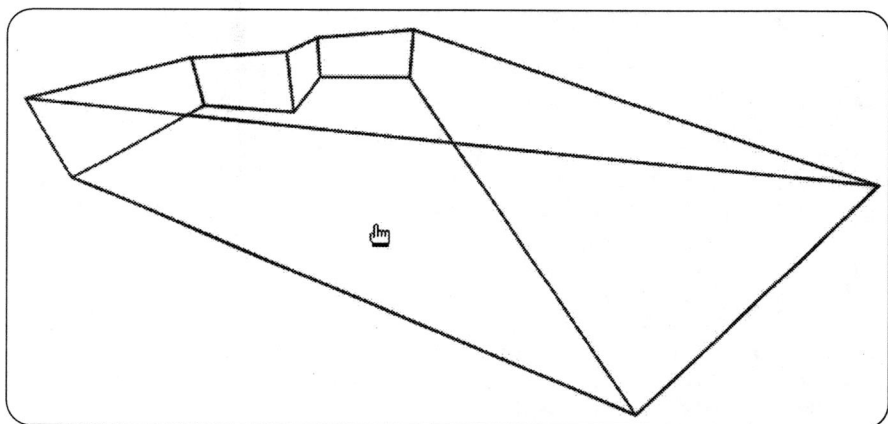

This example could be improved in many ways. For instance, we could develop a 3D file format importer to import 3D objects directly from applications like 3D Studio Max. We could also use the `beginFill()` and `endFill()` movie clip methods to actually shade the faces of our object, and we could use line styles and movie transparency to create a number of interesting visual effects. All of the 3D tricks we've seen in the last two examples merely scratch the surface of what is possible with Flash MX. The possibilities really are endless!

In this chapter we covered some basic 3D concepts and introduced the Trackball component. We demonstrated one movie that can rotate the vertices of a cube and used a simple parallel projection technique to render those vertices. We also introduced a simple polygonal model and used the movie clip drawing methods to render the edges using a perspective projection technique.

As 3D content becomes more prevalent in Flash, we're going to need to find new techniques to visualize three-dimensional information and, along the way, we'll have find new ways to interact with that information. The Trackball component provides a robust tool that we can use to explore Flash-based 3D programming and design.

Todd Yard:

After studying theatre in London, then working for several years as an actor in the US, Todd was introduced to Flash in 2000 and was quickly taken by how it allowed for both stunning creativity and the application of programmatic logic – a truly left-brain/right-brain approach to production–and has not looked back. He now works as Creative Director for Daedalus Media in New York City, which specializes in the creation of Flash-based corporate presentations primarily for clients in the investment banking industry. His more frivolous work and experimentation can be found at his personal website, www.27Bobs.com.

As his new line of employment makes it incredibly unlikely that Todd will ever accept a best acting Oscar, he'd like to take this opportunity to thank his parents for their support through the years, and to thank Lydian for her continued understanding as he sits hunched over a keyboard through many a night.

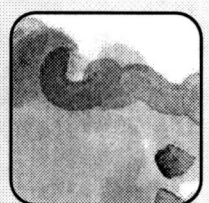
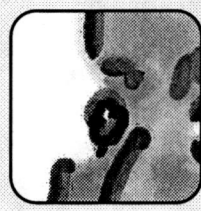

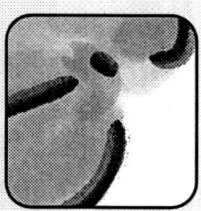

Component 20

Text Animations with PuppetStrings

The PuppetStrings components allow Flash designers to streamline the manipulation and animation of text elements in their movies. With PuppetStrings:transitions, you can create fantastic animation for strings of dynamic text without ever having to leave the Flash authoring environment. It's fast, easy, and capable of incredible results!

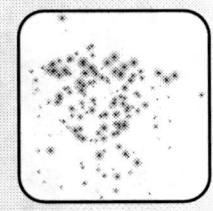
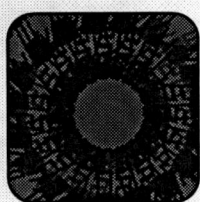

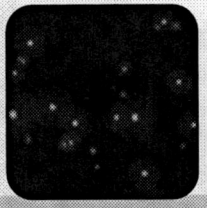

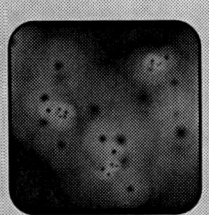

Flash MX offers a tremendous amount of control over text – much more so than its predecessor, Flash 5. Flash developers can now create and format text fields on the fly, as well as access and alter the properties we have already grown familiar with through the MovieClip object, such as position, scale and opacity. With all this added control, creating animated text sequences within the Flash authoring environment should be made easier, but it still can be a long, tedious process. That is where components come in.

The PuppetStrings components are actually three components in a set that I have been developing to deal with the dynamic manipulation and animation of text without ever having to leave the Flash authoring environment or open the ActionScript editor. Each component offers a separate functionality:

- **PuppetStrings:paths** – allows the developer to place and animate text on Bezier paths defined in its custom interface.

- **PuppetStrings:envelopes** – offers envelope distortion tools for text, allowing you to create effects such as perspective.

- **PuppetStrings:transitions** – allows the developer to quickly and easily animate a string sequence using the text field's common properties.

It is this final component, PuppetStrings:transitions, that we'll be exploring in this chapter:

The PuppetStrings:Transitions component is intended for limited, single - line text strings (don't try it with pages and pages of text!), and it works by taking the position and the text string from a dynamic or input text field placed on the stage, as well as text-formatting information from an instance of a TextFormat object. It then uses this information to create individual movie clips to hold each letter and animate them separately. The custom user interface (UI) built in to the component facilitates the setting and testing of all the individual properties that you can animate, in addition to giving you the option to change the registration points, the time and order of animation, and the type of easing for the animation of each property.

If you like this particular PuppetStrings component, be sure to check the other PuppetStrings components in the components section of www.27bobs.com. You can also check this site for updates to this component.

Using the PuppetStrings:Transitions component

This PuppetStrings component is set up almost completely from within a custom UI to make the animation process as simple and intuitive as possible. You'll find this in the Component Parameters panel in Flash when you have the component selected on the stage:

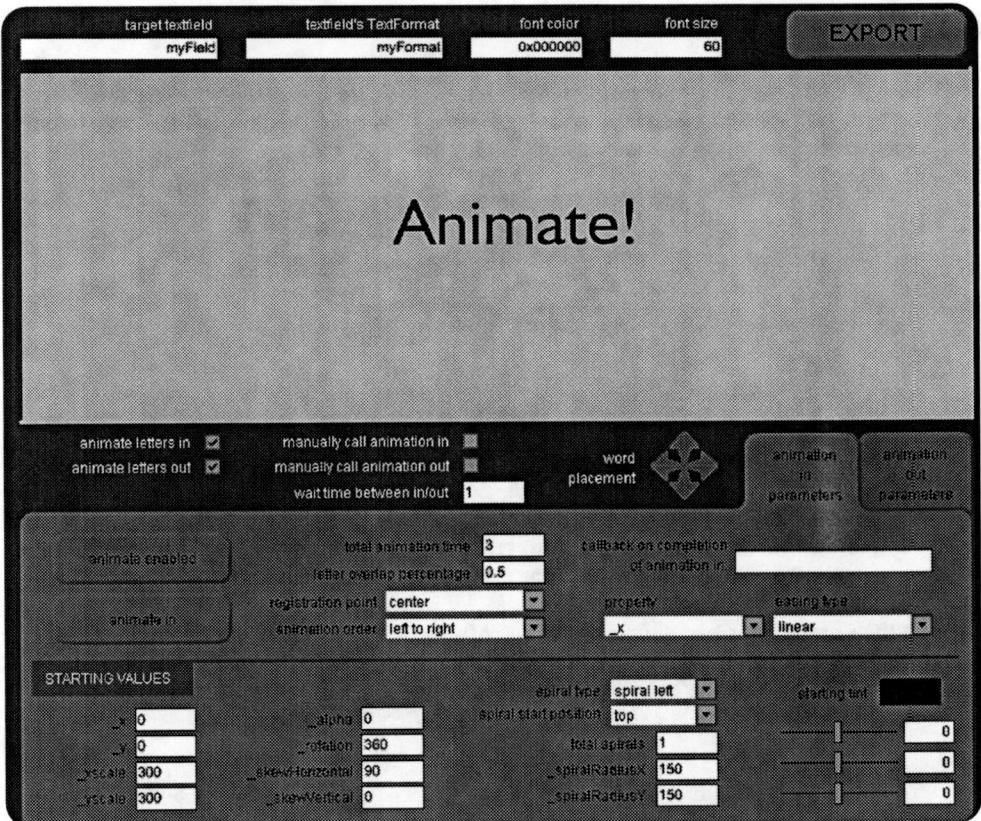

The animation window within the interface can give you immediate feedback on how a text effect will look so that you can quickly tweak values to get your desired result. I'll break the entire process down into steps in the next tutorial so you may see how to quick it is to get it working and start creating your own effects and transitions. I'll elaborate on these steps over the course of this chapter, and let you know about all the additional options.

Let's get started right away – you'll find the `PuppetStrings.mxp` file in the download, with which you can install this component using the Macromedia Extension Manager. There are also a number of example files in the download that you can refer to while reading this chapter. Remember, if you have Flash MX open, you'll need to close and reopen the application, and then the PuppetStrings set will appear in the drop-down menu of your Components panel. Now let's get it working!

Getting started

This section will serve as a quick lesson for using the PuppetStrings:transitions component. Refer to the file `quickStart.fla` while following this tutorial to see the component in action. If you are unfamiliar with components in general, or with using the TextFormat object in Flash MX, you should find that everything is fully explained in the following pages. If you want to know what's going on behind the scenes and how to configure this component for your own purposes, don't worry – it's all coming later in the chapter.

1. First of all, create a new Flash movie (CTRL/COMMAND+N) and name it whatever you want (or just take a look at `quickStart.fla`). Make three layers in this movie, naming them from top to bottom textfield, PuppetStrings, and TextFormat. The order of the layers is *very* important, so make sure your movie's layer structure is as follows:

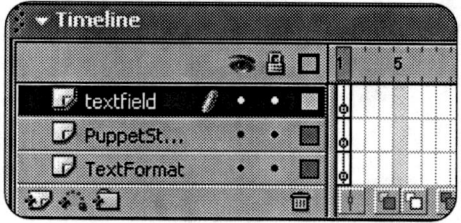

2. Now, we need to create an instance of the TextFormat object for the movie. This is usually accomplished through ActionScript coding, but there are certain procedures you will need to follow when using this method with the PuppetStrings component. Instead, so that we don't get bogged down with scripting right from the start, we'll create our TextFormat instance with the help of another handy component that takes care of all the code for us.

    In the Components panel, find the newly installed PuppetStrings subdirectory – here, as well as the PuppetStrings:Transitions component, you'll find the TextFormat_component. Drag it into the TextFormat layer. It doesn't matter whether you place it on or off the stage, since it will be invisible when the movie is published.

3. With the TextFormat_component instance selected, open up the Property inspector or the Component Parameters panel to view all of its parameters. The parameters listed here are all of the properties that you can assign to a TextFormat. You can use this component in any movie where you need to create a TextFormat through code, and the format you create will be attached to the _global object for access throughout your movie. For our purposes, set the TextFormat's formatName property to myFormat, the font to Impact (or an alternative of your choice), and the size to 60:

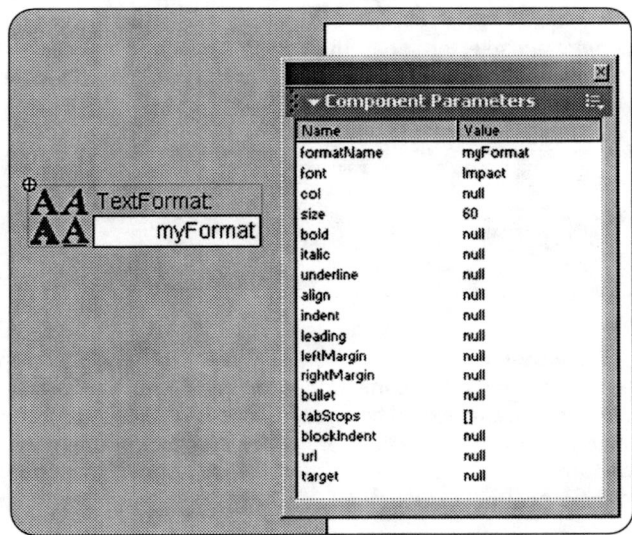

4. The next step is to create a text field on your stage. Go to the textfield layer and, using the Text tool, draw a single line dynamic or input text field on the stage and give it the instance name myField. Type Simple Sample, or whatever you want, into the field and format it to match the TextFormat we defined in the previous step (60 point Impact).

5. With the text field still selected, embed the font by clicking on the Character... tab in the Property inspector and selecting Only for both Uppercase Letters and Lowercase Letters.

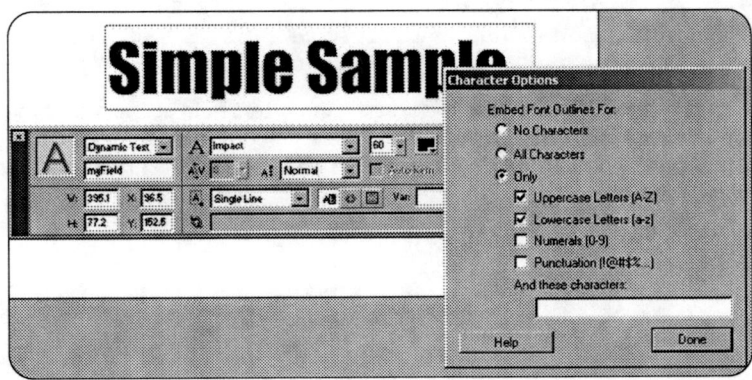

After accepting these changes and exiting the dialog box, we now have a TextFormat assigned and a text field to animate. Everything is in place ready to drop the PuppetStrings:Transitions component onto the stage and use it to create our animation.

6. Drag an instance of PuppetStrings:Transitions from the Components panel and place it on the PuppetStrings layer of the stage. Again, it doesn't matter where you place it on the stage, as it will be invisible when you publish the movie. Note for the time being that we are placing it on a layer *above* the TextFormat component. The reason for this will be explained very soon.

7. With the component selected, open the custom UI from the Property inspector by clicking on the button: Launch Component Parameters Panel (you can also open up this UI directly by selecting Window > Component Parameters):

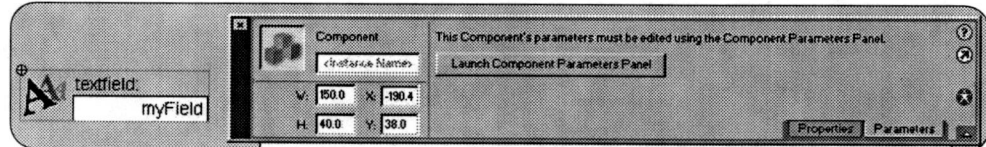

8. The UI might launch in a tiny window, so just resize it to fill your screen. In the input text fields at the top of the interface, define which text field and TextFormat are to be used in this animation. In our case that would be `myField` and `myFormat`, respectively. By typing the names of the format and text field, we are letting the component know which text field to animate using which format. If we did not specify these values our animation wouldn't be applied to anything in the authoring environment!

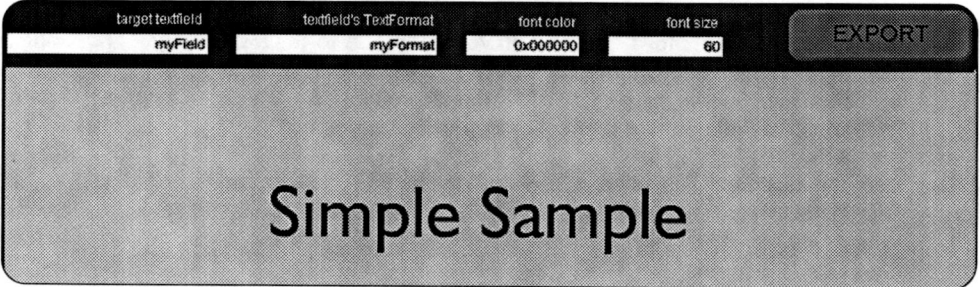

Next, change the font size value to 60 in the input text field at the top of the interface. You can also add/amend your text in the middle of the animation window – it's actually an input textbox, so simply hover your cursor over it to get an I-bar, select the current text and overwrite it with whatever you want.

9. Now comes the fun part! By changing the values in the properties fields at the bottom of the UI, we can create an animation. Let's start by changing the _xscale and _yscale values to 300. This will make the letters start at 300% scale and animate down to 100%. Next, change the _alpha value to 0 to make the letters of the word fade in during the animation. Finally, change the _rotation value to 360. By altering this value, our letters will rotate one full revolution during the animation. Note that at any step along the way, you can just hit the animate in button to see the effect that you've created so far.

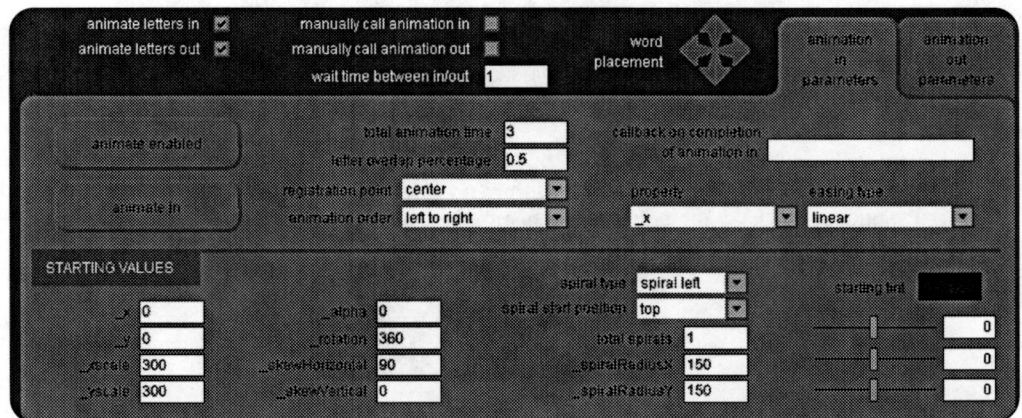

10. Next, change the _skewHorizontal value to 90 to skew each letter from 90 degrees to 0 as it animates. For another effect, set spiral left in the spiral type ComboBox, as seen above. This will cause each letter to spiral in, starting at a radius of 50 pixels on the x-axis and 50 pixels on the y-axis. To change this radius value, enter 150 in both the _spiralRadiusX and _spiralRadiusY input boxes. Go ahead and test all of our 'hard' work again!

11. All of the animation we have created thus far has been on the 'animation in' sequence, but we can also work on the letters as they 'animate out'. Let's try that now – click on the animation out parameters tab at the right of the UI. Changing the values here in this tab will affect the animation-out sequence of animation. The only value I changed here was to set the _skewVertical to –90. Do that now, then hit the animate out button to see what it does.

12. That's a nice effect, but we can make it better by doing two things. First, locate the registration point ComboBox and set it to right bottom. By default, a text field's registration point is at

the top left, so setting this to a different location allows us to move the 'hinge'. Second, let's change the order of animation from `left to right` to `right to left` in the animation order combo box. Test the animation again using animate out to see how the changes have worked:

13. If you click on the animate enabled button, you'll notice it only animates the animation in sequence. By default, the animation in is the only sequence set to play. To enable our animation out sequence, click on the animate letters out checkbox:

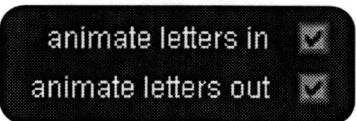

Clicking on the animate enabled button now, you should see the animation of both sequence.

14. The last step is to add some lag time between our animation in and animation out sequences. In the input field with the label wait time between animation in/out, type the number 1. This will put one second dead time between the two sequences, so one doesn't go right into the other:

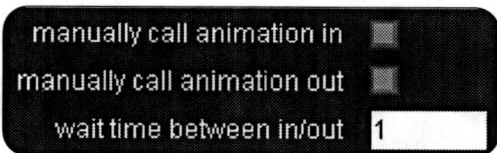

15. Now we can click on the Export button at the top right of the interface to send all of the necessary code back to the component in the authoring environment. A small window should pop up to let you know it is successful, at which point you can close the interface:

16. Finally, test your movie (CTRL/COMMAND+ENTER) and watch your animation – it's that easy! And if you had any trouble along the way, just refer back to `quickStart.fla` to see how it was put it together. Then read on for some elaboration on these steps and to learn more about what's happening behind the scenes.

Creating a TextFormat

In order to recreate each letter in a text field, we need to make sure Flash can access all of the formatting information of that text field. This is most easily accomplished by supplying a TextFormat instance for the component to use. There are two ways you can create this instance – the first is to create a TextFormat instance with ActionScript in the Actions panel. If you choose this option, then you must make sure that the instance is made a part of the `_global` identifier, which allows it to be accessed from anywhere in your movie. The following lines demonstrate the necessary code (you could place this code anywhere in your movie since it uses `_global`, but the best place is probably the first frame of the main timeline):

```
_global.animationFormat = new TextFormat();
animationFormat.font = "Arial";
animationFormat.size = 44;
animationFormat.color = 0xFF00FF;
```

You can find an example of using code to define the TextFormat in the file `quickStart_code.fla`.

After creating the TextFormat instance (on the first line above), you would then add whatever properties you needed to create your desired format. In actuality, you are only *required* to provide a value for the font property, as the font will need to be embedded for the animation to work. The easiest way to list a font name is to use the font's actual name (as you would find it in the Property inspector when the Text tool is active), as opposed to creating a font symbol in your Library and exporting it with a unique identifier. Either method will work, but I usually favor the former technique.

The only other factor to consider is that this TextFormat instance *must* be declared before the component is initialized and the animation is run. All this requires is that you place the above lines of code in a frame *before* the component appears in the timeline. If you create the format in the same frame as the component, the component will try to reference the format before the format has been created, effectively breaking the animation. Again, open the file `quickStart_code.fla` to see how I have set up the frames and layers for this method to work:

The second, and easier, option for creating a TextFormat instance is the option we chose for our first example (see `quickStart.fla`) – using the TextFormat_component that is also provided with the PuppetStrings component set. This is a simple component that you can drop into any movie to easily set

269

up a new TextFormat instance. The interface for the component is the standard drop-down list in the Property inspector (or a full list in the Component Parameters panel). Each TextFormat property is listed in this interface, as well as an additional property for the name of the TextFormat. The instance is automatically attached to the `_global` identifier.

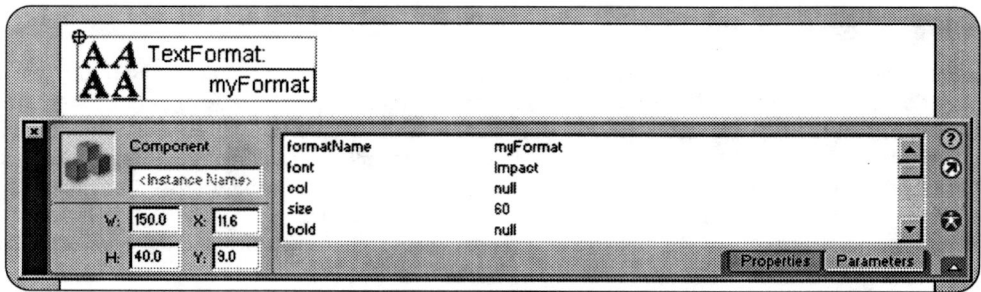

To use this component, drop it into your movie on a layer *below* whatever layer your PuppetStrings:transitions component is sitting on. This is important because, by default, a Flash movie is loaded into the player from the bottom layer up to the top layer. By placing the TextFormat_component in a layer below the PuppetStrings component, you allow for the TextFormat to be initialized before the PuppetStrings looks for it (of course, you could always reverse this loading order in your Flash movie's publish settings – File > Publish Settings...).

Once the TextFormat_component is in your movie, give it a formatName – this refers to the name of the TextFormat it creates, not of the component itself – as well as values for whatever properties you wish for your format (remembering that a value for the font property is always required). Any property you leave as `null` will not be included in your format. Don't worry about where (at which coordinates) you place the component, as it will be invisible when you publish the movie. Once you assign a name to the format, the Live Preview will update to show you the instance name. This is the way I created the TextFormat in `quickStart.fla`, so look there for a demonstration.

Creating a TextField

After a format is created, you need to create a text field instance on the stage. It is from this instance that the PuppetStrings component will get the text string and positioning on stage. Using the Text tool from the toolbox, create a dynamic or input text field and place it where you would like it on the stage, giving it a unique instance name. Make sure that you use the same values that you supplied to the TextFormat instance to manually format the text field (font, size, color, and so on).

270

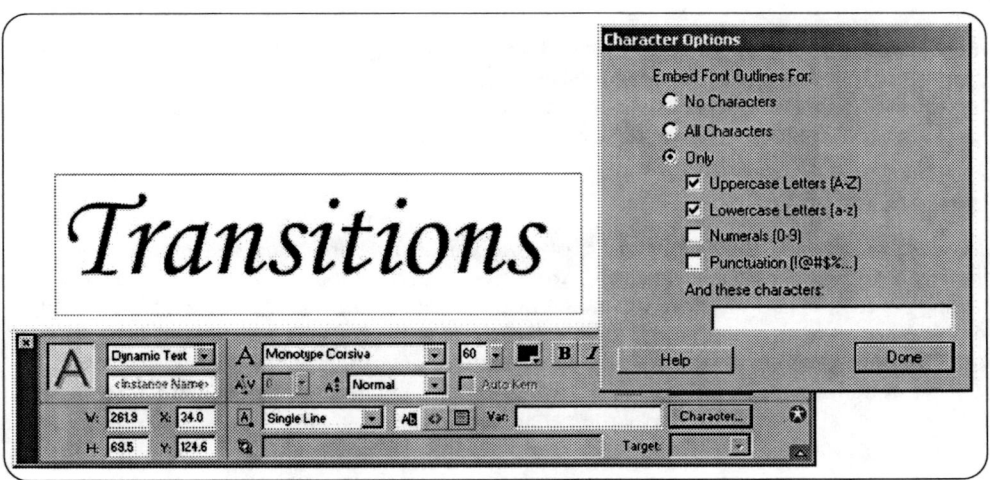

Finally, with the text field selected, click on the Character... button in the property palette and embed whatever characters you need to animate (for instance, if you are only using lowercase letters, just embed those instead of the entire font). This is one reason why embedding a font in this way is preferable to exporting a font from your Library, which automatically embeds the entirety of the font. Also, by embedding it in an actual text field on the stage, you can choose in which frame the font is loaded into the player.

Adding the component

This is by far the easiest step of all (amidst a number of easy steps!). Simply drop the PuppetStrings:transitions component onto the stage from the Components panel or from your movie's own Library if you have already used the component in your movie.

Place the component instance anywhere on the stage that is convenient. It is made invisible when published, so don't worry about it conflicting with your graphics. I usually place mine in a single column off the left side of the stage:

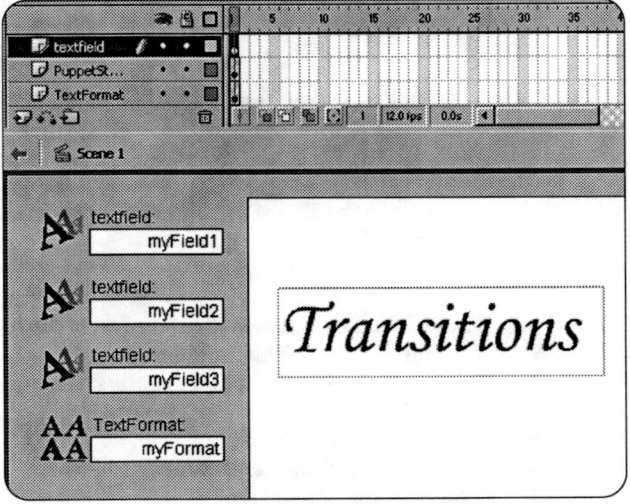

The only important thing to consider is which layer you place the instance on, as it needs to be loaded *after* your TextFormat instance has been declared (see the section on *Creating a TextFormat*, above). Placing your transitions component on a layer above your TextFormat_component is perfect. Again, refer to `quickStart.fla` for an example of the proper layer structure.

The custom UI

This is where we set up all the characteristics of our textual animations. With the PuppetStrings:transitions component selected, access the custom UI from the Property inspector. A new window will open up containing the custom user interface (at times it might be rather small, so just resize it as you need). There are no hidden menus or panels inside the interface, so at a quick glance you can see all of the available options. There is, however, a separate tab for setting the 'animation out' sequence, but it contains the exact same options as the 'animation in' screen. Look at the illustration below and the following bullet list for reference as we step through all the parameters in the interface:

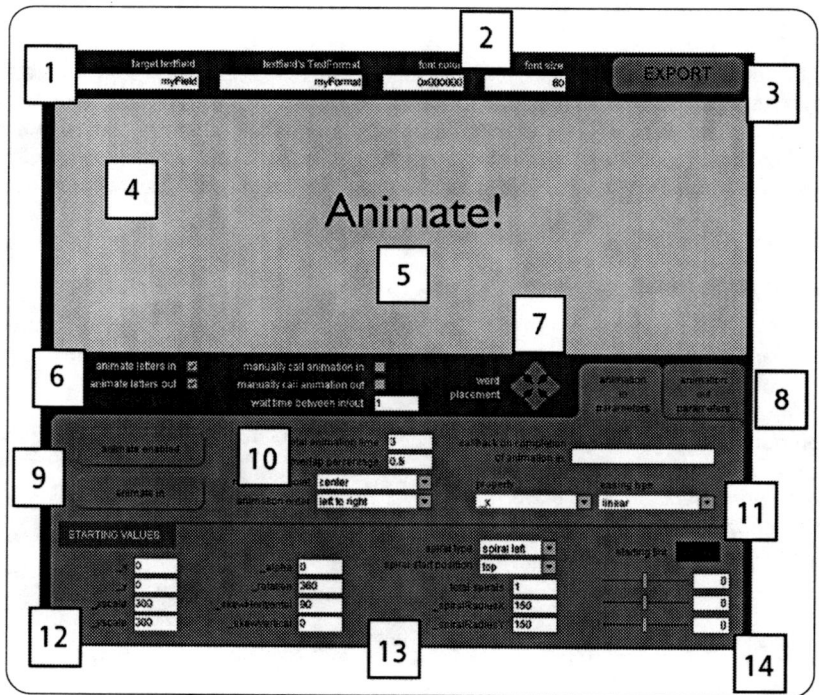

1. **TextField and TextFormat reference in authoring environment**
2. **Text formatting within custom UI**
3. **Export animation back to authoring environment**
4. **Animation window**
5. **Sample text to animate**
6. **General animation parameters**
7. **Translate text placement**

8. **Tab between animation in and animation out sequences**
9. **Animate current configuration**
10. **Sequence-specific animation parameters**
11. **Property-easing ComboBoxes**
12. **Standard animation properties**
13. **Special animation properties**
14. **Tint to animate**

TextField and TextFormat reference in authoring environment
Place the instance names for both your TextField to animate and its TextFormat within these input boxes.

Text formatting within custom UI
Specify the color and size for the animated text *inside the custom interface*. These do not affect the text you created in the authoring environment, but are provided for you to make the size and color of the sample text consistent with that in the authoring environment. This is necessary in order to give you accurate feedback as you sample your animations.

Export animation back to authoring environment
Once you have created your desired animation sequence, pressing this button sends all necessary information back to the component in the authoring environment. The component is *not* updated automatically, but only when this button is pressed (there is a lot of information to pass back and forth, so it is only done as and when necessary). Pressing the button should open a pop - up window to let you know the process of exporting is completed.

Animation window
This area displays the animation of the sample text.

Sample text to animate
This sample text field is used to show your current animation. It is actually an input text field, so you may enter whatever text you will actually be animating in your movie. If you know the specific text, it is recommended that you type it into the field, as the animation rate depends on the number of letters in the text field.

General animation parameters
These options allow you to set how an animation is run when the movie is published. To enable the animation in sequence and/or the animation out sequence, use the animate letters in/out CheckBoxes on the left. If you wish to call the animation sequences using code (for example, with an onMouseDown event) instead of having them run automatically, use the manually call animation in/out CheckBoxes. Finally, to specify a wait time in seconds between the animation in and animation out sequences (only if the animation out sequence is set to automatically play), place a value other than 0 into the wait time between in/out input box.

Let's take a quick look at an example of a practical application of these options. Perhaps you want to have the 'animation in' sequence play upon the component's initialization, but you want the 'animation out' sequence to occur only after the user has clicked the mouse. This might be the case when a page loads (and the animation in automatically plays), then remains static until the user clicks on another option, at which point the animation out sequence would play. To do this, you would deselect the manually call

273

animation in option and select manually call animation out. Then the only code necessary within your actual movie would be as follows:

```
this.onMouseDown = function() {
    titleAnimation.animateLettersOut();
};
```

Obviously this code depends on the name of the component instance – in this case I have named it `titleAnimation`. The animation out sequence would wait for this command before playing. You can see an example of this nature in `practicalPS.fla` – this file demonstrates how you might use the callback commands to enable more complex animations. Also, in `twoTextfields.fla` we demonstrate how two separate text fields can be animated using the callback functions, making it look as if a single text field has multiple animations assigned to it. For more information on what ActionScript commands are available for use with this component, refer to the *code interface* section later in this chapter.

Translate text placement

These arrows move the sample text field about the animation window in order for you to place it to better see your animation. Moving the sample text does not affect the placement of the text field in the authoring environment. You might want to move the sample text field if the actual text field in the authoring environment is placed at the bottom of the stage, and perhaps animates down from the top of the stage. Repositioning the sample text to a similar location in the UI will give you a better preview of the animation.

Tab between animation in and animation out sequences

You can set up two different animation sequences from within the custom UI: the **animation in** sequence will *end* with the text field at its set location on the stage, while the **animation out** sequence will begin with the text field at its set location on the stage. Use these tabs to toggle back and forth between the two sequences in order to set the values for the properties.

Animate current configuration

These buttons animate the sample text field within the animation window so that you can see how your current configuration will look. The animate enabled button will animate both the animation in and animation out sequences in the UI (if they are enabled, regardless of whether you have selected to manually call the animation in the authoring environment). The animate in/out buttons will animate the sequence for whatever parameters tab you currently have active (in or out).

Sequence-specific animation parameters

These parameters offer a number of options for both the animation in and animation out sequences (whichever is active):

- total animation time is the time in seconds for the active sequence.
- letter overlap percentage controls how soon a letter will begin to animate after the previous letter has begun to animate (a value of 0 will cause no overlap to occur, animating each letter at the same time, while a value of 1 will cause a letter to wait to animate until the previous letter has completed its animation).
- registration point allows you to set one of nine registration points for the letters in the string. Altering this value will be most evident when using scaling, skewing and rotation.

- animation order can be used to set the order for the letter animation to be left to right, right to left, or random.
- callback on completion of animation in/out input can be used if you would like a function to run upon the completion of an animated sequence – you'd simply place the name of the function into the box. You might utilize this to load a new page as soon as an animation sequence is completed, or perhaps start another animation sequence as soon as one has completed.

For a demonstration on how to use these features, check the `twotextfields.fla` and `practicalPS.fla` examples from this chapter's download directory. The *code interface* section, on the next page, covers incorporating callback functions with your text animations.

Property-easing ComboBoxes
These two ComboBoxes are used to change the easing type for the animation of each property in the sequences (each property can have a different easing, and each sequence is independent of the other). Use the ComboBox on the left first to specify which property you wish to set, and then use the ComboBox on the right to set its easing type (provided by Robert Penner's easing equations, available at www.robertpenner.com). The number of properties you can animate in combination with the number of easing equations gives you a myriad of effects to discover.

Standard animation properties
These fields show the values for the standard properties of a text field. By changing the values from their set positions, you create the animations. For instance, while in the animation in parameters tab, changing the _xscale and _yscale to 200 will cause the letters to scale from 200 to 100 during the animation in sequence. Similarly, setting the _alpha to 0 here will give you a fade up.

Special animation properties
Additional properties have been provided to give you more control over your animations. Lifaros (www.actionscript.cl) has created an extremely useful skewing function that enables the horizontal and vertical skewing of the letters here through the _skewHorizontal and _skewVertical properties (by the way, be sure to check out the image modulation components that Lifaros has created for this book – see Component 17). Alter these properties to create some great pseudo-3D effects:

Open up `PS_3D.fla` to see an example of this type of textual animation.

In addition, you can add spiral movement to the letters by changing a few properties – spiral type can be set to `spiral right` (clockwise), `spiral left` (counterclockwise), and `none` (but you must choose something other than `none` to enable any of the other spiral properties). You can then alter the spiral's starting position when animating in (you can as well for the animation out sequence, but since the two radii start at 0, you won't see any difference). This position can be at the `top`, `right`, `left`, or `bottom` of the spiral. Finally, you can change the maximum radius on both the x and y axes – keeping these equal will give a relatively circular spiral.

Note that each of the skewing and spiral properties can be assigned a separate easing equation as well, offering a large number of combinations and effects. The right angle of the letters in the file `practicalPS.fla` is accomplished by altering the easing functions for both the _x and _y properties.

Tint to animate

Finally, you can alter the tint of the letters at the start (for the animation in) or the end (for the animation out) of the sequence. These are *not* the RGB values for the letters, but correspond instead to the RB, BB, and GB properties when using the `setTransform()` color method, or the advanced options in the color effects. Because of this, the set color of your TextFormat directly affects how the tinting works (for instance, a red letter tinted with 255 blue will give you a purple letter). This is the reason why the font color text field is provided at the top of the interface so you may see how the tinting will act. Use either the color sliders or the corresponding input boxes to change a color value. The swatch above the sliders will update with the new tint.

The code interface

Because so much of the component is set up through the custom UI, there isn't much call to communicate with it through code. There are a few useful methods, though, and the component may be used to call user-defined functions upon the completion of the animation sequences.

Public methods

There are actually only three public methods for this component (discounting `init()`, which you may call when attaching the component to reinitialize it – more on that in the *Attaching the component* section below), and none of them takes any parameters:

- `animateLettersIn()` and `animateLettersOut()` are used to call their respective animation sequences. If, while in the interface, you have selected to manually call the animation, then you would use these commands to do so. You may also use these methods to run the animation multiple times (you do not need to specify anything from within the interface to enable this).

- `removeLetters()` removes the animated letters and returns your original text field to the stage. The component works by creating a number of single letter text fields inside nested movie clips. Your original text field is made invisible after its information is extracted. To remove these animated letters so you may once more access and affect your text field (perhaps to change the text or to allow the user to input text into it), use this method.

Callback functions

As mentioned earlier, you can specify a function to be called when an animated sequence is completed. There are input boxes in both sequence tabs of the custom UI called callback on completion of animation in/out where you can place the name of the function to be called (just the name, not the following parentheses). This can be after the animation in, animation out, or both (you can call separate functions upon the completion of each sequence). Then, in order for the function to be called, you need to make it a method of the component itself. For instance, if you entered the string `traceCompletion` in the callback box for the animation-in sequence, after you exited the interface you would first make sure you have named the component instance (in this example `letterAnimation`), then you would place the following code in your ActionScript editor:

```
letterAnimation.traceCompletion = function() {
    trace("Animation-in is complete!");
};
```

When the animation in sequence is completed, this function will be called and your Output window will open with the message "Animation-in is complete!". Simple!

Attaching the component

One of the reasons for the extensive custom UI of this component is that there are an awful lot of variables to set up in order to run an animation. Because of this, attaching the component to the stage dynamically at runtime through code isn't the easiest option. It's certainly possible, but you are forced to provide the newly attached component with what can steadily become a large number of properties. For instance, the following code creates a simple fade up of each letter over three seconds, with a 50% overlap for each letter. We've also added some scaling, rotation, and easing for the rotation, which adds even more lines:

```
// temporary object to hold properties
props = {};
// seconds for animation in
props.totalTime_in = 3;
// overlap % of each letter
props.overlap_in = .5;
// sets center registration point for each letter
props.registrationPoint_in = "center";
// initial _alpha of letters
props.startAlpha_in = 0;
// initial _xscale
props.startScaleX_in = 300;
// initial _yscale
props.startScaleY_in = 300;
// 360 degree rotation
props.startRotation_in = 360;
// sets an easing function for the rotation property
props.easingType_rotation_in = "easeInOutCirc";
// textfield to animate
props.targetField = "tf";
```

277

```
// TextFormat object
props.appliedTextFormat = "myFormat";
// enables animation-in sequence
props.animateIn = 1;
// attaches component and passes props object
this.attachMovie("PuppetStrings:Transitions", "transition", 0, props);
// removes temp object
delete props;
```

You can also see a demonstration of this code in the file codeInterface.fla. Notice that in this example, we add all the necessary properties to a custom object, which is then passed as an initObject (the fourth optional parameter) to the component in the attachMovie() method. You could also do the same in reverse, and then simply reinitialize the component:

```
this.attachMovie("PuppetStrings:Transitions", "transition", 0);
transition.totalTime_in = 3;
transition.overlap_in = .5;
transition.startAlpha_in = 0;
transition.startScaleX_in = 300;
transition.startScaleY_in = 300;
transition.targetField = "tf";
transition.appliedTextFormat = "myFormat";
transition.animateIn = 1;
// reinitializes to begin animation
transition.init();
```

As I said, this is probably not the best way to utilize the component, but it is possible. For a full list of all the properties you can access, refer to the file PuppetStrings_properties.html, included in the download – there are almost 70 listed here, with brief descriptions of their function and what data needs to be passed.

Taking it further

Because of the nature of the component (and the fact that I tried to add everything I could think of at the time!), it's not one that you might immediately think of extending. That said, here are a few ideas that I've considered for future versions, and that you might consider incorporating:

- Allowing the user to set separate animations for each letter.
- A randomizing feature (if the previous suggestion has been implemented).
- An additional ComboBox in the custom UI in which you could include preset effects.
- The ability to make multiple animations in a single sequence (for instance, move letters into a certain position, then fade out).
- Incorporate some getter/setter methods for the animation properties.

Flash was initially offered as an animation tool and, although it has since developed into an impressive web application tool, it still offers fantastic simplicity for the creation of motion graphics. In fact, some of the functionality that has been added ostensibly for websites and web applications (the creation and manipulation of dynamic text fields, and the addition of components) is just as useful when utilized for animation, as this component demonstrates.

The benefit of using such a component, as opposed to making frame-by-frame animations, or perhaps a third-party tool, should be evident after reading this chapter. There are, of course, a multitude of other applications. For instance, you could consider adding an animation for the title of a page in a dynamic slideshow – you'd simply reuse the same component for each title and just change which text field it is looking at, thus allowing consistency across the slideshow without having to animate each title separately. Consider a greeting to users visiting your website that uses a name stored in a local cookie, but keeps the animation consistent for each (perhaps to synch with a soundtrack). Consider a dynamic calendar that you update via an XML file – if you would like the date to animate in, wouldn't it be great not having to animate each day of the year?

These are just a couple of the ideas that I'm currently playing around with! Hopefully you'll find some interesting and original uses for this component – and I encourage you to take a look at its companion PuppetStrings components, available from www.27bobs.com. Sometimes developing in Flash is too much fun to be considered work!

Peter Elst

Born and raised in Keerbergen, Belgium I spent a significant portion of my early childhood copying pages and pages of code from computer magazines on the family Apple IIGS computer. With a bit of luck I managed to reproduce some blinking text, annoying sirens and other useful gadgets. As time went by I learned HTML and JavaScript and got the opportunity to help develop several large portal sites and work on a Flash advertising project. These experiences fuelled my interest in content management systems and multimedia development which are now my main areas of expertise. Together with my arty sister we founded Art Fundum, a company specialising in web development and multimedia applications, from which I recently resigned as business partner to pursue other interests.

To read more about me, hire me or download my latest Flash MX components you can visit: http://www.peterelst.com

Dedicated to my parents, and brother and sister for their never-ending support, and to my grandfather who recently passed away.

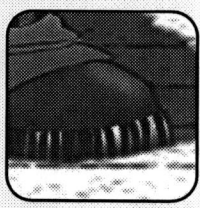

Component 21

StringThing

The StringThing component allows you to easily manage dynamic textfields. Using placeholder tags inside the text field it inserts the corresponding values taken from an external data source. It also has a very useful in-built auto-update functionality that checks the external datasource for changes and updates the text field if needed.

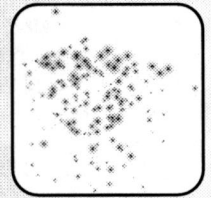

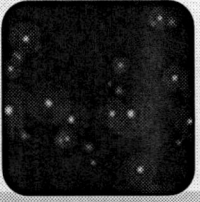

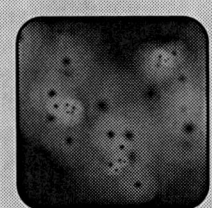

Have you ever had one of those days where nothing seemed to work right? No? Then you must be an incredibly lucky person! I seem to get such days on a regular basis (probably due to some karmic imbalance, I'm sure!), and on one of them I needed to solve a bug for a client. After some time, someone asked me what I thought was actually causing the bug in question, so I answered him frankly, "It's just one of those string things!" With a bewildered glare in his eyes and an unconvincing, "Oh yes, I see..." he shuffled off, and I returned to pulling my hair out.

That was the fateful day that I thought up the idea for the StringThing component. What if you could use some kind of tags as placeholders in a text field and have those tags replaced by values from an external data source? If I could get that to work, I'd never again have to worry about writing any code to fill in my text fields. This would also imply that I could just type everything inside a text field and use a tag wherever I want the value to come from a data source. Sounds pretty cool, huh!

Wait, it gets even better... why not have the component check if the values in the external data source have changed and, if that is the case, update the text automatically? I felt liberated at just the thought that I could soon do all these things without having to spend half an hour writing the code.

Lack of inspiration for a more descriptive name, and good old nostalgia made me keep StringThing as the name for this component and in the next few pages I'll give you some insight into how to utilize this component and implement it in your Flash projects.

What, how, when, and why?

So what exactly is the StringThing component? How, when, and why the heck should I use it? I can imagine these are some of the questions you're asking yourself at this moment! The basic concept of the component is quite simple – it manages dynamic text fields and provides a single, easy to use interface for loading and updating data from an external file. This allows you to effectively separate the content in your Flash project from its code and play around with it without constantly having to edit the ActionScript.

A typical situation where you would use the StringThing component is for text fields that contain both static and dynamic content. In my opinion, it's very useful in this scenario, especially when working as a team, and it can help simplify your project's workflow tremendously.

An example of what I often see happening when working in a team is that designers don't have a lot of technical background with ActionScript. After the design process has finished and the project is passed on to the technical team, they get to hear something like, "Oh yeah, that line of text in the text field needed to come from a database." Most likely some grunting and moaning noises will be heard in the background because what they then need to do is remove the text from that text field, split it up into parts where some dynamic data needs to come in-between, write the code that loads the data, check if it has loaded correctly, concatenate the static and dynamic strings together, and have that displayed in the dynamic text field. Phew!

Using the StringThing component you can make it much easier. Just tell the designers to write whatever text they want in the text field and use a placeholder tag wherever they want a value to be dynamic and come from a data source. The only thing that's left to do for the technical team is to look at what tags have been used in the text field, write a script that outputs the variables accordingly and hook up a StringThing component to that text field.

Out with the old, in with the new

For some of you who may not be familiar with loading external data into a text field this may all sound rather confusing, but it really doesn't have to be. Below I'll give two examples of how you would go about loading an external data source into a text field, the first one using the 'traditional' method, and the other one using the StringThing component. You'll find these examples within the `Basics` folder in the download, along with the code for all the other examples featured in this chapter.

Traditional method of loading external data into a dynamic text field

First of all you'll need to start with your external data source – this is typically a plain text file that consists of name/value pairs. Make sure you always keep this data source in the same directory as your Flash movie. Here's what our example file, `myData.txt`, looks like:

```
&title=Flash MX Components Most Wanted&review=Very good book! A
must-read for every Flash designer and developer.
```

Notice that that every variable name in the text field starts with an ampersand sign (`&`); this is needed so that Flash recognizes that you've just started a new name/value pair.

You would load this text into Flash MX as follows: first, draw a text field on the stage of your Flash movie and give it the instance name `myTextField`. Then, add the following ActionScript to the first frame of your main timeline:

```
loadText = new LoadVars();
loadText.load("myData.txt");
loadText.onLoad = function() {
      _root.myTextField.text += "Friends of ED book reviews!\n\n";
      _root.myTextField.text += this.title+"\n\n";
      _root.myTextField.text += this.review+"\n\";
      _root.myTextField.text += "Stay tuned for more reviews in the
next ➥couple of days!";
};
```

If you test this movie (`classic_method.fla`), you'll see that our text field is filled with both the static text we defined in the ActionScript and the `title` and `review` variables that are taken from the external data source (`myData.txt`).

The example above is not very difficult to understand for users with some ActionScript experience, but using the StringThing component you can make it *much* easier. The next example will show you how to do exactly the same thing as we did here, but without writing even a single line of code!

Using the StringThing component to load external data into a dynamic text field

We'll use the same external data source as we did in the last example (`myData.txt`), and again we'll draw a dynamic text field on the stage of our Flash movie and give it the instance name `myTextField`. The next thing we do is just type the following text inside the text field – noting the use of the **placeholder tags** (curly brackets) in {title} and {review}:

```
Friends of ED book reviews!

{title}

{review}

Stay tuned for more reviews in the next
couple of days!
```

Now we've got that ready, we just drag an instance of the StringThing component onto the text field (it will snap to the edge), set its Target textfield parameter to `myTextField`, and add `myData.txt` as a value for the Datasource. We'll go into more detail about modifying the other component parameters a bit later on in this chapter, so for now just leave them as they are.

If you now test this Flash movie (`stringthing_method.fla`) you should see that the placeholder tags are replaced by the corresponding values in the external data source, leaving the rest of the text in the text field intact:

```
Friends of ED book reviews!

Flash MX Components Most Wanted

Very good book! A must-read for every
Flash designer and developer.

Stay tuned for more reviews in the next
couple of days!
```

Using StringThing

Before you can use the component, the first thing you'll need to do is install it. This is not very difficult at all – on the CD-ROM that accompanies this book you'll find the file `StringThing.mxp` in this chapter's source code folder. If you have the Macromedia Extension Manager installed (see the Introduction to this book for more details), you can just double-click `StringThing.mxp` to install it. StringThing will then automatically appear in the Components panel of Flash MX the next time you run it.

Using the component is really quite easy, as you might have gathered from the previous example. You start off by drawing a text field on the stage, setting it to `dynamic text`, and giving it an instance name. The next thing you do is open the Components panel and drag an instance of the StringThing on top of your text field. You can then type your text inside the text field and wherever you want the text to come from a data source you simply use placeholder tags. For more details on using these placeholder tags, take a look at the *Datasource* and *Start tag and End tag* sections below.

Setting the component parameters

Now let's take a closer look at the component parameters. Most of these parameters have a default value that you can of course change, through the Property inspector, to best suit your needs:

Target textfield

This parameter refers to the instance name of the dynamic text field that you are assigning the StringThing component to. When you drag the component on top of a text field it will automaticly snap to the edge of that text field and set the Target textfield parameter to the instance name of the text field it is attached to.

If you change the instance name of your text field, make sure that you go back to the component parameters for the StringThing component and change the Target textfield parameter there as well to have it assigned to the correct text field.

Datasource

Datasource is the parameter that refers to the external data source you are using. This data source can be a plain text file or a server-side script (PHP, ASP, JSP, ColdFusion, and so on).

The thing you need to watch out for it that the data source file outputs in a name/value pair format. The delimiter for using multiple variables is the ampersand sign (&), and the equal sign (=) is used to assign a value to the variable. A typical data source would look something like this:

```
&variable1=value1&variable2=value2
```

In this example we have two variables: variable1 with value value1 and variable2 with value value2.

To get access to these variables inside the text field you need to make use of placeholder tags. When using these tags you must make sure that you are using exactly the same variable name as the one you used in the data source (note that it's case-sensitive). By default the start and end tag characters are set to { and }, thus when we would want to reference to variable1 of the example data source above, the placeholder tag would be {variable1}, or {variable2} to reference to the value of variable2 in the data source.

Start tag and End tag

The Start tag and End tag parameters are used to determine how a placeholder tag should look. These tags can consist of one or more characters. Make sure when setting these parameters that you don't use common characters that you might use inside your text field (for example, comma, exclamation mark, and so on), this could cause a piece of text to be mistaken for a placeholder tag, which would then cause the text field to be displayed incorrectly.

When enabling HTML for your dynamic text field, be sure not to use < and > as your start and end tags. The obvious reason for this is that Flash will mistake these placeholders for HTML tags and not retrieve the value properly.

Auto update

Auto update is a parameter with a Boolean (`true`/`false`) value. When you set the parameter to `true` the StringThing component will automatically check the data source at an interval specified in the Refresh rate parameter (see below). If any changes have occurred in the data source, the target text field will automatically be updated.

This behavior is very useful in situations where you would like to see the live status of a particular variable:;for instance, the number of visitors that are currently on your site, the number of items that are left in stock of a particular item, and so on.

If you don't expect the data in the data source to change very often, or you don't need the data to be dynamically updated in your Flash movie, you are better off setting this parameter to `false`.

Refresh rate

The Refresh rate parameter is only applicable if the Auto update parameter is set to `true`. This parameter lets you determine the interval (in seconds) at which the component checks the data source for changes.

When setting this value you need to take a few things into consideration. While it can be tempting to set the Refresh rate very low (that is, to have it frequently checking for changes to the data source), this is not always a good thing to do. For online projects you need to take into consideration the amount of data you need to load into Flash and your visitor's connection speed. Likewise, if you set the Refresh rate too low and the data source has not finished loading when it is triggered again to check for updates, it will not function properly. If this is the case no updates will appear, even though the data source may have changed.

We've now covered the basics of how to use the StringThing and setting its component parameters. For another simple example of using this component, take a look at `simpleStringThing.fla`, which you'll find in the `SimpleExample` sample files folder. This time our data source is a text file called `componentData.txt` – examine how the component parameters have been set up, and test the movie to see the result:

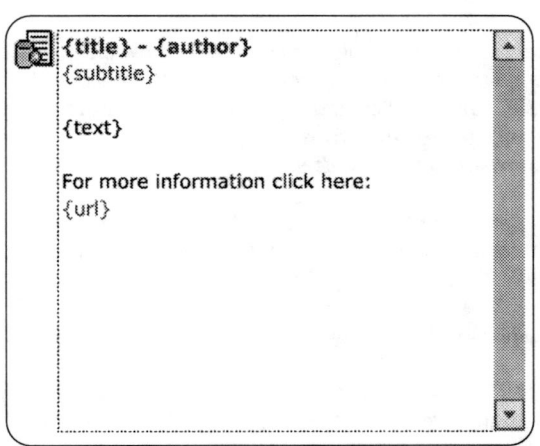
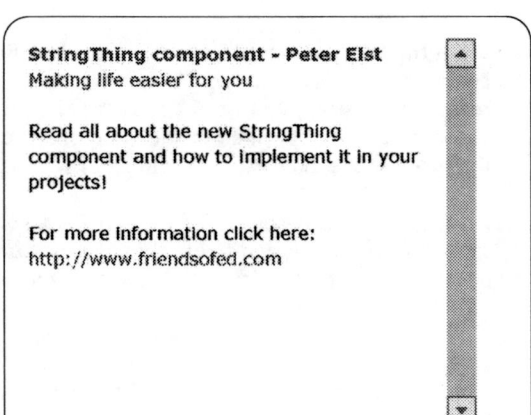

You've now pretty much mastered the basics of the StringThing component, so in the next few sections we'll look at some slightly more advanced examples, and how the StringThing can be useful in 'real world' situations.

StringThing in the real world

In the following case studies, we'll give a brief description of a realistic design scenario, followed by an outline of a practical solution using the StringThing component.

E-commerce application: online book sales

An online bookstore wants to promote and sell certain books in a short timeframe.

Solution

Start off by drawing a text field on the stage, setting it to `dynamic text`, and dragging an instance of the StringThing component on top (see `Booksale\booksale.fla`):

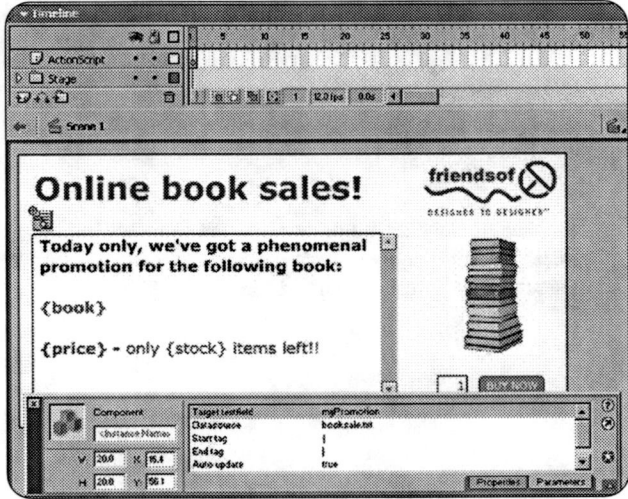

Write the text you want to appear in the text field and put placeholder tags where you want the text to come from the data source. These placeholder tags were covered a bit earlier on in the chapter, but to recap they basically consist of a start tag, the variable name, and an end tag (in that order). Both the start and end tags are specified in the component parameters for the StringThing, and the variable name is that used in the external data source, of which you want to retrieve its value.

Next, specify a Datasource for the text field. For a project like this one, it would most likely be a server-side script (ASP, PHP, and so on) that connects to a database and outputs the variables you want to import into Flash. The output from such a script would look something like this:

```
&book=Flash MX Most Wanted Components&price=$39.99&stock=10
```

Now set the Auto update parameter to `true` and the Refresh rate for the component to 30 seconds. And that's about it! In 5 minutes (or less) we've created an advertisement for an online bookstore, which is connected to an external data source and updates itself automatically:

Note that for this demonstration we're just using a local text file as our data source, but more advanced readers can add database connectivity to this example by playing around with the PHP script that I've provided in the download, in the `AdvancedBonus\Booksale` folder.

Multilingual content

A website wants to display articles in multiple languages, without having to create multiple versions.

Solution

As always, start off by drawing a text field on the stage, setting it to `dynamic text`, and giving it the instance name `myStringThing`. Then, drag 'n' drop a StringThing component on top of the text field (see `Multilingual\multilingual.fla`):

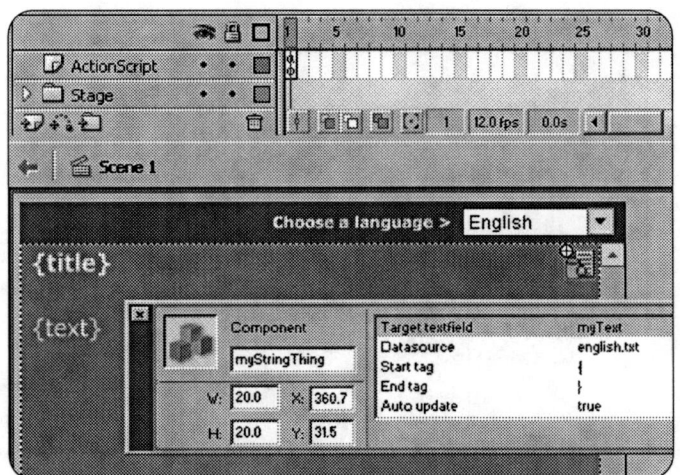

Next put a {title} tag and a {text} tag in the text field, and set the data source for the StringThing component to english.txt, which is the default language for this site (make sure you put all your text files in the same directory as your FLA for it to work).

To be able to change the language of our site, we'll drag a ComboBox component onto the stage and give it the instance name myLanguages. Next we set the labels to English, Français, and Deutsch, and the respective data values to english.txt, français.txt, and deutsch.txt. The ChangeHandler should point to the function setLanguage, which is defined on the root timeline and looks like this:

```
function setLanguage() {
    myStringThing.setDatasource(myLanguages.getSelectedItem().data);
}
```

The three text files that we use are basically one and the same file – they all have just two variables, title and text, and the only difference lies in the value we give those variables. Each text file assigns a different value to the variables for them to display the text in that respective language.

When using multiple languages in your Flash projects you might well come across some special characters. To have Flash display these special characters correctly you should add the following ActionScript statement on the first frame of your main timeline:

```
System.useCodePage = true;
```

Unless your external text file is Unicode encoded, you should always set this to true. This tells Flash to use the code page that is installed on your visitor's computer.

That's all that you'll have to do to create a multilingual application! The default language is set to English and if the ComboBox selection changes, the setLanguage() function is called. This changes the data source for the component, and the text field is then automatically updated:

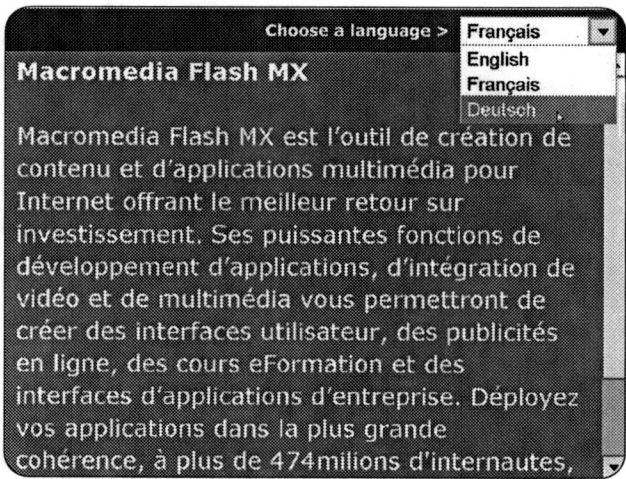

Personalizing your content

A supplier of digital images wants to add some personalization features to their site. Members to this site need to log in and then be presented with information taken from a database.

Solution

This is another situation in which the StringThing component can come in very handy. We want to get certain information from our database for a particular member that has just logged in, and display it in our text field (see Personalization\personalization.fla).

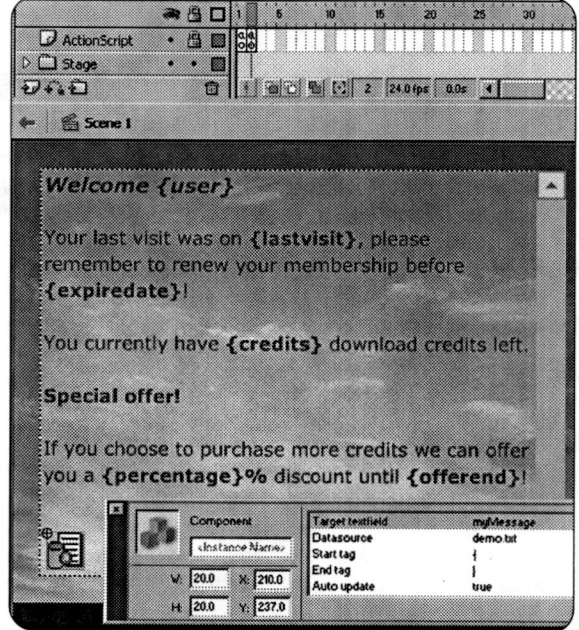

On the first frame of this Flash project we have a screen that prompts members to log in using their username and password. This frame also contains the following ActionScript:

```
stop();
loggedIn = false;
function login() {
    if(username.text == "demo" && password.text == "demo") {
        loggedIn = true;
        gotoAndStop(2);
    }
}
```

For demonstration purposes, I've hard-coded both the username and password as demo, but in a real world scenario the username and password would be sent to a server-side script, which would then query the database and send the results back to Flash (in the name/value pair format that you're no doubt familiar with by now). So the login() function checks if the username and password are demo and, if so, the variable loggedIn is set to true, and Flash is told to go to the next frame.

On this second frame we've got the following code:

```
stop();
if (loggedIn == false) {
    gotoAndStop(1);
}
```

This makes sure that the loggedIn variable is set to true, otherwise it goes back to frame 1 (this is very important to disable visitors from using the forward option in the right-click Flash menu, and thus being able to see the site without the need to log in).

If we look at the stage of personalization.fla on frame 2 of our Flash movie, as shown above, we can see it contains a text field that has an instance of the StringThing component attached to it. Again, for demonstration purposes the data source for the component is set to demo.txt, but in a robust real world example this would most likely be a server-side script that outputs the variables for us. Inside the dynamic text field some text has been entered, as well as several placeholder tags.

Note that the data we are loading into this text field does not need to be actively updated so we set the Auto update parameter to false. If you test the movie, you'll see that we've got a nicely implemented StringThing component in this membership-based site:

The scope of this chapter does not allow me to go deeper into this subject, but for those interested in building further on this functionality I've included a PHP script in the download in the AdvancedBonus\Personalization folder to experiment with. Also included is a modified

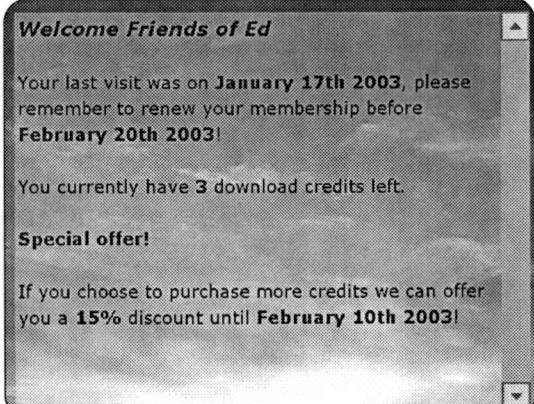

Welcome Friends of Ed

Your last visit was on **January 17th 2003**, please remember to renew your membership before **February 20th 2003**!

You currently have **3** download credits left.

Special offer!

If you choose to purchase more credits we can offer you a **15%** discount until **February 10th 2003**!

version of this example FLA. It's also probably worth your while reading the following section on *Extending the component*.

Extending the component

In this section I'll give some tips on how you can extend the StringThing component to add more functionality and mould it into a form that suits your particular projects. Don't feel discouraged if you don't understand everything here the first time around as it's mainly aimed at developers with an intermediate-to-advanced knowledge of ActionScript. If you want to see exactly how the component's code fits together, select the Edit... option of the component in the Library, and check out the ActionScript on frame 1 of the component's main timeline.

When extending the component it is useful to know what public methods are available, and what they can do for you. Accordingly, I've included an overview of these methods and a short description of their function in the following table:

Method	Description
setTextField()/getTextField()	Set/get the target text field for the component
setData source()/getData source()	Set/get the data source for the component
setText()/getText()	Set/get the text for the target text field
setHtmlText()/getHtmlText()	Set/get the HTML text for the target text field
setAutoUpdate()/getAutoUpdate()	Set/get Auto update for the component (true/false)
setRefreshRate()/getRefreshRate()	Set/get the Refresh rate (in seconds) for update checks

Adding your own functionality

Sometimes you might not want to simply get a value from an external data source, but get the *result* of a specific function. For example, you might want to have the current date or time displayed in the text field.

Adding that functionality is not very difficult, you just need to include some extra lines of code in the `replaceText()` method definition in the component's code (the suggested new lines of code are shown in bold):

```
StringThingClass.prototype.replaceText = function() {
var newText = this.oldText;
for (var i = 0; i<this.vars.length; i++) {
        var from = this.vars[i];
        var to =
➡this.textData[this.vars[i].cutEnds(this.beginChar.length,
➡this.endChar.length)];
        var result = eval(to);
        if(typeof(result) == "function") {
```

```
                    to = result();
            }
        newText = newText.replace(from, to);
    }
    if(this.targetText.html) {
        this.targetText.htmlText = newText;
    } else {
        this.targetText.text = newText;
    }
    if (!this.intervalID && this.refresh) {
        this.intervalID = setInterval(this, "update",
this.refreshrate);
    }
};
```

What these few extra lines of code do is the following:

- Evaluate the variable data that is loaded into Flash
- Check if that evaluated data is a function
- If it is a function, run it and use the return value in the text field

Let's say you have the following function on your main timeline (see also
Extending\RunningFunctions\eval.fla):

```
function getTime() {
    var today = new Date();
    return today.getHours()+":"+today.getMinutes();
}
```

The function getTime() creates a new instance of the Date object which is stored in the variable today, and we have the function return the result of the getHours() and getMinutes() methods, essentially just displaying the current hour and minute taken from your visitor's computer.

To have the result of this function displayed in the text field, set up the data source like this:

```
&time=getTime
```

If you use the {time} tag in the text field with the StringThing component and link it up to this data source, the current time will be shown.

Of course, you can do much more than simply display the date or time, you can have any function executed using this function. However, remember that the component needs a return value from the function to display in the text field, otherwise the tag in the text field will just appear empty.

Retrieving and overwriting variables

There might be some situations where you want to overwrite the data you read into Flash, or you just need an easy way to retrieve the value of a placeholder tag in the text field. To achieve this we'll need to add two getter/setter methods to the component class code – take a look at the modified component code in `setData-getData.fla`, which you'll find in the `Extending\RetrieveOverwrite` directory of the sample files:

```
176  StringThingClass.prototype.getRefreshRate = function() {
177      return this.refreshrate/1000;
178  };
179  // setData and getData methods
180  StringThingClass.prototype.getData = function(varname) {
181      return this.textData[varname];
182  }
183  StringThingClass.prototype.setData = function(varname,varvalue) {
184      this.textData[varname] = varvalue;
185      if(!this.targetText.html) {
186          this.targetText.text = this.oldText;
187      } else {
188          this.targetText.htmlText = this.oldText;
189      }
190      this.replaceText();
191  }
192
193  Object.registerClass("StringThing", StringThingClass);
194  #endinitclip
```

Line 179 of 194, Col 31

The `getData()`/`setData()` methods retrieve/overwrite the value for a specific variable that was loaded into Flash by the StringThing component. A good example of how you could use these methods is to include a reference to a photograph in the external data source and then use `getData()` to retrieve that particular value. The data source would then include something like this:

```
&photo=myPhoto.jpg
```

Below (and in `setData-getData.fla`) you can see how a function retrieves that photo variable from the StringThing component and uses it to load that particular image in a movie clip:

```
function loadPhoto() {
    myPhoto.loadMovie(myStringThing.getData("photo"));
}
```

One thing to remember with the `setData()` method is that it does not overwrite the external data source; it only overwrites the internal variable. If you've set the component's Auto update parameter to `true`, your changes will be undone when the next update event occurs.

Wrapping it up

The StringThing component is undeniably a great tool to use in a wide range of situations. At first sight you might think it's just a nice gizmo that simplifies the development process, but it is much more than that. You can have the component update your text field on the fly when your data source changes, which is indeed a very powerful and hands-free feature. This feature alone is a good enough reason to use the StringThing component in your Flash projects.

The examples presented in this chapter are just a few ideas of some of the possible situations in which StringThing could be used. Obviously, it should by no means be limited to just those scenarios. Readers with a bit of ActionScript experience can start extending the component by adding their own methods to the component class and attempt to simplify the development process even more. I'd certainly encourage everyone to get their hands dirty and start playing around with the code!

Index

The index is arranged hierarchically, in alphabetical order, with symbols preceding the letter A. Many second-level entries also occur as first-level entries. This is to ensure that you will find the information you require however you choose to search for it.

friends of ED particularly welcomes feedback on the layout and structure of this index. If you have any comments or criticisms, please contact: feedback@friendsofED.com

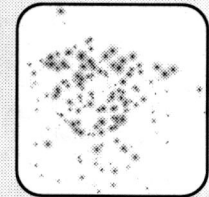

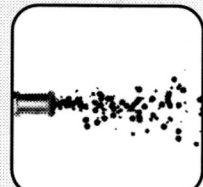
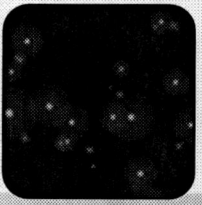

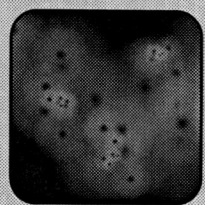

A

Advanced PHP for Flash (book) 19

B

brightness 131

C

Calliscope (tutorial) 94-98
  child movie clip 95
  component assets folder 95
  component parameters 96
  createTextField method 95
  idea movie clip 95
  parent movie clip 95
ColorPicker (tutorial) 130-140
  capturing user events 139
  color modes 130
  colorChange method 137
  ColorPickerGlobal component 132, 135
  component methods 138
  component parameters 134
  Free Transform tool 133
  get/set HSB methods 138
  getBrightness method 138
  get/set ColorScheme methods 135
  getHEX method 138
  getHue method 138
  get/setPadding methods 134
  getRed/Green/Blue methods 138
  get/setRGB methods 137
  getSaturation method 138
  hexadecimal color 130
  HSB color 130-131
  modifying component appearance 133
  onChange events 139, 140
  onClose/Open events 140
  positioning component on stage 133
  preview color swatch 132
  setChangeHandler method 136, 137, 140
createTextField method 95

D

Data Grid (tutorial) 188-193
  COLUMN element 191
  component enhancements 193
  component parameters 191-192
  HEADER element 190
  ITEM element 190
  keyboard commands 193
  LIST element 190
  scrolling Data Grid 193
  sorting Data Grid 193
  XML data source 189
Debreuil, Robin 30
DraggablePane component 44
drawing API 57, 171, 248. See also Virtual Trackball (tutorial)

E

event calendar (tutorial) 8-21
  adding events 11-12
  component parameters 9-10
  generateXML method 19
  getDisplayedMonth/Year methods 19, 20
  get/setEvent methods 14, 20
  getXMLscript method 20
  HTML formatting for events text 12
  modifying component style 13-15
  resetMonth method 20
  ScrollBar component 13
  setButtonTitles method 20
  setTextFormatting method 20
  setXMLscript method 20
  showDay/Month methods 20, 21
  storing events in XML files 16-19

F

files:
  3D_example1 - 2.fla 251, 255
  actionscript101 - 201.fla 211, 213
  ApplyTint.fla 139
  bacteria.fla 167
  BasicUse.fla 176
  booksale.fla 287
  brick_wall.jpg 59
  brute_force.fla 215
  cal1_within.swf 96
  cal2_cycle.swf 96
  cal3_abstract.swf 97
  cal4_redmoebius.swf 97
  cal5_spatial.swf 97
  cal6_Kalligram.swf 97
  calliscope.mxp 94
  changing_colors.fla 14
  classic_method.fla 283
  codeInterface.fla 278
  ColorPicker.mxp 132
  ColorPickerExample.fla 132
  componentData.txt 286
  ContainerDemoLayout.swf 175
  data.xml 190
  deutsch.txt 289
  dgrid.fla 191
  dgrid.mxp 191
  english.txt 289
  eval.fla 293
  EventCalendar.mxp 9
  events.xml 17
  event_calendar.fla 9
  explosion.fla 164
  FLiquidMatrixComp.mxp 224
  FoED-GameSelector.mxp 144
  français.txt 289
  FSkewedMatrixComp.mxp 231
  FVideoPlayer.fla 74
  FVideoPlayer_skin.fla 77
  FVid_properties.fla 77
  generatexml.php 19
  image1.jpg 84
  imported_video.fla 72
  index.html 82
  inkjet.fla 166
  InsetsExample.fla 182
  InteractiveDemo.swf 174
  LayoutManager.fla 176
  liquid_monkey_01 - 4.fla 226, 227, 228
  LoadStyle.fla 114
  ManualAdjustmentExample.fla 180
  MBW_Component_Set.mxp 44
  monnone.mxp 83
  monnone_scroller.fla 85
  multilingual.fla 288
  MultipleContainers.fla 181
  MultipleMCs.fla 139
  multiple_loaders.fla 218
  myData.txt 283
  myImages.xml 83
  newsTicker.fla 35
  newsTicker_buttons.fla 39
  palettes.fla 168
  pens.fla 171
  personalization.fla 290
  poetry.fla 169
  practicalPS.fla 275
  preloader.fla 205
  PS_3D.fla 275
  PuppetStrings.mxp 264
  PuppetStrings_properties.html 278
  quickStart.fla 264
  quickStart_code.fla 269
  rad1_base.swf 100
  rad2_variation.swf 102
  rad3_spiral.swf 102
  rad4_spiral_green.swf 102
  rad5_spiral_orange.swf 102
  rad6_spiral_greenshell2.swf 102
  rad7_spiral_purple.swf 102
  sample1 - 4.jpg 200

selector1 - 2.fla 147, 149
selector3_skin.swf 152
setData-getData.fla 294
simple.fla 198
simpleStringThing.fla 286
sketchpad.fla 59
sketchpad_sky.swf 58
skewed_money.fla 233
skewed_monkey.fla 232
skewed_redgalaxy.fla 232
slidingPanel.fla 119
slidingPanel_Examples.swf 119
snow.fla 166
StringThing.mxp 284
stringthing_method.fla 284
Style1 - 2.fla 114
TabControl.mxp 106
TabControlExample.fla 110
testClip movie clip 147
TextEditor.fla 24
textEditor.mxp 24
ToolTipSample01 - 04.fla 48,
50, 51, 52
tornado.mxp 198
trail1_simple.swf 99
trail2_stardust.swf 100
trail3_swarm.swf 100
trail4_streamer.swf 100
trail5_streamer_coil.swf 100
trail6_unruly.swf 100
trail7_metallicSpring.swf 100
trivia.swf 150
twotextfields.fla 275
video_player.mxp 74
XMLparse.fla 238
xmlStaticDemo.swf 17
*Flash MX Designer's ActionScript
Reference* (book) 85, 241
Flash UI Components Set 2 8
fonts 95
Foundation PHP for Flash (book) 19
Free Transform tool 133
FStyleFormat object. See tool
tip (tutorial)

G

Game Player Selector (tutorial) 144-151
BarLength graphic symbol 151
BlankNumbersMC text box 151
change methods 149
component methods 148
component parameters 144-148
MarkerSkin graphic symbol 151
PlayerEntry text box 151
removeChoices method 149

return methods 148-149
skinning component 151
Slider MC movie clip 151
TeamTitle text box 151
TitleBar text box 151
globalStyleFormat object. See tool
tip (tutorial)

H

Hall, Branden 30, 196
hexadecimal color. See
ColorPicker (tutorial)
HSB color. See ColorPicker (tutorial)

I

image scroller (tutorial) 82-91
animation within loaded clips 88
breaking apart text 87
component parameters 89-90
Monnone Engine movie clip
84-86
resizing images 87
suitability of loaded SWFs 87-88
theEngine/Image/Url
variables 84, 85, 86
XML functionality 83, 86
importing video into Flash MX
(tutorial) 71-73
converting video to movie clip 72-73
Import to Library dialog box 71
Import Video Settings dialog
box 71-72

J

JavaScript 34
JPEG files 196

L

Layout Manager (tutorial) 174-185
addComponent method 179, 184
attachMovie method 179
component methods 184-185
component operation 175
Container class 176-179, 182-183
container offset feature 180
creating initialization object 177
custom layouts 183
doLayout method 180, 184
dynamically updating component
arrangement 182-183
FlowLayout algorithm 175
FlowLayout class 176, 178,
179, 181, 183

FlowLayout constructor method 185
getInsets method 182, 184
getMaxheight/width methods 184
hgap/vgap variables 182
Insets constructor method 185
layoutContainer method 183
LayoutManager.fla 176
manual adjustment feature 180
ManualAdjustmentExample.fla 180
multiple containers 181, 182
setLayout method 178, 184
setMaxheight/width methods 185
update method 182
Lifaros 275
lightness 131
liquid image modulator
(tutorial) 224-230
attachMovie method 228
component parameters 225-226
crazy button 229, 230
horizontal and vertical sliders 226
Image linkage ID input text field 226
normal button 229, 230
Step buttons 226

M

Macromedia Extension Manager 3
Microsoft Visual Studio 24
Moock, Colin 24
mouse toys 94. See also Calliscope
(tutorial); TrailerMaker (tutorial);
Radiolaria (tutorial)
movie loading. See Tornado (tutorial)

O

object-oriented programming
(OOP) 2, 29-30

P

Particle Emitter (tutorial) 157-171
bacteria example 167
component parameters 158-162
disordered jet example 166-167
dynamically creating
emitters 162-163
explosion example 164-165
falling snow example 165-166
graphical customization 163
maxDust variable 165
myword variable 170
neoObject particle emitter 162
particleBody movie clip 163, 168,
169
ParticleComponent component 157

ParticleEmitterComponent
component 157, 164
pens example 170-171
poetry example 169-170
random palettes example 168-169
particle systems 156. See also Particle
Emitter (tutorial)
pattern generators 94. See also
Calliscope (tutorial); TrailerMaker
(tutorial); Radiolaria (tutorial)
Penner, Robert 275
Photoshop 131
PHP. See XML news ticker (tutorial)
Property inspector 9
PuppetStrings:Transitions
(tutorial) 263-278
adding component 271-272
adding time lag 268
Animate current configuration
buttons 274
animateLettersIn/Out methods 276
animating text 267
animation in/out tabs 274
Animation window 273
attaching component to stage 277
callback methods 277
code interface 276
component enhancements 278
component methods 276
component parameters 265
creating text field 265
creating TextFormat object instance
264, 269-270
embedding font 271
Export animation back to authoring
environment button 273
Property-easing ComboBoxes 275
removeLetters method 276
Sample text to animate input text
field 273
specifying text formatting within custom UI
Text formatting within custom UI
parameter input box 273
TextField/Format reference in
authoring environment input
boxes 273
Translate text placement
controls 274
user interface 263, 266, 272, 274

R

RadioButton component 121
Radiolaria (tutorial) 100-102
component parameters 101
RGB color. See ColorPicker (tutorial)

S

Schoneveld, Stuart 24
ScrollBar component 13
shared objects 8, 16, 65
sketchpad (tutorial) 58-66
brushSize movie clip 62, 63
changing background alpha value 60
clearBut movie clip 62
colorPicker movie clip 62, 64, 65
component parameters 61
frame rate 60
graphical customization 62-65
Library images 59
lineSize variable 63
padActive variable 63
recorderBit movie clip 62, 63, 65
sketch component 60
Sketch_interface folder 62
undoBut movie clip 62
user interface 58
skewed image modulator
(tutorial) 231-233
component parameters 231
FSkewedMatrixClass component
class 231
FSkewedMatrixComp.mxp 231
holder movie clip 231
horizontal/vertical offset sliders 231
sliding panel (tutorial) 118-126
CEventManager class 119, 121
component parameters 120-125
CTabbedPanel class 119
default panel designs 122, 123
open/close methods 126
StringThing (tutorial) 282-295
classic_method.fla 283
component enhancements292
component methods 292
component parameters 285-286
e-commerce application 287-288
get/setAutoUpdate methods 292
get/setData source methods 292
get/setHtmlText methods 292
get/setRefreshRate methods 292
get/setText methods 292
get/setTextField methods 292
getHours/Minutes/Time
methods 293
installing component 284
loggedIn variable 291
login method 291
multilingual content
application 288-289
password variable 291
personalizing content 290-291

placeholder tags 283
replaceText method 292
retrieving and overwriting
variables 293-294
setData-getData.fla 294
setLanguage method 289
text/title variables 289
username variable 291

T

TabControl (tutorial) 106-114
addTabs method 109
component methods 108
component parameters 107
creating tabbed content 110-111
customizing component 112-113
defaultTab1 - 2 107
get/set ActiveTab methods 109, 111
get/set AutoWidth method 109
getTab methods 109
loadMovie method 114
myContentMovie movie
clip 111, 112
removeTabs methods 109
setColorScheme method 114
setTabLabel method 109
setTextFormat method 114
swapTabs method 109
tabChange method 111
TabControlGlobal component
106, 113
text control 24, 262. See also
PuppetStrings:Transitions (tutorial)
text editor (tutorial) 24-29
component enhancements 29
customizing component 26-28
editing symbols through Library 29
setBackground methods 27
setButton methods 26-27
setTextColor method 27
setTitle method 27, 28
setToolbar methods 27
Title option 25
user interface features 26
Visible? option 25
text fields. See StringThing (tutorial)
TextFormat object 24. See also text
editor (tutorial)
tool tip (tutorial) 44-53
code hint menu 46
component methods 49-50
component parameters 46
component properties 47-48
customizing component 46, 50, 51
disappearOnMouse methods 49

embedding font 51
FStyleFormat object 52
FtoolTip component 44
globalStyleFormat object 52, 53
methods and properties
documentation 47
resetToDefault method 49
setHandler methods 49
setFade methods 49-50
setFont method 50
setShadow methods 50
setTargetMC method 50
setTimeDelay method 50
start/stopDragToolTip methods 50
style format properties 52
waitForMouseStopBool method 50
Tornado (tutorial) 197-221
adding component
dynamically 211-213
alignment controls 207-208
attachMovie method 211, 213
component features 218-219
component limitations 219-220
component parameters 199-200
DraggablePane component 218
exclusive /non-exclusive forcing of
movies 214-215
External movie path box 203
Flash 5 version 221
forceButton_mc movie clip 215
global transformations 209
installation 198
installing testing server 202
integration with other components
216-217
layout functionality 207
Live Preview feature 200-201
loading in and laying out external
movies 201
Movie Container Clips section
204, 205
moving component with movies
loaded 204
myCallback method 210, 211
myPreloader method 210
onPreload event handler 205,
206, 207
placement controls 207-208
preloader clips 205
preloader.fla 205
refresh methods 218
relative transformations 209
returning/non-returning
forces 214-215
ScrollPane component 216, 217, 218
setFunc methods 211

Show Background/Foreground
CheckBoxes 209
start/stopLoader methods 220
trailing slash mark 202-203
transformation controls 208-209
using multiple Movie Loader
components 218
_root property problems 220-221
TrailerMaker (tutorial) 98-100
component parameters 99
trailClip method 98

V

video 70. See also Video Player (tutorial); importing video into Flash MX
(tutorial)
compression and editing 73-74
Video Player (tutorial) 70-78
component enhancements 78
component methods 76-77
component parameters 75-76
component specification 70-71
converting video to movie clip 75
getLoop/Vol methods 76
pause/play/stopVid methods 76, 77
resizing panel 75
setLoop/Vol methods 77
skinning component 77
Virtual Trackball (tutorial) 248-259
begin/endFill methods 258
canvas movie clip 256, 257
component methods 249
component parameters 250-251
drawing 3D polygon 254-258
getQuaternionRotation method 249
getRotationMatrix method 250
increment method 249, 257
myPoint movie clip 252
parallel projection 251
perspective projection 254
setProperty method 253
transformVertex method 249, 254

W

Wan, Samuel 30

X

XML (eXtensible Markup Language) 85,
236-238. See alsoData Grid (tutorial);
event calendar (tutorial); image scroller
(tutorial); XML news ticker (tutorial);
XML to ActionScript parser (tutorial)
XML news ticker (tutorial) 34-40
component enhancements 39-40

component parameters 35
component structure38-39
fadeTicker method 39
init method 39
loadData method 39
loading from external data source 37
moveOn method 39
pause/runTicker methods 39
PHP server-side script 37-38
processData method 39
start/stopTicker methods 39
unpauseTicker method 39
XML data structure 37-38
XML to ActionScript parser
(tutorial) 236-245
accessing data in arrays 242
And add... menu 241
component parameters 239
Find nodes named... menu 241
Preview option screen 244
XMLtoASparser component 236

Printed in the United States
81642LV00001B/19-44